NEW GUINEA ON THE THRESHOLD

New Guinea on the Threshold

Aspects of Social, Political, and Economic Development

edited by
E. K. FISK

UNIVERSITY OF PITTSBURGH PRESS

Library of Congress Catalog Number 68-21625

First published in 1966 by Longmans, Green and Company, London, England, and the Australian National University Press, Canberra, A.C.T.

Published in the United States of America, 1968, by the University of Pittsburgh Press

Foreword

THE AUSTRALIAN administered Territories of Papua and New Guinea have become a major interest of the Australian National University, and in particular of the Research School of Pacific Studies within that University. As a result of this interest there is now a considerable body of scholars, in a wide range of disciplines, who have spent many years in the study of New Guinea and its problems.

There has resulted a great deal of specialized writing, but New Guinea and its problems have recently come to the notice and interest of a much wider audience throughout the world, whose needs are not adequately met by what a specialist writes for his fellow specialists. I therefore suggested to Mr Fisk that he attempt to bring together some of these specialists in the writing of a book that would serve as an 'intelligent man's guide' to Papua-New Guinea and some of its more interesting problems and prospects. The result is a lively book, in which a group of leading specialists look at the present situation in Papua-New Guinea from the point of view of their own specialty, and consider what this bodes for the future, and in particular for the next decade or so.

There are of course gaps in the coverage of the book as not all the experts were available to write for this book at the appropriate time. There are also a few points of dispute between the experts themselves, which may detract somewhat from the consistency of the book, but add substantially to its interest.

New Guinea (more and more used to cover the two Territories, Papua and New Guinea) today constitutes the largest, if not the most populous, of the remaining non-self-governing territories of the non-Communist world. It includes some of the most recently contacted primitive races known to mankind; and it is still possible, in some areas, for anthropologists to study stone-age man living virtually undisturbed in his natural stone-age environment. Add to the primitive economic systems the vast range of languages and the social and political fragmentation so prevalent in the Territories, and it is not surprising to find a bewildering but fascinating range of problems. Many of these problems are as yet little understood by more than a few, but they have begun to capture the interest and attention of many people in many countries throughout the modern world.

Some of this growing interest and attention has been politically motivated. Whatever the motives of some participants in the debate it is likely, nevertheless, that this same debate has awakened many people to the strange and difficult responsibility that, by the accident of history, has fallen upon Australia.

One purpose of this book is to inform and encourage debate and discussion amongst interested people, both inside and outside the United Nations, and also in New Guinea itself. The 'Threshold' referred to in the title is clearly a reference to the development of self-government and independence. All chapters have a relevance, some less directly so than others, to the task of 'guiding' New Guinea to the point of the decisions which will finally spell self-government and, not necessarily immediately concurrent, external independence.

Dr West gives us the historical setting and warns against anachronistic judgments about past policies formed in an earlier day in which the development of self-government and independence were not seen as matters of urgency. Mr Fisk develops a theme of 'primitive affluence' which, under pressure of change to a western style economy, will not readily or quickly become viable. Its external dependence on Australia for capital and skills will increase rather than decline before there emerges a 'national economy' able to support a politically independent and self-governing national unit. Dr Brookfield indicates that the 'comfortable' subsistence economy has been possible because population has not widely pressed on resources. But at a new level of living standards, which will accompany the adoption of a monetary economy, a major redeployment of population (especially urban) will occur and will need careful oversight. Dr Shand shows that major new rural industries have developed in recent years and plots for the course of economic development needed to lessen external dependence.

Dr McArthur warns us that our knowledge of the population in terms of vital statistics is so slight as to make nonsense of precise planning of schooling and other social measures. Readers of other chapters will realize, however, that inadequate data do not get us 'off the hook': we have for example to develop an educational policy within the framework of the best guesses or judgments we can make about the structure of population.

Professor Spate deals with the complex educational problem which has quite suddenly become critical at the tertiary rather than primary level. He discounts the attempt in some quarters to pose education and economic development as antithetical in priorities for the use of public resources. Readers will be interested in the marginally different views on the role of native languages expressed by Professor Spate and Dr Wurm. Both stress the need for English as the language for secondary and tertiary instruction, when the requirements of abstract thought are clearly beyond the vernacular languages. The latter's chapter is a wise reminder to the reader of the basic difficulty of developing a sense of nationhood in a country with some 700 recognizable languages.

Dr Paula Brown deals with the process of social change and for many readers her treatment of 'cargo cults' will be of great interest and value. Other contributors (especially Professor R. S. Parker) use the general description of cargo cults as reflecting problems of 'hopeless envy' or, less unmanageably, 'ignorance and wishful thinking' by indigenous groups about the apparently magical affluence of the European. Dr Reay deals with a too neglected subject: the role of women in the changing New Guinea. She shows the difficulties and opportunities ahead and also explains why some mainland organizations (e.g. Girl Guides) transplant well and others do less well.

Dr Bettison deals sympathetically with the problems of the expatriate in New Guinea. He shows the dilemmas in assimilating two alien cultures in one country. He stresses the ambivalence of the Australian who does not claim innate superiority over the indigenes as human beings and recognizes the justice of developing New Guinea for New Guineans while, at the same time, he finds it difficult to adjust his daily life to take full account of both these points.

Professor Parker provides two essential chapters. Together they serve to differentiate between legislation and government. Significant power to legislate has been given to the new House of Assembly, but administration is still largely in the hands of ex-patriates. The road to full self-government is still a long one in terms of skills and experience to be acquired whatever the legis-lative and temporal time-table turns out to be.

Professor Parker shows reticence, a reticence perhaps surprisingly evident on the part of other contributors, too, on the subject of target dates for political and administrative independence. The writer of this foreword shares this reticence and sees nothing to be gained by dramatic announcements of early dates as targets for self-government and independence. Professor Parker poses the relevant questions but the tenor of the book as a whole is a healthy reminder of what remains to be done. Any early target date would either embarrass the proposers by proving unpracticable or embarrass the New Guineans who, they have been assured, alone will determine their readiness.

It has not been my intention to review the book but simply to indicate its promise as an 'intelligent man's guide' to the nature and problems of Australia's responsibilities in Papua and New Guinea. All the writers record something of the substantial progress of the last two decades but none is brash enough to belittle the task ahead. I have said the book is 'lively' in its presentation of the subjects dealt with; but it is also sobering in that none can escape the conclusion that Australia's responsibilities in New Guinea are both serious and difficult.

I commend the book as a contribution to understanding: I hope it will find its way into administrative and political circles in New Guinea and Australia, into our schools and universities, and into business houses. Not least I hope the book will come into the hands of influential readers in those other countries who today form our critics and whose friendly and constructive help will be necessary in fulfilling the task Australia, and now the New Guineans themselves, have undertaken in promoting the advancement to nationhood of the two Territories.

J. G. CRAWFORD
Director, Research School of
Pacific Studies

Canberra
January 1966

Acknowledgments

Our debts of gratitude are many: to all those residents of Papua-New Guinea, official and unofficial, and too numerous to be named individually, who have helped each of us in so many ways during our visits to the Territory. To them all we extend our grateful thanks.

We wish also to express our appreciation to Hunter Douglas (Australia) Limited for the grant it made towards the cost of publication; to the Department of Territories for permission to use the photographs reproduced in plates 1-8; to Mr W. F. M. Straatmans for the use of the photos in plates 2 (centre) and 3 (below) from his private collection; to Mr Hans Gunther and his colleagues in the Cartographic Section of the Research School of Pacific Studies for the maps in Chapter 3 and the endpapers; and, finally, to Mr Howard Liu, for his assistance in compiling the index and for many other points in the making of the book.

E.K.F.

Notes on Contributors

Bettison, D. G., PH.D., Associate Professor of Anthropology, Simon Fraser University, Vancouver: formerly Senior Fellow in the Research School of Pacific Studies, Australian National University, and Executive Officer of the New Guinea Research Unit of that School. Dr Bettison is a sociologist and has published widely on African problems as well as on those of New Guinea. He was also editor of the *New Guinea Research Bulletin*.

Brookfield, H. C., PH.D., Professorial Fellow in Geography, Research School of Pacific Studies, Australian National University. Dr Brookfield is known for his work on the Geography of Oceania and as author (with Dr Brown) of *Struggle for Land*.

Brown, Paula, PH.D., Senior Fellow in Anthropology, Research School of Pacific Studies, Australian National University. Dr Brown has made a special study of the Chimbu people of the Eastern Highlands of New Guinea and is author of numerous articles in this field as well as joint author of *Struggle for Land*.

Fisk, E. K., M.A., Senior Fellow in Economics, Research School of Pacific Studies, Australian National University. Mr Fisk has published on the rural economy of South-East Asia as well as on the economic theory of primitive societies and on the economy of Papua and New Guinea.

McArthur, Norma, PH.D., Professorial Fellow in Demography, Research School of Social Sciences, Australian National University. Dr McArthur is known for her work on the Demography of Oceania and has published a special study, *The Populations of the Pacific Islands* in 8 parts (Australian National University, Canberra).

Parker, R. S., M.EC., Professor of Political Science, Research School of Social Sciences, Australian National University. He has since 1962 been a member of the Interim Council of the Administrative College of Papua and New Guinea, and is well known for his published works on Australian politics and administration.

Reay, Marie, PH.D., Senior Fellow in Anthropology, Research School of Pacific Studies, Australian National University. Dr Reay is known particularly for her work in the Western Highlands of New Guinea, published in her book *The Kuma* and in many journal articles.

Shand, R. T., PH.D., Senior Research Fellow in Economics, Research School of Pacific Studies, Australian National University, has made a special study of cash cropping in Papua and New Guinea over the last four years. His published works include a number of articles on the agricultural economics of New Guinea.

Spate, O. H. K., PH.D., Professor of Geography in the Research School of Pacific Studies, Australian National University, is well known for his works on India and Fiji. He has been associated with research in New Guinea for many years and was recently a prominent member of the Commission on Higher Education in Papua and New Guinea, whose report was published in Canberra 1964.

West, F. J., PH.D., Professorial Fellow in Pacific History, Research School of Pacific Studies, Australian National University. His book on Sir Hubert Murray is being published by Oxford University Press in 1966.

Wurm, S. A., PH.D., Professorial Fellow in Linguistics, Research School of Pacific Studies, Australian National University. He is known for his contributions to Oceanic Linguistics, and in particular for his recently published accounts of the linguistic situation in New Guinea.

Contents

Figures

Plates

Abbreviations

A.B.C.   Australian Broadcasting Commission.

ANGAU   Australian New Guinea Administrative Unit.

ASOPA   Australian School of Pacific Administration.

B.A.E.   Bureau of Agricultural Economics.

C.P.D.   *Commonwealth Parliamentary Debates.*

CSIRO   Commonwealth Scientific and Industrial Research Organization.

Currie Report   *Report of the Commission on Higher Education in Papua and New Guinea.*

ECAFE   Economic Commission for Asia and the Far East.

F.A.O.   United Nations, Food and Agriculture Organization.

H.A. Deb.   *House of Assembly Debates.*

I.B.R.D.   International Bank for Reconstruction and Development.

N.I.D.   Royal Naval Intelligence Division.

N.G.A.R.   *New Guinea, Annual Reports,* see Australia 1921-40, 1946- .

P.A.R.   *Papua, Annual Reports,* see Territories 1905- .

Roy. Com.   Australia, 'Report of the Royal Commission . . . Papua'.

T.P.N.G.   Territory of Papua and New Guinea.

Tariff Report   Australia, Tariff Board Reports.

I

The Setting

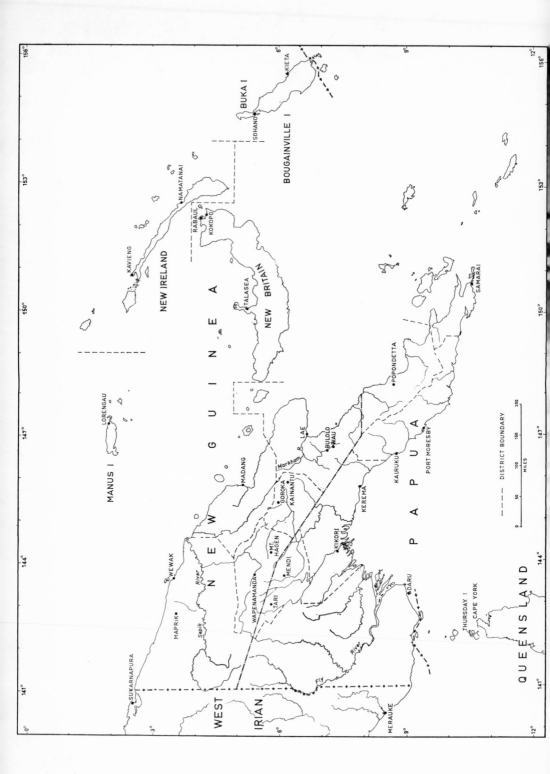

1

The Historical Background

F. J. WEST

PAPUA and New Guinea, administered jointly since 1946, came under Australian control in different ways and at different times. The former, a British Crown colony, was transferred to the new Commonwealth of Australia by Royal Letters Patent in 1902 and formally accepted when the Papua Act was proclaimed in Port Moresby on 1 September 1906. The latter, the German colony of Kaiser Wilhelmsland, was captured by an Australian expeditionary force in 1914, ruled by a military administration for six years, and first retained under civilian control as a Class 'C' mandate under the League of Nations and then as a Trust Territory under the United Nations in 1946. The differences in the method of their acquisition affected the course of Australian rule, for in both colonies the Australian government inherited a pattern of administration and of unofficial enterprise, but such differences between the two Territories, although contemporaries often supposed them to be great, were in fact relatively minor. The physical and social characteristics of the two colonies are so similar that the broad pattern of European control has been the same. The differences in the time of acquisition are more important, however, because the assumptions and beliefs which were made about colonial rule by those responsible for its administration differed in 1921 from those of 1906. And these assumptions led to a different perception of the problems involved as well as setting limits to their solution.

When Australia assumed the government of Papua, it did so in the context of an argument about the best policy to be pursued. The participants in this debate saw matters in two broad categories. One was the duty to protect the natives. In its extreme form this end of policy was asserted by the Reverend James Chalmers of the London Missionary Society in Papua. At the time of annexation he had said: 'The smallest amount of government and interference will be the best, and any attempt to Anglicise the natives or their customs should be strictly prohibited' (Chalmers 1887:105). Such a policy,

3

as the first governor of Papua realized, could not be seriously urged upon a metropolitan government which was paying the cost of administration, but Chalmers reasserted his opinion after seven years of colonial rule: 'New Guinea is never likely to become a land fit for colonising. Its position and climate are both against it; and in addition to this . . . Every native right would, I fear, be an impediment to colonisation' (Chalmers 1887:104). Chalmers represented a tradition of thought about colonial rule which concerned itself with the protection of the aboriginals, and it was the sole view which many in Australia ascribed to the British administration of Papua. In this belief, when the colony came under Australian control an additional policy was proclaimed: development.

In 1906 the Royal Commissioners who sat to recommend a policy for the Territory declared that the hour had struck for a forward policy. Any future administrator should 'put behind him most of the late Crown Colony traditions' and 'be determined that every officer under him will work with singleness of purpose in the interest of legitimate white development of whatever kind' (Australia 1907:xcviii). They believed, as did most Australians with any interest in Papua, that it was a potentially rich and profitable possession whose resources could and should be unlocked, and that incidentally in this process of development the Papuans would benefit because they would have models of European industry to imitate and by working for Europeans they would acquire both skills and habits of industry without which they would suffer the fate of other aboriginal races and die out. As Hubert Murray, the first Australian Lieutenant-Governor of Papua, told his brother Gilbert in 1908: 'white civilisation is not incompatible with the well-being of the natives', adding that if they did not work they were 'doomed' (Gilbert Murray n.d.). It is easy to be cynical about the belief that development and the best interests of the natives were complementary, but even in missionary and philanthropic circles it was generally agreed that hard work was the principal means by which the native could achieve his religious and social salvation, although these circles might deny that this hard work should be performed for a European settler or entrepreneur.

Thus at the outset of Australian rule there was a dual policy: of development, which meant the encouragement of European enterprise; and of protection, which meant that Papuans working for Europeans to assist development must be shielded from cruelty, ill-treatment, and injustice.

By 1921 these assumptions and the optimism with which the dual policy was regarded had changed. In part this was due to Papuan experience. World War I had dealt Papuan trade a grave blow, and in any case it had become obvious that whatever resources existed could not be developed quickly or easily. Murray had begun to give a more positive stress to native policy (West 1963:292), as a consequence both of attempting to bring the whole of the colony under control and of his awareness that since European development was slow, native development was necessary to the prosperity of Papua. In part the change was due to external factors. It was generally believed by the men who drew up the peace treaties that the Germans were unfit to rule colonies; that their treatment of natives had been harsh. The Covenant of the League of Nations proclaimed that the control of native peoples formed a 'sacred trust' of the civilized powers which administered colonies, with a clear implication that there would come a time when these people who could not yet stand on their own feet under the strenuous conditions of the modern world would be able to do so. Again, it is easy to be cynical about the effect of high-sounding declarations on practice, but at least there was a proclaimed standard and a system of inquiring into its achievement. Whatever the failures of colonial governments, consciousness of native interests took on a more positive form. Protection from abuses and civilization as an incidental effect of European activity began to be replaced by more positive efforts to civilize primitive peoples and by doctrines of the paramountcy of native interests. There was still, however, no sense of urgency, no sense of time running out, and no elaboration of 'welfare' measures of the kind that came with the Colonial Development and Welfare Acts of 1940 and onwards.

Granted the assumptions and beliefs men had about colonial rule (for it is idle to blame them for being of their own time and place), these different stresses in the dual policy had different consequences in practice. While development by European capital and skill seemed the chief need, both to make the Territories self-sufficient and to yield a profit to those who risked their money and their lives there, the crucial issues of government were land and labour policy, together with ancillary needs like communications— roads and bridges, ports and wharves—which they implied.

There was always an undercurrent of hope about the mineral resources of Papua. Writing in 1912, Murray described the minerals as hardly touched (J. H. P. Murray 1912:316). He had in mind gold, copper, coal, and oil, all of which were known to exist, but in unknown quantities. If the oil discovered on the Vailala in 1911 were as extensive as was reported, he looked forward to the tripling of his revenue. But these were still hopes, and the real development of Papua was thought to be agricultural. There was great optimism about the range of crops which could be grown—the Royal Commissioners had supplied a long list including coffee, tea, cinchona, sisal hemp—but in practice development early concentrated on two: copra and rubber. Both required land for plantations and labour to work them.

New Guinea was a somewhat different case. When Australia took control, the plantations which grew chiefly copra had already been established, first under the aegis of the Neu Guinea Kompagnie and then under Imperial German administration (Rowley 1958:51). At the end of World War I these plantations were expropriated and made available on generous terms and as freehold to Australian settlers, and it was not until the Highlands were discovered and brought under control after World War II that land policy became a problem on the scale it had been in Papua (West 1956:163). Then too New Guinea mineral resources were spectacularly revealed by the Edie Creek gold strike, which outshone the agricultural attractions of the territory. These circumstances made labour policy, not land, the principal aspect of development, but the allied problems of communication were no less acute when development was stressed.

Land policy was the first major issue to be tackled under the Australian administration of Papua. In 1906 the area of land leased to Europeans was some two thousand acres and the amount of freehold land alienated to Europeans was twenty-two thousand acres during the eighteen years of British government (Legge 1956: 140-2). The Papua Act abolished freehold because of Australian experience with land speculation, but to promote settlement the Land Ordinance of 1906 provided for leasehold grants on extremely liberal terms. Leases were granted for periods up to ninety-nine years, rent free for the first ten years. No limitation was placed upon the area which could be taken up. Free survey was provided, and the nominal deposit demanded with applications for land was refunded when the lease was taken up. To prevent speculation, however, strict improvement conditions were laid down which prescribed the nature and the extent of cultivation and of stocking of leases, and failure to comply with these conditions led to forfeiture of the land.

This liberal ordinance did its work, measured by the crude test of land held by settlers. Over forty thousand acres were leased during the first year of Australian rule, a figure which went up to nearly a quarter of a million acres in the following year and reached 364,088 by 1911. Thereafter the land boom stabilized. In part the improvement conditions came into effect, with the result that by the time of the outbreak of war in 1914, 174,355 acres had been forfeited, and the amount of land in the hands of private Europeans stabilized at a quarter of a million acres. Of this, by 1911, very nearly sixteen thousand were actually under cultivation, and over double that amount when war came. In part the levelling off of land settlement was due to government policy. Estimating that the encouragement the ordinance offered had been successful, in 1909 survey fees were charged and the scale of deposits was increased according to the area applied for, in 1910 rents were charged within the first ten years and at the same time a limit was placed upon the amount of land that could be taken up as an individual lease.

What was achieved was sufficient, thought the government, to provide the basis for the profitable development of Papua, to achieve that self-sufficiency which both the Australian and Papuan administrations regarded as an attainable end of policy; and both in Australia and in Papua the day was expected when the Australian subsidy (before World War I ranging from £20,000 to £30,000 a year plus certain smaller special grants for roads, wharves, and government plantations) would be unnecessary.

Only one serious obstacle appeared. Land was available, but where was the labour to work it? If, for instance, the Ceylon figure of three boys per acre was appropriate, from the beginning of development a serious labour shortage existed, granted that the government had a duty to protect the natives. The Native Labour Ordinance of 1907 provided for recruiting by licensed recruiters who, having found labourers, must bring them before a government officer to have an indenture made up. The officer must satisfy himself that the men were willing to work, that a fair remuneration would be offered and duly paid, that there was no reason to expect ill-treatment, and that at the end of the contract the labourer would be returned to his village. The ordinance went on to prescribe the conditions of work. The length of engagement could not exceed eighteen months for a miner or carrier nor three years for an agricultural worker. Regulations prescribed the payment of wages, conditions of housing, scale of rations, and medical care. Murray later described this indenture system as a near relative of slavery, but he defended its retention in Papua as a protection for the native, who was safeguarded from compulsion or fraud, and as protection for the employer, who had a criminal remedy for breach of contract by his labourers (J. H. P. Murray 1925:110-21).

Such an elaborate labour code, policed as it was with some care, could not in itself produce the men required. Even if the figure needed to work the land in cultivation could be reduced from that deemed necessary in Ceylon, there was still an apparent shortage. The importation of Asiatic labour, although it was from time to time considered in official circles and permitted in the case of 'labourers of special skill', was never seriously contemplated even when there were grave doubts in 1910 about the adequacy of the Papuan supply. Estimating the total population at something like 200,000, the Papuan government thought that 10 per cent of this number was the outside limit of available manpower if Papuans were to be saved from turning into a landless proletariat. Yet faced with this threat of a labour shortage, the government was still optimistic; it thought that numbers would prove adequate for the degree of settlement which had occurred and it ascribed any particular shortages to the shortcomings of individual employers and the resulting unwillingness of Papuans to engage for particular individuals. But it was the labour question, nevertheless, which produced the belief that Papua could not be developed in a single generation, that development would not be quick but gradual. And it was the labour question, too, which caused the Papuan government to attempt to bring the whole of the colony under control and to stress the native administration aspect of its policy.

The acquisition of New Guinea did not present the Australian government with the necessity to evolve a land policy. Under Neu Guinea Kompagnie rule some 700,000 acres had been sold or leased to companies or to individuals, of which some 26 per cent was planted. Under the terms of the Versailles treaties, when these properties were expropriated and then offered for sale principally to ex-servicemen, the purchaser not merely bought the property on very favourable terms but also acquired the best title vested in the previous owner, which meant, since land under the Germans had been sold rather than leased, freehold tenure in most of the settled area of New Guinea. The Australian Administration indeed retained the law of its imperial predecessor that only the government could buy land from natives, and it also provided safeguards to prevent forced or fraudulent land purchase by establishing the tests of native willingness to sell and of consideration of present and future native needs, but a major part of land settlement had already taken place and that land was alienated. Under the new Australian ordinance leasehold land was gradually taken up on much the same terms as Papuan land, by 1939 reaching the figure of 134,000 acres. Of these two types of landholding, the major part remained freehold, and of both something over a quarter of a million acres was actually planted by 1939, an area of cultivation equal to the total amount of settlement in Papua.

New Guinea's labour problem was correspondingly greater. There had been complaints of shortages under the German régime when there was no necessity for a government officer to determine whether a recruit had engaged voluntarily and when the punishments for defaulting labourers included flogging, imprisonment with chains, and curtailment of food. Under Australian rule, an ordinance very similar to the Papuan one was introduced, although there were some differences of detail such as the length of the term of engagement, which was three years for agricultural labourers and two years for other classes, the fixing of a minimum wage at five shillings a month where the Papuan ordinance prescribed no minimum, and a working week of fifty-five hours where the Papuan was fifty. Regulations in New Guinea laid down working conditions, payment of wages, ration scales, and medical care and treatment, as well as controlling the stages of recruitment from engagement in the village to repatriation at the end of the contract. In general the New Guinea labour policy was somewhat less liberal than the Papuan, but the extent of European enterprise exerted much greater pressure in the Mandated Territory.

About 17,000 natives were working for Europeans when the Australians occupied New Guinea, and the military administration employed 31,000. Under civilian control the figure fell slightly, but the great gold strike sent it up to over 40,000 in the decade before World War II. New Guinea faced the same basic problem as Papua. In the latter the plantations were concentrated into two districts, the Eastern and Central; in the former the bulk of European enterprise had taken place in the offshore islands of New Britain and New Ireland. This concentration of settlement ruled out an adequate local supply of labour and so a labour supply had to be found, engaged, transported to its place of work, regulated there, and returned to its place of origin under an elaborate labour code designed to protect both employers and employees. But in New Guinea, unlike Papua after its early years, demand always outstripped supply, and the urgency of opening up new country, especially the Highland valleys which were discovered in the 1930s, always impressed itself upon European settlers and government alike (West 1958:98).

Land and labour lay at the root of development, the success of which was judged in Australia primarily by the Territories reaching self-sufficiency. To make this possible, the plantations had to be connected to ports by adequate communications, and wharf and shipping facilities had to be secured. The internal problem of communications was harder in Papua than in New Guinea. The plantations of the Mandated Territory were situated on the coast not too far from reasonable natural harbours, but the Papuan ones had less easy natural access. The question of external shipping was beyond the control of the local governments, depending upon Commonwealth negotiations with such companies as Burns Philp, which to all intents and purposes exercised an unpopular monopoly, and upon exemption from the operation of the Commonwealth Navigation Act, which was applied to both Territories in 1921 and for five years imposed disadvantageous conditions upon their trade. Internally Papua never reached that self-sufficiency which was aimed at. Although its revenue from duties on exports and imports rose from £42,000 in 1907 to double that figure before World War I and to three times as much in the most prosperous years before World War II, it was never more than a half to two-thirds of the total expenditure of the government. New Guinea was better off. It never needed a Commonwealth subsidy, and with the gold strike of 1926, which eventually produced an export value of almost two million pounds a year, its local revenue was always four times as much as the Papuan and very often much greater; by 1939, for example, the revenue of the New Guinea administration was over the half million mark when Papua's, including the Commonwealth grant, was barely £190,000. This comparison is somewhat unfair to the Papuan efforts at development, because the windfall of the gold strike in New Guinea obscured the basic similarity in agricultural development (Mair 1948:99).

The mainstay of European enterprise and therefore of the government's revenue was copra. In Papua rubber at first seemed promising, but before the trees had really come into production there was a world depression in prices which eliminated Papuan producers, and only a system of Commonwealth bounties kept the industry alive until it revived a little just before World War II. Copra until the depression was the mainstay of development, making up half of the export value of the colony, but this too suffered from the drop in world prices, and by 1940 had fallen to but one-eleventh of Papua's exports. The Mandated Territory's development was even less healthy, depending agriculturally almost exclusively upon copra. Some rubber and coffee were planted but they were experimental crops rather than any serious contribution towards agricultural production. Copra made up 95 per cent of exports up to 1925 and half from that date until it was displaced by gold in 1931; but even when gold was reaching its highest value, copra still made up 36 per cent of the value of exports. This lack of diversification made the economies of both Territories somewhat precarious. If minerals were not discovered, or when they were worked out, the revenue of the two governments depended upon the price in the world market of one tropical product which was easy to grow and which did not demand a highly skilled labour force. The final result of development policy before World War II suggested failure rather than success, a fact recognized explicitly by Murray and implicitly by the government of the Mandated Territory. They blamed external circumstances of war and depression rather than the meanness or lack of interest of the Commonwealth of Australia, recognizing that Australia itself suffered from these world calamities, and that in any event, as a country itself still needing development, it was in no position to put many resources into Papua and the Mandated Territory of New Guinea.

If this were true of development policy upon which the prosperity and therefore any other policies depended, it was still more true of the second great aim of Australian government: the protection and then the civilization of the natives. At the outset of Australian rule in Papua, protection was a negative matter of either doing nothing or at least minimizing the effects of development policy. It was protection from the evils which might attend land and labour policy and elsewhere had done so. In this sense of protection, safeguards had been inserted in the land and labour ordinances. The basic safeguard was, of course, that native rights were left undisturbed by annexation; all land, that is, did not become Crown land with the natives tenants-at-will. Land could only be bought from Papuans by the government, which would only do so if the owners were willing to sell and if the land they were willing to sell was surplus to their present and likely needs. In fact, as Murray pointed out in 1912, whenever a native made a claim that land had been bought from others while he was really the owner, the government allowed his claim as a matter of course and the land was bought once again. Murray was confident that no injustice had been done, partly because of this attitude of the government which worked on the most liberal interpretation of the principles, partly because 'there is far more land than is ever likely to be wanted either for natives or for Europeans, so that the land problems which have caused so much trouble elsewhere are not likely to arise' (J. H. P. Murray 1912:344).

This optimism was justified in general, although there were cases of hasty or too rapid land purchase which caused local discontent, but the demand for land in Papua was never so great that a land shortage or widespread hardship to the natives was a serious risk. The same principles in New Guinea, especially when, with the settlement of the Highlands after the war there was greater pressure for white settlement, revealed their complexities more clearly (West 1956:165). The first difficulty obviously lies in the concept of ownership. From the beginning it was apparent that there was no clear-cut, precisely-defined body of land law in native society but rather a range of custom and a large number of individuals who had rights in any particular piece of land. Hence, of course, Murray's stress on finding all of the owners. But even if all rights were traced in this way and all claimants paid, this still left untouched the possibility that the land might in time past have been controlled by another group which had been dispossessed in fighting and which, because the government had now established law and order, could not regain its land. With an area like the Central Highlands, where to a much greater extent than Papua each group had a long and chequered fighting history, the starting-point of actual possession when the government arrived to impose peace in itself caused some injustice, quite apart from the often complicated circumstances of any particular case. Willingness to sell land, as a criterion of protection for the natives, is thus only a reliable principle if the right to sell the land can be clearly established; and this is notoriously difficult.

'Present and future needs' of native groups is also a difficult criterion. It depends upon the end of policy aimed at. If the natives are to be peasant proprietors, as Murray envisaged, or if they are to be encouraged to grow cash crops as the Mandated Territory believed after World War I, or if they are to establish co-operatives as in the policy after World War II, their land needs are obviously quite different. These needs in any case depend upon the system of cultivation used. The traditional method of cultivation requires one kind of area; cultivation for a European market quite another. The imponderable factors involved mean that any decision about future needs is a matter of the assumptions made about the future of the Territories, and before World War II, and for some time afterwards, these were never systematically examined. When Papua was taken over, the Prime Minister might say casually that its future was as a State of the Commonwealth of Australia; when the Mandated Territory was taken some kind of self-government might be envisaged; but the idea of independence and the need for economic development of native land impose quite different estimates of land needs. In other words the protection incorporated in the terms of land policy, which has remained in the ordinances since 1906 and is still pointed to as part of the policy of protecting native interests, was not in itself a protection; it depended upon the general situation in the colony, upon the European demand for land, and upon the government's conception of its duty.

So too did the protection of the natives which was prescribed in the labour legislation. Here the willingness of a labourer to engage was not difficult to determine, but the number which could be safely engaged was. When Murray first discussed the problem he was concerned with the total percentage of the population available as a labour force. He placed this at 10 per cent, which he admitted might seem rather high. He was also aware that if labourers remained away from their villages for long periods, they might turn into a landless proletariat by being unable to readjust to village life, which might in any case crumble if too many adult males were away. The length of time could be and was policed, but the percentage of adult males was rather more difficult, as it was later in the Mandated Territory. Such a criterion depended upon having an accurate census and upon labour being indentured and not free; only so could the figures be carefully checked. The demand for labour in Papua never made the matter acute; usually there were more labourers offering than were needed. But in New Guinea the gold strike of 1926 led to widespread over-recruitment. As in Papua, the figures for the whole territory were good, but in any particular group more men might be taken than was safe if the aim of the government to preserve village life and to avoid the creation of a landless proletariat or an urbanized working force was to be achieved. In general the labour legislation, like the land policy, avoided hardship or injustice (although in particular cases these certainly existed because of the concentration of European enterprise), but its success was due as much to the disasters that overtook European development and so restricted the demand for both land and labour. The real complexities of protection from the effects of land and labour policy it was never necessary to unravel, and the protection from individual abuses seemed to have been successful.

This limited view of protection as the prevention of ill-treatment and the avoidance of disruptive effects of land and labour policy

·The Commodore of the Australian Squadron reading the proclamation of annexation at Argyll Bay, Papua, 1884

Modern ceremonies are more crowded: Highland natives at Mount Hagen Show, 1965

Above *Women cultivating subsistence gardens, Lufa*

Above *The subsistence economy provides food and housing for most of the population at a level of primitive affluence*

Right *The Bougainville-Iwi road under construction. By investing unpaid surplus labour the subsistence sector contributes substantially to public capital formation*

upon native society has been an enduring one throughout Australian rule in Papua and New Guinea, but protection came to mean more than that; it came to mean more than a duty of civilizing a primitive people by the incidental contacts of native and European which the land and labour policy involved. Every European might be, as Murray said, a focus of civilization, but the government had a positive duty. Obviously the possibility of European enterprise had always depended upon the suppression of raiding, murder, and violence, but the labour shortage in both Papua and New Guinea led to the attempt to bring the whole of both Territories under control simply to increase the available supply, although there was an equal acceptance that the duty of a colonial power was to elevate a barbarous race; and this implied the extension of government control and then the civilization of the natives by way of medical care, education, and economic development (*P.A.R.* 1912: 1-15).

Control was the first element in the native policy of the two governments. In Papua, Murray began systematically to examine and then to pacify the considerable unknown areas of the colony from 1912. In New Guinea, the administration began slowly to extend the German area of control on the coast and the major off-shore islands to the interior, taking its big leap forward in the early 1930s when it started to establish law and order over the great Highland valleys. The Papuan government prided itself on the methods of peaceful penetration it employed, with the strictest control over the use of firearms by its officers, and it often used to contrast this with the less strict methods of the Mandated Territory. But the broad pattern of native administration was the same. One or more government officers with an escort of armed native police entered a new area, established a base camp, and then by a series of patrols began to assert government influence, preventing fighting, arresting murderers, and gradually enforcing the Native Regulations, which imposed standards of hygiene, sanitation, cleanliness, and so on upon the villagers. In both, the transitory effects of patrol visits were supplemented by a system of appointed local native officials, in Papua called village constables and in New Guinea *luluais* and *tultuls*, whose duty it was to represent the government, to convey and enforce its orders, and to report any infringements of its laws. Both faced two major difficulties. One was the fact that the nature of village society compelled the government to repeat its work every few miles because of the absence of widespread political or social unity; the other was the absence of any highly organized system of rank and the corresponding difficulty of finding and using men of influence to assist the work of control and the beginnings of civilization. The process of pacification and control was thus slow, its advance limited by the number of officers available for the work and by the difficult position of the local native officials who, if they were men of influence in traditional society, might be reluctant to support measures which might weaken their authority or, alternatively, might grasp the greater powers government office offered them, and become tyrants. Or perhaps a native group, not wishing to expose a man of influence to the kind of indignity he might sometimes suffer from a government officer, would put forward a nonentity who could do little to influence them or help the government. The result was what Murray called the dreary round of prosecutions for infringement of the law and the replacement of weak or inefficient native officials. Only from 1951 was this native authority system slowly replaced by local government councils (Healy 1961a:167).

The imposition of government control was a slow business. By 1939 Murray thought that the whole of Papua was known, but there were still considerable areas like the Southern Highlands which were uncontrolled. So too in the Mandated Territory. The Central Highland valleys were not brought under control until the 1950s, and even then there were areas which had never seen a white man. In any case, the suppression of fighting and the enforcement of European law and order were only the first step. To replace the excitements and the occupations of traditional life, both governments were well aware that something had to be substituted; but what could be substituted was a matter of the resources at the disposal of the administrations in men, money, and materials.

Lack of money and manpower in both administrations was most clearly revealed in health and education policy. The task of providing schools for the child population was tremendous, quite apart from the technical difficulties of the kind of education which was needed. Granted the elementary need for literacy, the Papuan government thought that technical and industrial education of the kind provided by the former mission school at Kwato was what was wanted. The idea was to make better agriculturalists or artisans out of the Papuans, not to provide a literary education, and before World War I Murray was exploring the possibility of technical schools. He did this in consultation with a missionary, and this was typical of the main effort of the Papuan government. This particular scheme was overtaken by the war but the approach remained. Faced with a task beyond its own resources, the government adopted a policy of subsidizing mission schools at a certain standard and with an authorized curriculum, and this educational effort, until after World War II, was the government's principal contribution to the formal education of the Papuans. Its extent cannot really be measured because figures for the total numbers of children at school were not collected, but in 1940 the number of pupils examined was 3,319, at a cost to the government in subsidies of something like £8,000. The figure expended on education in the Mandated Territory was higher. In 1922, £19,000 was spent on government schools, although this amount was never approached again before the war, when it had fallen to the Papuan figure. In Mandated New Guinea, however, the government established its own schools and had nothing to do with the missions, to which it tended to be antagonistic, in part at least because so many missionaries were German. The latter by 1939 had some 69,000 pupils, while the government schools, except for a small technical school opened in Rabaul in 1922, were all at the elementary level. By 1939 the total number of pupils in official schools was 385, and with the exception of the school opened at the Chimbu post in the Highlands as part of the extension of control, they were all in 'urban' areas (Reed 1943:187). The Mandated administration was criticized for its education policy by the Mandates Commission of the League of Nations as the slowest of any territory under mandate, but in both Papua and New Guinea the effort was hampered by the smallness of the amount raised by native taxation (due to the unfavourable economic circumstances) and by the belief that any education must be vocational, must be directed towards making better villagers in order to raise the general standard of living before any more ambitious education could be undertaken.

In both Territories too there was a general belief that health was a more urgent task than education. Correspondingly more money was made available, and in both Territories it was spent in two main ways: on hospitals in the major administrative centres, and on the employment of European medical assistants to make patrols, either by themselves or with an administrative officer in the course of his visits. These services were supplemented in Papua from 1926 by native medical assistants who had some elementary training but whose chief use was to report serious cases of epidemic or individual illness for European treatment; in the Mandated Territory the equivalent office of the medical *tultul* was inherited from the Germans and retained. Even so the resources available for an attack upon the major diseases of malaria, respiratory infections, dysentery, and hookworm were not great. For most of the period before World War II there were but two hospitals in Papua, at Port Moresby and Samarai, although New Guinea spent more money than Papua (some £90,000 in 1939) and in addition opened native hospitals at each government station and sub-station. These government activities were supplemented by the medical work of the missions and by a few private firms, but the effort tended to be concentrated upon the areas close to European settlement and enterprise.

This limitation of effort was due neither to indifference nor to assumptions about the place of natives in general development (for the obligation to improve health and medical care was firmly accepted) but to shortage of money. Both education and health were regarded as matters of native welfare which should at least

in part be paid for from native taxation, which was introduced into
Papua in 1919 (with the proceeds paid into a trust fund exclusively
used to benefit the Papuans), and by a head tax levied in New
Guinea since German times. But this revenue implied native
economic development. Money to pay tax could be earned as
wages by labouring for Europeans, but the indentured labourer was
himself exempted from payment. Those who did not labour had to
find their tax money by their own industry. To a limited extent this
came from market garden produce supplied to European centres
like Rabaul from the people of the Gazelle Peninsula, but the major
part of it came from cash crops. In 1918 the Papuan government
introduced the Native Plantations Ordinance, which provided for
the compulsory planting of land, just as an earlier regulation had
provided for the compulsory planting of coconut trees. In New
Guinea, when civil administration was set up, a Director of Agriculture was appointed who conceived it his duty to encourage native
production. Both policies eventually came down to the encouragement of copra production, although other experimental crops were
tried without much success: rice and coffee in Papua, cotton, maize,
and ground-nuts in New Guinea. All of these attempts, although
they might be backed by penalties for failure to plant and then to
clean and weed plantings, depended upon arousing native enthusiasm, maintaining it while trees or crops came into bearing, and
then marketing the produce. A situation of competition with
European enterprise never arose, but the technical and incidental
difficulties were discouraging enough. The world market never
helped native economic development in the years before World
War II, and the resources of the administrations never allowed of
skilled technical help and guidance on any significant scale. Coconuts were easy enough to grow, but the quality of the copra and its
sale were quite a different matter. In neither Papua nor New
Guinea did pre-war native production for sale on a European
market provide more than a small proportion of the total budget.
Health and education policy were not completely financed out of
this money, and there were welfare benefits to the natives from
other aspects of administration, but the positive aspect of protection
and civilization was referred to these figures as indicators of what
could be afforded.

Resources in money set limits to the possibility of elevating a
barbarous race, which Murray defined as the principal duty of the
colonizing power, but resources in men were equally important
and in equally inadequate supply. Moreover the initial availability
of men to get the land policy under way and then to carry out the
labour policy was as important for development as it was for native
policy. Two difficulties were always present in both Papua and
New Guinea. The first was the actual recruitment of personnel:
whether men could be persuaded to go to the Territories at all. The

second was the quality of those who were recruited: whether they had the special skills needed for particular work as well the more general qualities of character and temperament required of colonial service officers.

Recruitment presented a problem from the very first in Papua. At the time of the land boom in 1909 there was a peculiarly great difficulty in attracting qualified surveyors to expedite the granting of leases, but even the clerks were hard to come by. With the policy of development, the Papuan public service expanded from some fifty officers in 1906 to one hundred and twelve by 1909, but many of these men were not up to the work and just before World War I Murray thought that although the service was better than it had been, it was still very 'sloppy' (Gilbert Murray n.d.). He did not think that uncomfortable conditions were solely responsible for the difficulty of getting men, nor that the low rate of pay—some £250 p.a. for an Assistant Resident Magistrate, for example—was a handicap, since the country offered the lure of adventure, but he thought that the absence of a pension and of free medical treatment deterred recruits. For the specialist posts like doctors the salary was not enough and the accompanying administrative work caused difficulties. And there was always the risk that those who did come were men unable to get on in more civilized countries by reason of personal defects or incompetence. Just before World War I a pension scheme was drawn up, but it was only after a good deal of agitation in the early 1920s that such a scheme and a revised scale of salaries were actually put into effect. This scheme made the Mandated Territory's administration somewhat easier so far as recruitment went, but even so there was no ready supply of men to join either of the services until the depression in Australia produced a large number of applications at a time when they could not really be afforded. The public service of Papua and New Guinea was never really attractive to able men, and although many outstanding officers joined, there were many unsatisfactory ones.

This in itself was serious enough, for the standard of entry was not high in terms of education, and the training given was what could be picked up by experience in Papua and a short course below university level in New Guinea. For work in the field as a patrol officer these low standards might be compensated for by character, but for specialized services like agriculture, education, and health, they produced what was essentially an amateur approach. The supervision of native planting, for example, was never (until after World War II) carried out by an expert in tropical agriculture, after the first Director of Agriculture in New Guinea retired, and in general the number of university graduates or their equivalent was always very low. The bulk of the work of both development and protection was thus carried on by officers whose approach was amateur, however much field experience they may have had, and since the methods of implementing policy invariably depended upon such men, the achievements were always likely to be limited. Land purchase, for instance, depended upon an officer's sympathy with and ability to get inside the native situation in any particular group; labour policy depended upon the acuteness and patience of any particular officer; and the choice of native officials rested upon an officer's familiarity with the internal affairs of his people. The absence of any high standard of entry and the lack of any comprehensive system of training after joining the service, coupled with a haphazard organization of the service itself, which in Papua depended very largely on Murray personally and in New Guinea operated rather as rival departments than a co-ordinated government, all put a premium on the abilities of individual officers to offset organizational defects. In the nature of things they could not wholly succeed, and with many of them frustration turned to resignation and indifference. Murray at least could inspire his officers; the Administrators of the Mandated Territory, retired generals, were men of lesser calibre.

Between lack of financial resources and lack of adequate personnel neither of the two proclaimed ends of Australian policy was realized before World War II came to eliminate civil administration. Development policy had produced a one-crop economy exposed to the fluctuations of the world market. Protection had produced a native society which was preserved in its traditional villages and hamlets but suffering from the frustrations revealed in the widespread cargo cult movements which affected native groups at a certain stage of European contact. The principal achievement of the governments of Papua and New Guinea was the initial one of any colonial power: the establishment of law and order over much of the Territories by peaceful penetration, the most fundamental action of colonial rule. The latter stages of colonial government, of the diversification of the economy and the general raising of primitive standards, had been only lightly tackled; and it is for this relative failure in the later stages of development and welfare that the two governments have been blamed in recent years.

Not altogether fairly. Most of contemporary or near-contemporary criticism has been of failure to develop anything like a viable economy, of failure to educate and civilize the Papuans to something like a point of 'self-government take-off', so that now, in the 1960s, Papua-New Guinea is not ready for independence. Put in this way the criticism is misplaced. Leaving aside the external factors of war and depression which hindered the progress of the Territories and over which neither the local governments nor the Australian government had much control, this kind of criticism blames the situation in which an underdeveloped metropolitan country which needed its own capital and manpower could not or would not afford to use some of these resources for its colonies. It blames too the motives of men involved in colonial policy and practice. Such judgments are thoroughly anachronistic; they blame the men and the times before World War II by the standards of the post-war world. It is fairer to criticize by comparison with other colonies, to point to a lack of willingness to experiment compared with parts of Africa. It is fair to criticize techniques of colonial policy which did not profit by contemporaneous experience elsewhere. But before World War II, there was no sense of time running out for colonial rulers anywhere in the colonial world, and 'God made New Guinea on Saturday night'.

II

The Economy

2

The Economic Structure

E. K. FISK

THE PURPOSE of this chapter is to consider briefly some of the main structural features of the economy of Papua-New Guinea, and to examine their implications for economic policy over the next ten years or so.

The economic structure to be examined is, in many respects, quite unusual. There is a vast, stagnant, but surprisingly affluent subsistence sector, upon which has been grafted a rapidly expanding but still relatively small monetary sector, within which economic growth is taking place at an encouraging rate. There are two major divisions of the economy which, both as sources of income and as origins of growth, completely dominate the whole: namely, agriculture (and the related activities of animal husbandry, forestry, and fishing), on the one hand, and the expenditure of public authorities on the other. Of these, the latter is the greatest single source of Territory cash incomes, and this is dependent almost entirely on Australian financial aid. There is the commercial and industrial sector of the economy, which plays a vital, but subsidiary, part in the economic life of the Territories, and this in turn is almost completely dependent on non-indigenous skills and capital for its operation. Finally, there is an investment pattern in which the indigenous contribution is considerable, but almost entirely non-monetary: in which by far the largest monetary investment is in the public sector and is dependent on external aid for finance: in which private monetary investment is mainly provided by the non-indigenous resident or the overseas investor. These special features of the economy are examined in some detail below.

The overall picture that emerges is that of a low income country in which virtually all of the population have as much food as they want, are housed adequately by their own traditional standards, and have ample leisure for feasting, ceremonial, and other pastimes. It is an economy that is potentially viable and self-sufficient at a level of primitive affluence, but which is almost entirely dependent

23

on external aid, and on the importation of foreign skills and
capital, for any advance beyond that very primitive level.

This advance has already made considerable progress, and the
foundations upon which economic independence may ultimately
develop have already been laid. The formation and growth of
indigenous skills, local capital, and internal government revenue
is already taking place under the strong encouragement of government development activity. However, this development activity
itself greatly increases the demand for capital, skills, and public
expenditure, and it will be a considerable time before the supply
of these from internal resources can begin to match the growing
demand. In the meantime, the degree of dependence on outside
aid and resources is likely to increase rather than decline.

THE SUBSISTENCE AND MONETARY SECTORS

In discussing the economy of Papua-New Guinea, the distinction
between a subsistence and a monetary sector is analytically useful,
and will be used repeatedly in this chapter. However, it first must
be emphasized that in many respects this is an artificial division
and distinguishes between types of activity rather than between
types of people. During recent years the monetary economy has
spread geographically very widely over the Territories, so that there
are now relatively few people who never handle money at all. On
the other hand, for the great majority of the indigenous people of
the Territories, the use of money remains an irregular and peripheral
factor, rather than an essential part of the business of living. For
these people, therefore, the greater and the most fundamental part
of their economic activities takes place in the subsistence sector
and without the use of money, whilst a smaller and less basic part
takes place in the monetary sector.

Most people in the Territories do in fact operate in both sectors
of the economy, and when it is said that the subsistence sector is
predominant in the economy as a whole, this merely means that
more productive activities are undertaken outside the framework
of monetary exchange than within that framework. It does not
imply, as might have been the case twenty-five years ago, that most
people take no part in monetary exchange.

This straddling of the two economies by indigenous people is
becoming increasingly common in Papua-New Guinea, even among
the indigenous wage-earning labour force. In 1963, the indigenous
wage-labour force was estimated at 81,000 and their dependants at
about 178,000 (Territories 1964a: Table 3.1). It would be wrong,
however, to assume that these 260,000 people are therefore removed
from the subsistence sector into the monetary sector. This is by no
means the case, and in fact hardly any of the dependants, and only
some of the wage-earners themselves, obtain their basic food requirements through the market. These are still obtained in the main

from subsistence gardens cultivated by dependants and relatives of the wage-earner, and the money income is used to purchase goods and services not available from subsistence production. Traditional foods, such as yams, sweet potatoes, sago, and taro, are seldom purchased by indigenes for their own consumption.

The monetary sector of the economy of Papua-New Guinea therefore covers only a minor segment of the total economy of the country. Of the total goods produced and consumed in the country, nearly two-thirds are not exchanged for money in any form, and the number of people who are wholly or mainly dependent on a money income for the basic essentials of life is probably less than 100,000, or less than 5 per cent of the total population.[1] This small proportion is, moreover, made up very largely of non-indigenous people on relatively high incomes and with a high standard of living. For the great majority of the indigenous people a money income is not a means of livelihood, but rather a means of access to non-essential exotic goods and services not available in the tribal way of life. As such, a money income is very acceptable and highly desired, but it can be dispensed with at any time without undue hardship either to the wage-earner or to his family.

This fact is an important consequence of the large size of the subsistence sector, and of the relative freedom from hunger and extreme poverty for which it is responsible. It is basic to the understanding of the problems and prospects of the economy as a whole.

Importance of the monetary sector. On the other hand, the subsistence sector, however affluent it may be within the limited range of goods and services that it can produce, is almost by definition a stagnant sector.

In most of Papua-New Guinea, serious pressure of population on the land has not yet developed, and productivity per unit of labour is high in traditional agriculture. To meet their subsistence requirements, most producers need to use only a modest proportion of their resources of labour and a part of their resources of land. The balance is available to produce a considerable surplus, but in the absence of monetary exchange, and the trade that it facilitates, there is no point in producing more sweet potatoes, yams, and taro than they can consume. In most of Papua-New Guinea, therefore, the *pure subsistence* producer has developed economically almost as far as his non-monetary economic system permits. His level of production *per capita* is stagnant at the point where he is producing as much of what he knows how to produce as he can

[1] The number of people who, whilst not being dependent on money for the essentials of living, nevertheless have some money income for expenditure on non-essentials, is of course very much larger. The actual number would be a guess, but it would certainly include 80 per cent of the adult population.

consume with satisfaction, and within a closed subsistence system there is little more that he could expect to do.

In this situation, economic growth, with an increase in the level of consumption and standard of living, is only possible by introducing new goods and services into the consumption pattern. This in turn requires either the diversification of subsistence production to include the new items (a possibility of very limited scope under normal conditions), or access to the products of the outside world through the medium of trade and exchange. This means that, generally speaking, the spare resources of the subsistence sector cannot readily be used for raising the standard of living or for sustaining economic growth, without participation in the monetized sector of the wider economy.

For this reason the expansion of the monetary sector is of vital importance. Even in 1965, by far the greater part of the resources of land and manpower in Papua-New Guinea is retained in the subsistence sector; but significant growth is only possible in the monetary sector: so that the expansion of the exchange economy into and throughout the subsistence sector is a necessary precursor to the economic development of the country.

The potential of the subsistence sector. As some succeeding sections of this chapter show, certain essential resources for economic development are exceedingly scarce in Papua-New Guinea and economic development at an acceptable rate will only be possible if these resources can be heavily augmented from overseas by external aid. This is true in particular of financial resources, capital goods, and skilled manpower. On the other hand, substantial resources of land and labour are available within the economy itself, mainly in the subsistence sector.

These resources are already very substantial, and can be greatly augmented by relatively simple means (Fisk 1962). The potential for development concealed in the subsistence sector is therefore very considerable indeed. In the immediate future, it is probably by far the greatest source from which the Territories themselves can contribute to their own development. The need is for this potential to be released and made available for capital formation, export production, the provision of additional services, and other productive uses. This requires not only the expansion of the exchange economy along the lines already discussed but also in many cases an actual call upon the resources of the monetary sector for some essential element to augment the land and labour supplied. This will be discussed in more detail in a later section of this chapter.

In Papua-New Guinea, therefore, the resources of the advanced monetary sector, scarce as they are, have a dual role to perform. They are required for the operation and expansion of the primary, secondary, and tertiary industries of the advanced sector itself, where indeed they provide the greater part of the inputs necessary for production. They are also, however, required to perform the equally important role of releasing the great development potential of the subsistence sector and making it available for increasing production. In this latter, often almost catalytic, role the monetary resources of the advanced sector may be expected to bring greater returns in overall development than in any role within the advanced sector itself.

THE PREDOMINANCE OF AGRICULTURE

The economy of Papua-New Guinea is very heavily based on primary production, in which mining and quarrying now plays a relatively small part. A very rough indication of the degree of dependence on primary production can be obtained from the latest national income estimates (Territories 1964a) for the year ended 30 June 1963. These indicate cash primary production income at £12,960,000 and subsistence sector income at £83,343,000. In addition, wages, salaries and supplements amounting to £36,456,000 include a substantial proportion derived directly from primary production enterprises. Only a rough estimate of the proportion of this latter can be attempted on the data readily available, but the figures would appear to be roughly as follows:[2]

Non-indigenous wages and salaries from primary production, year ended 30 June 1963	£2,600,000
Indigenous wages and salaries from primary production, year ended 30 June 1963	£6,500,000
Total	£9,100,000

Adding together primary production income, subsistence income, and wages and salaries gives a total of roughly £105,400,000 of an estimated gross Territory product of £146,965,000, or 71 per cent, derived directly from primary production.

In terms of the numbers of people employed, primary production is even more predominant. The estimated labour force of the monetary sector in 1963 was 96,661, comprising 81,468 indigenous and 15,193 non-indigenous. Of these, 39,053 indigenous and 1,256 non-indigenous, or a total of 40,309, were engaged in primary industry. The estimated labour force of the subsistence sector, which may be taken to be solely engaged in primary industry, was 543,511.

[2] Classification of wages and salaries by Industry is available only for incomes given in assessments issued under the Income Tax Ordinance (Territories 1964a: Table 1.4). In Papua and New Guinea this is almost synonymous with non-indigenous wages and salaries. Indigenous wages and salaries from primary production have been estimated by applying the proportion of the total indigenous labour force engaged in primary production (Territories 1964a: Table 1.13) to the total Indigenous Wages, Salaries and Supplements (Territories 1964b: Table 1.17).

Accordingly a total of 583,820 out of an estimated total labour force
of 624,979, or 93 per cent, were engaged in primary production
(figures from Territories 1964a: Table 3.1).

In the monetary sector of the economy, this emphasis on primary
production is less pronounced, but it is still significant. In terms
of gross Territory product, £22,060,000 of the total estimated for the
monetary sector £63,622,000, or 35 per cent, derives directly from
primary production. In terms of employment, 42 per cent of the
labour force earning wages or salaries are employed in agricultural
enterprise, in addition to which there is a large but undetermined
number of indigenous people earning cash incomes from the sale
of crops grown on smallholdings. The actual numbers can be
nothing more than an informed guess, but the Minister of Territories, with the advantage of the full resources of information of the
Administration to assist him, estimated in 1962 that about 250,000
indigenous smallholders were obtaining a cash income in this way
(Hasluck 1962b:10). If this estimate is even approximately correct, it
is clear that of the 300,000 to 350,000 indigenous people of Papua-
New Guinea who earn a money income, only between 10 per cent
and 14 per cent do so in industries other than agriculture.

Finally agriculture and forestry are the source of virtually the
whole of the country's export earnings. Some details of exports are
given in Table 3.3 and are discussed in a subsequent section, but
it is clear that apart from foreign aid, and in the absence of some
as yet undiscovered bonanza such as very large resources of
mineral oil for export, Papua-New Guinea will be dependent
mainly on agriculture and forestry for its overseas earnings for many
decades to come.

Papua-New Guinea must therefore be considered as a primary
producing country, not only in the present and in the immediate
future, but probably for a considerable time. As development
progresses the share of the gross national product contributed by
secondary and tertiary industries will increase, but this development is starting from a very small base, and there is as yet nothing
to suggest that agriculture and related primary industries will be
supplanted as the main source of the national product in the foreseeable future.

THE PUBLIC SECTOR

Within the monetary sector of the economy the part played by
public authorities in Papua-New Guinea is very large indeed. For
the year ended 30 June 1963 gross current and capital expenditure
by all public authorities was estimated at £35,171,951 (Territories
1963a: fol. 81). For the same period, gross Territory expenditure
for the monetary sector as a whole was estimated at £81,521,284,
of which £7,999,315 comprised non-marketed production consumed
by salary- and wage-earners and their families, leaving the actual

Picking coffee in Luluai Ninji's garden at Mount Hagen

Cash cropping in the Boana area. Right of the houses a small indigenous coffee holding

Kukukuku children at the Australian Lutheran Mission primary school, Menyama, in 1961

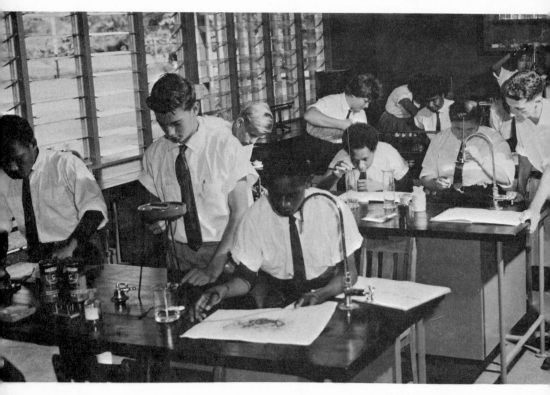

A science class at the Rabaul High School

monetary expenditure at £73,521,929 (Territories 1964a:Appendix, Table II). Therefore, very nearly half of the total monetary expenditure in Papua-New Guinea was derived directly from public authorities. Moreover, during recent years there is evidence that this proportion has been increasing.

Another significant feature of the public sector is its heavy dependence on external aid, which to the time of writing (1965) has come almost entirely from the Australian government. In the year ended 30 June 1963 nearly 71 per cent of the gross current and capital expenditure by public authorities was financed by the Commonwealth government of Australia. Actual figures are given in Table 2.1.

The I.B.R.D. (1965) report envisages a very substantial increase in public expenditure over the next five years, and if its programme is followed this will increase both the relative importance of the public sector and its degree of dependence on external, and particularly Australian, financial contributions. Unfortunately the figures quoted in the I.B.R.D. report and programme are not directly comparable with those given above as they refer to the budget of the Administration only and exclude, for example, the very substantial direct expenditure by Commonwealth government departments and instrumentalities in Papua-New Guinea. However, the programme envisages an increase in annual Administration expenditure from an average of £22,900,000 for the five-year period ending 30 June 1963 to an average of £50,200,000 for the five-year period ending 30 June 1969, involving a decrease in the proportion financed from internal revenue from an average of 31·7 per cent to an average of 27·5 per cent (I.B.R.D. 1965:56).

In the economic life of Papua-New Guinea the importance of the public sector, and the degree of dependence on external finance, is greater even than these figures would indicate. With public expenditure contributing approximately 50 per cent of the total monetary expenditure in the Territories, a very substantial proportion of private income is derived indirectly from that expenditure. This is particularly so in the secondary and tertiary industries. Moreover, a large portion of government internal revenue, whether in the form of direct taxation, indirect taxation, or the sale of services such as electricity and water, derives directly from government expenditure, and in particular from the salaries paid to officers of government and its instrumentalities.

The implications of this are of the utmost importance to the understanding of the economic structure of the Territories. The actual degree of dependence on financial contributions from the Australian government is surprisingly great. For example, taking the figures for the year ended 30 June 1963 from Table 2.1 below, elimination of the Australian government contribution of £24,890,000

TABLE 2.1   Territory of Papua and New Guinea

Contribution of Public Authorities to Gross Monetary Expenditure
Year ended 30 June 1963

Gross Monetary Expenditure		£73,522,000
Australian Aid		
Commonwealth grant	£20,000,000	
Commonwealth departments, etc.	£4,890,000	
TOTAL	£24,890,000	
Internal Revenue		
Taxation	£5,843,000	
Earnings of departments	£3,181,000	
TOTAL	£9,024,000	
Other Sources of Expenditure, mainly internal		
Loan fund	£898,000	
Local Government Councils	£345,000	
Cash and investment	£13,000	
TOTAL	£1,256,000	
Public Authorities		
Gross current and capital expenditure		£35,170,000

would not merely have reduced public expenditure in the Territories by that amount; it would also have eliminated a large proportion of the internal revenue and other sources of finance, so that total public expenditure might well have had to be reduced from £35,000,000 to about £5,000,000, even assuming, as is most unlikely, that primary production incomes were not affected by the reduction of government activities and services. This in turn would have reduced gross monetary expenditure by considerably more than the £30,000,000 decrease in public expenditure, with the result that the national income in the monetary sector of the Territories (in which sector alone, as we have seen, significant economic growth is possible) would have been reduced to a small fraction of its actual level. This means not only that all significant economic growth, but even the maintenance of significant economic activity in the advanced monetary sector, is still, and will remain for many years, dependent on the continuation of substantial financial assistance from the Australian or some other external government.

Public investment and the infrastructure. Apart from the sheer magnitude of public financial transactions in relation to the total transactions of the monetary sector, the public sector is important

TABLE 2.2 Territory of Papua and New Guinea
Gross Expenditure by all Public Authorities
Year ended 30 June 1963
(£'000)

	Current Expenditure	Capital Expenditure	Total
Monetary Sector			
General services	8,793	566	9,359
Development and conservation of natural resources	3,327	1,645	4,972
Transport and communication	3,822	2,610	6,432
Other services (especially housing)	534	2,165	2,699
Social services (mainly education and health)	6,745	1,773	8,518
Public debt	126		126
Public works (not elsewhere included)	277	1,728	2,005
Miscellaneous	724	336	1,060
Total Monetary Expenditure	24,348	10,823	35,171
Subsistence Sector			
Non-monetary community investment, replacement, and maintenance	10,100*	4,500*	14,600

Source: Monetary Sector, Territories 1963b: fols. 77, 79, 81, Subsistence Sector, Territories 1964a: Table 3.9A.

*This is an estimate of the labour contributed without payment by the indigenous rural population in the construction, maintenance, and replacement of village or tribal community works, district roads, rest-houses, airfields etc., and council works, valued at the 1963 general rate for casual labour of 6s. a day. There is no means of determining how much of this contribution was of the nature of an addition to capital (as e.g. new road and track construction) and how much was replacement and maintenance. For purposes of illustration, however, the total has been divided between current and capital expenditure in the same proportion as the monetary expenditure of public authorities.

for the type and quality of its contribution to the economic structure. This is not the place for a detailed analysis of the activities of public authorities in the economic sphere, but some mention must be made of the special role of the public sector in providing the infrastructure necessary for economic activity and growth. The size and the vital nature of this contribution must be appreciated if the importance of maintaining and expanding the level of public expenditure is to be understood.

The public sector contributes to the infrastructure of the economy in several ways. Firstly, it invests directly in roads, port facilities, aerodromes, water supplies, power, and other services necessary to the economic activity of the country. Secondly, it invests in the provision of services that contribute to the facility with which economic activity can take place; these range from the basic service of maintaining law and order to the provision of education, the maintenance of public health, and agricultural extension services. Thirdly, it makes investment in buildings, plant, stores, and equipment necessary to enable such services to be provided. Fourthly, it undertakes the maintenance of this investment so that the facilities provided continue to be available over time. Fifthly, it channels some of the non-monetary resources of the subsistence sector so as to make a substantial contribution to the infrastructure, as when it helps villagers to construct a road or schools with their own labour. Some idea of the magnitude and direction of this contribution from the public sector is given by Table 2.2.

EXTERNAL TRADE AND THE BALANCE OF PAYMENTS

The external transactions of Papua-New Guinea indicate a number of interesting and important features of the economy. To examine these, the overall position of the balance of payments will first be considered, and then the composition of the import and export elements will be analysed.

The balance of payments. There is a most useful table in the Statistical Appendix to the World Bank Report (I.B.R.D. 1965:437) which summarizes the main items in the balance of payments on current account for six selected years. The figures for three of these years are given in Table 2.3.

The first point to be noted in this table is the very heavy dependence on Transfers. Less than half of the credits in the balance of payments accounts are derived from earnings of the Territories. Moreover, in recent years the proportion of total credits derived from earnings has declined, from 49 per cent in 1956-7, to 43 per cent in 1960-1, to 39 per cent in 1962-3. Although earnings have increased during the period, and may be expected to continue to increase, the assistance given by the Australian government has increased even more rapidly, as indeed has the much smaller, but still considerable, assistance given through mission finance.

TABLE 2.3   Territory of Papua and New Guinea
Balance of Payments—Current Account,
Selected Years
(£'000)

	1956–7	1960–1	1962–3
Credits			
Goods and Services			
Exports (Territory produce f.o.b.)	11,810	14,257	16,359
Copra Fund interest	91	144	153
Transfers			
Mission finance	496	560	963
Commonwealth grant	9,645	14,797	20,000
Net direct Commonwealth expenditure	2,078	3,922	4,759
Total credits	24,120	33,680	42,234
Debits			
Goods and Services			
Imports (f.o.b.)	18,487	24,236	25,800
Net freight and insurance	1,482	3,086	3,011
Net foreign travel	1,255	2,055	2,069
External cost of management and insurance	410	720	807
Other services (net)	1,410	1,875	2,572
Interest and dividends paid abroad	750	2,434	3,192
Total debits	23,794	34,406	37,451
Balance on current account	326	−726	4,783
	24,120	33,680	42,234

Source: I.B.R.D. 1965: Statistical Appendix, Table S.10.

This is another aspect of the dependence of the economy on outside financial assistance. In the previous section the level of economic activity in the advanced sector of the economy was shown to be determined to a very great extent by the level of Australian aid to the Territories. Here it is apparent that the ability of the Territories to obtain the goods and services they require from the outside world is similarly dependent. These two aspects are, as it were, the two faces of the same coin, and the prospects of such dependence being removed or substantially reduced in the near future are as remote in the field of external transactions as they are in the field of public finance or internal economic activity, and for the same reasons.

Table 2.3 also shows that, on the Debits side, imports (f.o.b.) represent only about 70 per cent of the Territories' requirements for overseas funds. Apart from freight and insurance, it is notable that foreign travel, interest and dividends paid abroad, other services, and external cost of management and insurance are all important and growing items in the balance of payments account. This is a feature of another type of dependence—dependence on expatriate skills and entrepreneurship to operate the advanced sector of the economy—which will be discussed further below.

Exports. For its earnings in the outside world the economy of the Territories depends, as we have seen, almost entirely on the export of primary produce. Papua and New Guinea export very little in the way of services as distinct from goods to the outside world. There is some tourism, a certain amount of re-export trade, and some servicing of transient ships and aircraft, but these as yet are small items, as Table 2.4 indicates.

TABLE 2.4   Territory of Papua and New Guinea
Value of Exports by Major Commodities
Year ending 30 June (£'000)

Commodities	1957	%*	1961	%*	1964	%*
Copra and copra products	7,090	60·0	7,758	54·5	7,133	38·7
Rubber	1,149	9·7	1,292	9·1	1,226	6·7
Cocoa	462	3·9	1,666	11·7	3,421	18·6
Coffee	183	1·5	1,106	7·8	2,681	14·6
Peanuts	48	0·4	280	2·0	272	1·5
Crocodile skins	64	0·5	128	0·9	451	2·7
Timber products	1,178	10·0	1,174	8·2	1,775	9·7
Gold	1,231	10·4	681	4·8	660	3·6
Other	405	3·4	171	1·2	798†	4·3
Total Territory produce	11,810		14,257		18,417	
Re-exports	1,268		2,349		2,083‡	
Total Exports	13,078		16,606		20,500	

Source: For years 1957 and 1961, Territories 1963a: Table No. 31B; for year 1964, T.P.N.G. 1964f: Table 7.

*As percentage of Total Territory Produce exported.

†Includes whole coconuts, passionfruit products, gums and resins, cutch, marine shell, and other items.

‡Figures not given in source quoted, but obtained from the Economic and Statistical Section, Department of Territories.

However, Table 2.4 illustrates also several other important features. Exports of Territory produce have grown substantially during the seven-year period covered by the table. What is more, the pattern of exports has become more diversified. Whilst the value of copra and copra products exported remained roughly constant over the three years cited, its importance, measured as a percentage of total exports of Territory produce, declined from 60·0 per cent to 38·7 per cent over the period. Similarly rubber, with total exports approximately the same in each of the three years, declined from 9·7 per cent to 6·7 per cent of the total. Gold (and gold alone) declined both in total value and in relative importance. The growth in the total value of exports has come mainly from the rapid expansion of cocoa and coffee, which between them were responsible for 33·2 per cent of the total in 1964, as compared with a mere 5·4 per cent in 1957. Peanuts, crocodile skins, and timber products have also contributed significantly, though on a smaller scale, to the increase in export values.

The prospects for further expansion of these exports, together with the new crops tea and pyrethrum, will be discussed in detail by Dr Shand in Chapter 4. It is sufficient here to indicate the pattern, which is one of steadily expanding exports, almost exclusively based on agriculture and forestry, but becoming increasingly diversified within that limitation. Moreover, there is little to indicate that this pattern is likely to change substantially within the next ten years or so. Expansion and diversification is likely to continue, as Dr Shand shows, but mainly within the field of agricultural and forest products.

Imports. An important feature of the economy is the characteristic division of the primary produce of the Territories into two broad classes: produce for export and produce for local consumption. Generally speaking, produce for local consumption, with the exception of quite small quantities of truck crops, fish and betel nut, etc., is not exchanged for money. Estimates made by the Department of Agriculture, Stock and Fisheries suggest that only about 54,000 tons of cultivated subsistence foods were sold for cash in 1961-2, out of a total production of about 2,900,000 tons, or less than 2 per cent (T.P.N.G. 1963e). As a corollary to this, a very large proportion of the supplies to the monetary sector is imported, and there is a very strong tendency for imports to grow as the monetary sector expands. This is illustrated in Table 2.5.

This table reveals a number of interesting characteristics. First is the remarkable rate of growth of the total value of imports during the seven-year period, an increase of 80 per cent. Secondly, there is the fact that the growth of imports has very nearly kept pace with the increase in gross Territory money income. Unfortunately, national income estimates for 1964 are not yet available, and the estimates for the year 1957 are not strictly comparable with those for 1961-3, but the general order of increase in gross Territory money income from 1957 to 1963 seems also to be of the order of 80 per cent. This is substantially more than the rate of growth of the total Territory product, which includes the very large, and

TABLE 2.5   Territory of Papua and New Guinea
Value of Imports—Selected Commodity Groups
(£'000)

Commodities	1957	%	1961	%	1964	%
Food, drink, tobacco	5,923	31·5	7,480	28·3	9,557	27·2
Clothing, textiles, footwear	1,588	8·1	2,565	9·7	3,244	9·2
Drugs, chemicals	1,393	7·1	1,646	6·2	2,248	6·4
Transport equipment	1,408	7·2	2,300	8·7	2,849	8·1
Petroleum products	1,053	5·4	1,242	4·6	1,600	4·5
Metals, metal manufactures and machinery	4,749	24·3	6,461	24·4	8,290	23·5
Total Imports	19,580		26,464		35,227	
Gross Territory product— monetary sector	28,900		41,900		52,500*	

Source: Territories 1963a: Table 38; T.P.N.G. 1964f: Table 6; Territories 1964a:
Appendix, Table I (part I), excluding 'Non-marketed Production'; White 1964:
Table 9.3.
   *1963.

relatively stagnant, subsistence sector, but it confirms that imports,
quite naturally, are influenced by the expansion of money incomes
only, and not by total incomes.

Thirdly, the table shows a remarkable consistency in the proportion of total imports made up by each class of commodity. This
is particularly significant in the context of great change and expansion in the monetary sector of the economy during these seven
years. The proportion made up by food, drink, and tobacco has
declined a little, and examination of the figures for earlier and
intervening years suggests that there is, in fact, a definite though
gradual trend in this direction. On the other hand, figures for 'Other
manufactured goods' and 'Miscellaneous' (excluded from Table 2.5
as figures for 1964 are not available) show a slight tendency to
increase, from 17 per cent in 1957 to 18½ per cent in 1962, suggesting some minor diversification of the import pattern. Generally
speaking, however, the pattern has remained remarkably constant.

Within this pattern there is another concealed pattern that helps
to explain the import characteristics of the economy. Imports can
be divided roughly into goods for personal consumption and goods
for production and business purposes. Consumption goods can
again be roughly divided into those mainly consumed by the
indigenous people and those mainly consumed by expatriates.
Canned fish and rice, for example, which are imported in large
quantities, are mainly consumed by indigenes, whereas fresh meat,
dairy produce, fruit and vegetable imports are mainly consumed by
expatriates. The percentage of imports falling under each of the
above three categories for 1963 and 1964 are given in Table 2.6.

TABLE 2.6   Territory of Papua and New Guinea
Classification of Imported Goods by End Use*
(Nine months ended March 1963 and March 1964)

Type of Use	Total Imports
	per cent
Indigenous consumption goods	21
Expatriate consumption goods	26
Production and business	53

*At the time of writing, the latest detailed trade statistics available were for the nine months ended March 1964 (T.P.N.G. 1964e). From these the values of all the important commodities imported during the nine months ended March 1963 and March 1964 were recorded under the heads 'Indigenous Consumption', 'Expatriate Consumption', and 'Production and Business', as appropriate, making an *ad hoc* division between headings in cases where more than one heading was involved (as for example textiles and flour, which are consumed in considerable quantity both by indigenes and expatriates). The figures for the two years were identical.

No pretence can be made that the results given in Table 2.6 are accurate, but they are sufficient, perhaps, to indicate the rough order of importance of the three categories in the import pattern of the Territories. They are, in any case, adequate to illustrate the manner in which expansion of the monetary sector, and hence the opportunity for further growth, is dependent on the expansion of exports; they also indicate certain fields in which that dependence might be reduced.

Indigenous consumption goods are the main incentive for the indigenous population to take part in the monetary economy, and they therefore play a vital role in the expansion of the monetary sector. As most of the indigenous people obtain their requirements of traditional food and other consumption goods without the use of money, incentive goods must be of a different kind. The present pattern is thus that they spend their cash incomes very largely on imported goods that are either luxuries or improvements on their traditional counterpart. For example, storable high value grain foods, storable protein foods, refined sugar, processed tobacco, textiles, made clothing and footwear are important incentive goods to the indigenous population and only available in quantity through the monetary sector of the economy. Until and unless these can be produced locally in the Territories, increasing imports of such goods will be a *sine qua non* for economic development.

Expatriate consumption goods are in general the goods necessary to maintain the high standard of living demanded by the expatriate population as a condition of their remaining in the Territory. In general, the indigenous population is as yet inadequately equipped with the entrepreneurial, administrative, and technical skills necessary to operate and expand the advanced sector of the economy. Until this can be remedied, economic growth is dependent on the attraction of increasing numbers of expatriates to live in the Territories, and in the absence of any system of compelling such services, the supply of such high, even luxury, quality goods will have to increase rather than decrease.

Import replacement. Granted that an increase in the supply of indigenous and expatriate consumption goods is essential, it does not necessarily follow that the imports of these commodities must increase in proportion indefinitely. With an expanding market there are fortunately a number of fields in which import replacement by local production does seem perfectly possible and reasonable. For example, in the year ended June 1963 the Territories imported 156,000 cwt of refined sugar, valued at £507,000 (Territories 1963c). Sugarcane is indigenous to the Territories, and when consumption reaches a figure sufficient to make a local mill an economical proposition, large-scale production may be practicable. Fresh meat, dairy produce, storable grains, amongst many others, are also possible fields for large-scale import replacement.

COMMERCE AND INDUSTRY

Commerce and industry play a large, but subsidiary, part in the monetary sector of the economy. White (1964:Table 8.1), in his valuable study of the social accounts of the Territories, estimates the total income produced in 1960-1 by what he calls 'Commercial Enterprises' to have been £13,569,000 made up as follows:

European labour income	£6,578,000
Native wages and keep	851,000
European surplus	6,140,000
Total	£13,569,000

However, in his definition of 'Commercial Enterprises' White has excluded that part of secondary industry mainly engaged in the processing of primary products for export. Such processing comprises an important part of the secondary industry of the Territories, and if the income generated in the processing of copra, coconut oil, coffee, cocoa, rubber, and timber for export were added, it is clear that industrial, commercial, and transport enterprises form a very substantial part indeed of the activity of the advanced sector of the economy.

Nevertheless it is equally clear that these industries, and their development, play a subsidiary role to the two main sectors of the economy, primary industry and the public sector. The commercial and industrial sector provides many of the services necessary for the primary sector to operate. It distributes the goods and services demanded by the employees of the primary and government sectors in exchange for the money they earn. It adds value to the agricultural and forest products exported from the Territories, and in recent years has to an increasing extent added value, through processing and partial manufacture, to goods imported for consumption in the Territories. However, apart from processing locally-produced primary products, there is virtually no development of manufacture for export and there seems to be little prospect for such development in the foreseeable future. There is no indication of the juxtaposition of rich mineral resources and cheap power necessary to provide the Territories with a comparative advantage over other countries for the development of heavy industry, and skilled labour is, and will remain for a considerable time, a very scarce and therefore expensive factor.

Imported skills. The commercial and industrial sector has been, to date, even more dependent on imported skills and imported capital than the other two major sectors of the economy. The figures given at the beginning of this section show this very clearly. Of the £13,569,000 estimated by White as the total income produced by commercial enterprises, only 6 per cent accrued to indigenous participants, and the whole of that was in the form of wages and keep.

This dependence on imported skills and capital will decline as indigenous participation in the monetary economy increases and as the supply of indigenous people with higher secondary and even tertiary education increases. However, the rate of decline may be expected to be very slight for a considerable time. Although it is in a sense a subsidiary sector, commerce and industry must expand at least in proportion to the expansion of the other sectors of the economy. Its failure to do so would soon place an effective check on the development of other sectors. For example, the development of a substantial cattle industry in the Territories, as recommended by the World Bank Mission, is entirely dependent on the provision of adequate facilities for the slaughter, preservation, distribution and marketing of the meat and other products produced. Government development programmes depend upon commercial enterprise to provide and distribute the goods and services necessary to make living conditions acceptable for its skilled staff and to undertake a great deal of the building and construction associated with such programmes. Over the next ten years or so the commercial and industrial sector of the economy must expand at a rapid rate and its demand for capital and skill will increase greatly.

On the other hand the supply of indigenous capital and skills, though they should increase substantially, may be expected to be attracted more in the first instance to the primary and public sectors of the economy than to the commercial and industrial sectors.

Indigenous savings, in particular, may be expected to show a preference for primary industry, in the form of new plantings of cash crops and the opening of new land, as the channel of investment in which they have the greatest understanding. Exceptions will be in the form of ancillary industries and services, such as road transport serving agricultural areas as has already been noted in the Gazelle Peninsula (Epstein 1964), and co-operative, small to medium processing plants. There will also be a gradual but steady increase in small-scale, indigenous retail enterprises. However, there seems little doubt that for the next ten years at least the bulk of new investment in commerce and ·industry, and in particular in the larger-scale units, will be dependent on non-indigenous sources of finance.

Indigenous skills, in the form of men and women with higher secondary and tertiary education, may on the other hand be expected to be attracted strongly towards the public sector. This is a common, and very natural, tendency in most countries moving towards political independence. The needs of the public services are very great, and the opportunities for secure tenure and for advancement are correspondingly attractive. In addition, the public service offers status and authority of a kind that is particularly attractive to the indigenous people of a nation working towards political independence. For this reason, so long as the supply of skilled indigenous people remains short of demand, indigenous participation in the more senior ranks of commerce and industry may be expected to grow more slowly than the rate of growth of the sector as a whole.

Therefore, if the expansion of the commercial and industrial sector is to be maintained at the rate necessary to service a growing economy, it is clear that a considerable expansion of non-indigenous capital and skills invested in this vital sector will be required over the next decade or so. Without such expansion a serious check to the development of the economy as a whole will rapidly develop.

INVESTMENT

Some aspects of the pattern of investment in the Territories have been touched on in previous sections. Some comment on investment itself is necessary, however, to bring together some important features of the overall investment pattern and to indicate their significance for the future development of the economy.

In the modern world we tend to think of investment in terms of money capital used to procure an increase in the production of goods and services. It may be applied in many forms, as in the construction of new roads and airports, the purchase of tractors or motor vehicles, the construction of hydro-electric schemes or irrigation works, the building of shops, offices, factories, or houses, or the purchase of stocks for trading. Investment need not necessarily involve a money transaction, however, and in an economy with a very large and relatively affluent subsistence sector, non-monetary investment can be a very important factor in development. This is the case in Papua-New Guinea, and in this analysis the distinction between monetary and non-monetary investment will be useful and revealing.

We have seen that the estimated population of the subsistence sector of Papua-New Guinea in 1963 was one and three-quarter million, out of a total population of a little over two million. Whilst many subsistence producers have some money income from the sale of cash crops, etc., the amounts are relatively small and often irregular. There is also thought to be considerable hoarding of coin and notes within the sector, and there have been instances in which surprisingly large sums have been raised quickly by groups of village people for investment in occasional projects that have captured their interest and imagination. Nonetheless, in relation to its population, the investible monetary resources of the subsistence sector are small. With the spread of cash cropping and participation in the monetary economy these resources will increase, but in terms of the needs of the economy as a whole it will be a considerable time before monetary investment from this sector can be expected to play a significant part in the economic growth of the country.

Non-monetary investment. On the other hand, the investible non-monetary resources of the subsistence sector are very large. These resources comprise surplus labour and, to a lesser extent, surplus land, over and above that required for normal subsistence production. The labour is available at low opportunity cost, in most cases at the cost of sacrificing some of the already quite abundant leisure, and in many areas there are still quite substantial resources of land available at the cost of the labour necessary to open it up and bring it into production. Moreover, this surplus both of labour and land can be, and at times is, substantially increased by the introduction of improved techniques and tools. This process has been discussed in detail elsewhere (Salisbury 1962; Fisk 1962, 1964).

In this way, the subsistence sector contains a very substantial and important investment potential. It is, in fact, potentially the greatest domestic source of development capital immediately available in the Territories. Some of this potential is already applied to investment, both private, as in opening up and planting new land or replanting old crops, or building canoes, fish traps, etc., or on community or public works, such as village tracks and improvements, district roads, rest-houses, airfields, and council works such as school buildings, clinics.

The size of this potential is undoubtedly very great at the present time but difficult to quantify in meaningful terms. In the *National Income Estimates for 1960-63* (Territories 1964a) an attempt has been made to calculate the rough order of magnitude of this component of the national income. The figures include work on maintenance and replacement of existing assets, as it was impossible to

distinguish labour contributed for this from labour contributed for
the construction of new works. Rough as they are, the figures
suggest that in 1962/3 non-monetary community investment, replacement and maintenance was of the order of £14,600,000 whilst
non-monetary private investment, replacement and maintenance
was about £4,230,000, making a total of nearly £19,000,000 altogether. Large though this figure may be, it is quite certainly only a
relatively small proportion of the total investment potential available
in the subsistence sector if the conditions for its utilization could be
fully met.

There is not space to discuss in detail what the conditions for full
utilization of this potential are. It must suffice to indicate that the
main ingredients are adequate incentive, technical guidance, and
usually some leavening component from the monetary sector (e.g.
cement, nails, tools, seed). It is also important to note that very
often the effective utilization of non-monetary investment depends
on its effective combination with substantial elements of monetary
public investment, as when indigenous labour is augmented by
road-building machinery and materials, and that the two are best
regarded as complementary rather than as possible alternatives.

Monetary investment. Details of monetary investment are also
difficult to obtain. The national income estimates give details of
gross domestic capital formation (Territories 1964a:223) but, following Australian income tax practice, a great deal of private investment in primary industry is treated as current expenditure. For our
purposes, therefore, the figures there given understate the total of
private capital formation, possibly by some £300,000 to £400,000.
Bearing this in mind, the figures given for 1963 are as follows:

Gross Domestic Capital Formation (Monetary Sector)

1. Private	£6,089,690
2. Missions	295,189
3. Public authorities	
Administration	8,272,926
Native Local Government Councils	217,446
Commonwealth departments and instru- mentalities	2,015,000
4. Increase in value of stocks	76,136
Total	£16,966,387

On this basis, the rough order of contribution to gross capital
formation in the monetary sector is Public authorities 62 per cent,
Missions 2 per cent, Private 36 per cent.

The source of finance for this capital formation is clear for the
public sector. This investment derives in the main from the Australian government, either through its grant to the Territory

Administration or through direct expenditure of Commonwealth government departments. Mission capital formation is also dependent to a considerable extent on external finance, as is evidenced by Table 2.3 which showed mission finance in the balance of payments as a net credit transfer of some £963,000 in 1963.

However, the source of capital formation in the private sector is less clear. There are indications that there has in fact been a substantial net outflow of private capital during recent years. White's estimates suggest a net outflow of around £4,000,000 a year over the three-year period ended June 1961, although these figures, being residuals, are unavoidably imprecise. It is certain that there has been some inflow of new private capital from Australia and overseas, countering the gross outflow from Territory profits, but it is virtually impossible to trace these movements. What does seem clear is that private enterprise in the Territories has in general been highly profitable during recent years and that a large part of gross private investment represents the re-investment of part of these profits, the balance having been repatriated to Australia.

The future trend of investment and capital formation in the Territory will depend on a number of things. First, the size of the Commonwealth grant, which will not only determine the trend of public investment to a large extent but will also influence the size of private investment by determining the general level of economic activity in the economy as a whole. Second, the confidence of the individual expatriate in his future in the country, whether as investor, entrepreneur, or employee, will greatly influence the investment climate in the private sector. Third, external factors, such as commodity prices on world markets, will affect the profitability of most investments in the Territories and their attraction to private capital whether from within or without the Territories.

Many of these factors can be influenced by government intervention at various levels. Two aspects of government intervention in particular require careful investigation in the immediate future. One is the role of government in facilitating the supply of credit to the private sector, which involves not only assistance in the form of finance as recommended in the I.B.R.D. report, but also institutional changes to facilitate the operation of such credit (e.g. in the form of land titles). The other is the role of government in fostering the confidence of the foreign investor, whether by some form of investment insurance, or by guarantees of different natures, or by tax and other concessions that raise the profit and thus the degree of risk acceptable in such investments.

An Assessment of Natural Resources

H. C. BROOKFIELD

THE NATURE OF 'RESOURCES'

THE INHABITANTS of a montane valley in the centre of New Guinea, viewing their productive resources in the third quarter of the twentieth century, might and sometimes do evaluate them in such terms as these: 'Our land is too cold for coffee; our mountains are steep and good roads cannot be built over them; our rivers lack gold and are barren; our forests have all been cleared and we have no timber; we have no means of making money.' Yet this valley has fertile soils, a healthy climate without frosts, droughts, or great heat, and it supports population densities far higher than those found in other parts of New Guinea. No one goes hungry, and in former times a skilful agriculture made possible the production of a surplus of food for ceremonial payments and feasts, and of pigs which could be traded for stone axe blades, shells, plumes, and fur ornaments, which were highly prized as wealth. Had previous generations made, or been able to make, a comparison of their productive resources with those of other parts of the country, they might have rated themselves wealthy indeed.

Both views are true, and their contradiction illustrates the difficulty facing any attempt to catalogue and assess the natural resources of a country. Inevitably we find ourselves speaking of 'rich' and 'poor' areas, of 'abundance' and 'scarcity' of resources. These are value-loaded terms, which we use in relation to a particular level of technology and understanding of resource-use, to particular types of production aimed at yielding a particular standard of living. In a territory such as New Guinea, with so wide a gap between the primitive way of life and the far higher living standards which are the conscious or unconscious aim of all, this problem of evaluation becomes particularly acute. Thus we shall find that there is little land in New Guinea suitable for large-scale mechanized production using massive machinery, while on the other hand there are very large resources indeed of timber and of potential power.

But the power resources are almost wholly unused and only a fraction of them can be employed in the foreseeable future; it is difficult to market the timber, and in looking at land we must observe the successful use made of much land that would be quite useless by the techniques employed in Australia. To view resources in their whole context we must take account of social structure, of the values held by the people, of the world market for particular crops, and of the factors limiting New Guinea's access to that market, including the innumerable links of commerce, investment, and legislation that bind the economy of New Guinea to that of Australia. Such a view would take us far beyond the scope of this essay, but it provides a context that must be borne in mind throughout.

Viewing the resources of New Guinea in the 1960s, then, we must take account of a few simple considerations. The overwhelming majority of the population depends on the land—perhaps 95 per cent of the people. The internal market for industrial produce is limited, and most of this market is, for a variety of reasons, more readily and cheaply supplied from overseas than it could be by local producers. There is a wealth of agricultural, handicraft, and collecting skills available in the country, but a poverty in technical skills suitable for use in the machine age. Consequently, even though by any international comparison the land resources of the country are not rich, it is the land that is New Guinea's most important resource. Indeed, nearly all comprehensive resource assessment that has been carried out has focused overwhelmingly on the land, and this essay will be no exception.

Among existing assessments, which include one outdated and now best-forgotten survey by the present writer (Brookfield 1958), the most important are those produced for specific areas within the country by survey teams of the Division of Land Research and Regional Survey of the Commonwealth Scientific and Industrial Research Organization (CSIRO).* Some more local assessments have been made by soil scientists, and by other individuals and groups, but the CSIRO surveys are by far the most important source of information, both on fact and method. It is, then, with a review of the CSIRO surveys that we must begin.

THE CSIRO SURVEYS

The first CSIRO survey in Papua-New Guinea was carried out in the Buna-Kokoda area of the Northern District of Papua in 1953. Since then survey teams have visited the Territory in most years,

* Grateful acknowledgment is made to the Division of Land Research and Regional Survey, Commonwealth Scientific and Industrial Research Organization, Canberra, for permission to study and draw on unpublished material, and for comment on the text of this chapter. Particular acknowledgment is made to G. A. Stewart, Chief of Division, and to H. A. Haantjens. However, responsibility for all statements made in this essay, including interpretations made from CSIRO material, remains my own.

and by the end of 1964 had covered most of the Central Highlands, a wide tract of country in northern New Guinea from the
middle Sepik to east of Madang, two areas in northern Papua, the
Port Moresby-Kairuku coastal strip, and Bougainville Island. A
number of interim reports have appeared, and the first of a series of
final reports was published late in 1964.

The essential characteristic of what has been called the Australian
Land Research method is the integration of different disciplinary
approaches in order as to describe, classify and assess 'land' as a
whole, including 'the whole vertical profile at a site on the land
surface from the aerial environment down to the underlying
geological horizons, and including the plant and animal populations,
and past and present human activity associated with it' (Christian
1964:390). The basis of the method is a classification of land into
land systems defined as 'a composite of related units . . . throughout
which can be recognised a recurring pattern of topography, soils
and vegetation' (Christian and Stewart 1953:11). Land systems are
built up of described but generally unmapped land units, defined

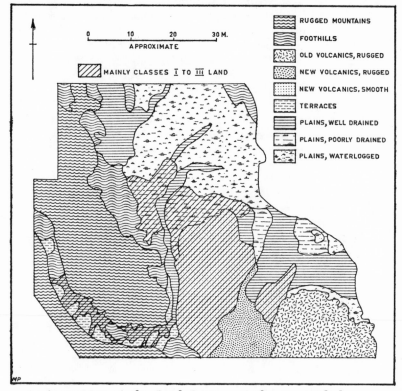

1 *A grouping of the Land Systems of the Buna-Kokoda area,
Northern District, Papua. From a map in* Lands of the Buna-Kokoda
Area . . . *(Land Research Series No. 10), by courtesy of CSIRO.*

as 'having similar genesis and can be described similarly in terms of the major inherent features of consequence to its land use—namely topography, soils, vegetation and climate' (Christian 1958:76).

This method, despite its rather unfortunate rigidity as a frame for description and analysis of land resources, has been skilfully applied in a wide variety of environments. Techniques have been refined over the years, and means found of introducing more analysis and rather less description. Like the survey methods as a whole, methods of assessing land potential have evolved over the years. Early assessments were not based on any very formal system. Recently the Division of Land Research has adopted a modification of a method developed in the United States by Klingebiel and Montgomery (1961), which is based not on possibilities but on the degree of limitations to land use, subclassified according to the type of such limitations. Klingebiel and Montgomery divided land into eight broad classes, of which the first four are suitable for cultivation with increasing degree of limitation, the next three suitable only for pastoral activity, range, or woodland, and the last unsuitable for any form of commercial plant production. The advantage of the system is that it is neither a productivity rating nor a rating of suitability for particular crops. Haantjens (1963) has suggested some modifications for use in New Guinea, and these have been incorporated in the most recent survey reports.

An example may be taken from survey data. Fig. 1 is a condensation of the land system map of the Buna-Kokoda area into a small number of landform types, distinguished according to terrain, lithology, and drainage condition. Of these, the areas distinguished by cross-hatching contain mainly land in classes I to III,[1] some of the

[1] Explanation of Klingebiel-Montgomery notation:
   I   Good land, level or gently sloping, suitable for agriculture without special limitations.
   II Good land, not level, requiring some special adaptations.
   III Moderately good, requiring intensive special measures to improve and maintain productivity when cultivated. Intensive drainage may be needed for tree crops where imperfectly drained.
   IV Fairly good, best maintained in perennial vegetation, but can be cultivated occasionally or in a limited way if handled with great care.
   V   Nearly level, productive soils, but unsuitable for cultivation because of other factors. Good for pasture or for forestry.
   VI Subject to moderate limitations for pasture and forestry.
   VII Subject to severe limitations for pasture and forestry. Severe erosion or other hazards.
  VIII Unsuited for any purpose
   S1 low chemical fertility
   S2 shallow soils
   S3 slowly permeable soils
    e erodibility
   st stoniness
    d poor drainage
    f flooding

largest tracts of such good land in the whole country. They include
land systems of three types: the footslopes of the Mt Lamington
volcano, steeply sloping alluvial plains in the Kokoda valley, and
rather poorly drained but readily improvable plains below the
footslopes of Mt Lamington. All the mountain country, together
with the whole of the old volcanic mass of the Hydrographers'
Range, the summit area of Mt Lamington, and the extensive alluvial plains in the north of the area are classed as of low potential,
with most land in classes VII and VIII. The balance of the area
falls into classes IV, V, and VI, though there are some pockets of
land in classes I and II.

In the Western and Southern Highlands (Wabag-Tari area) there
is a more intricate pattern. Thirty-nine land systems are distinguished, mostly widely scattered over a large area of country and
intermingled with other land systems. The Tambul land system, to
take an example at random, is developed on Pleistocene stratified
fluvial clays locally covered by volcanic ash. Most of its twenty
square miles is level, but there are some deeply incised streams,
liable to landslipping on the flanks. The occurrences of this system
lie between 6,800 and 7,300 feet and are all occupied and cultivated.
The plains constitute the largest land unit of the system, covered
with humic olive ash and brown clay soils, under gardens or sword-
grass regrowth. This land is in classes IId and IIId, except on
marginal slopes, where classes IIe and IIIe occur. There are some
boggy areas of small extent, with peaty soils in classes VII and VIId.
The steep slopes of dissected valleys form a land unit of very small
extent, with humic brown clays, but very liable to landslipping:
these are areas in classes VIIe and VIII. Finally there are some
very small flood plain channels, with fine-textured recent alluvium,
in class IV S3. Such intricacy is found in almost all land systems in
all areas surveyed.

These examples serve to bring out the value of methods employing land classification, taking into account all variables, as a basis
for assessment. But they also show the enormous complexity of
the problem and the very wide differences both in empirical
assessment and in intrinsic potential that may be found in very
small areas. This fact should provide a caveat in attempting more
generalized assessment on a wider, Territorial, basis, but none the
less such an attempt must be made. Unfortunately the CSIRO
surveys are, by their detailed nature and by their attempt to evaluate a range of variables, not amenable to ready extrapolation. In
order to obtain a Territory-wide basis of resource assessment, then,
we must go back to first principles, and seek more generalized
data on terrain, surface rock (lithology), soil, and climate. Maps
showing such generalized distributions have been prepared for this
essay, and are discussed below. Some comment on the sources of
data for these maps is to be found in the appendix.

THE BASIS FOR A TERRITORY-WIDE CLASSIFICATION OF LAND RESOURCES

Terrain. It is a commonplace that New Guinea is a mountainous island, with a scarcity of plains, rolling hills, and downland. This rather subjective view is true if seen from an Australian, English, or American viewpoint: a New Zealander or a Japanese would find less to remark on, and, indeed, the proportion of plains and rolling hill country to the total area of New Guinea is probably similar to that found in New Zealand. This much is clearly brought out in Fig. 2. Apart from the two extensive plains, in Western Papua and in

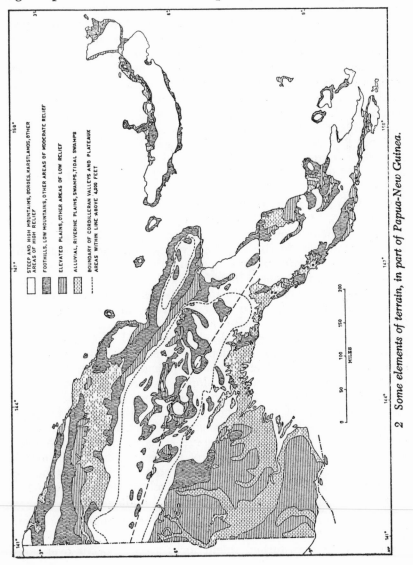

2 *Some elements of terrain, in part of Papua-New Guinea.*

STEEP AND HIGH MOUNTAINS, GORGES, KARSTLANDS, OTHER AREAS OF HIGH RELIEF

FOOTHILLS, LOW MOUNTAINS, OTHER AREAS OF MODERATE RELIEF

ELEVATED PLAINS, OTHER AREAS OF LOW RELIEF

ALLUVIAL, RIVERINE PLAINS, SWAMPS, TIDAL SWAMPS

BOUNDARY OF CORDILLERAN VALLEYS AND PLATEAUX AREAS WITHIN LINE ABOVE 4,000 FEET

MILES

the Sepik basin, there are important areas of low to moderate relief almost all along the south coast of Papua, in the Northern District of Papua, in the country around Madang and Rabaul, and at altitudes between 4,000 and 6,500 feet in the central cordillera. These areas of moderate relief are important: not less than 75 per cent of the population of the Territory is to be found living on these tracts of land.

The plains fall into two main groups: especially in the Fly and Sepik-Ramu valleys there are very extensive areas of permanently or seasonally waterlogged land. Many smaller coastal lowlands also have waterlogged tracts, some forested, some under swamp grass, some in coastal locations carrying mangroves. Within these water-logged areas, especially close to the rivers, are raised levees which carry some permanent occupation, but in the absence of drainage techniques, except in a few parts of the central cordillera, these are in the main negative areas, carrying little settlement. A second group of plains is in the main above flood level: some few are erosional, cut in firm 'country rock', but most are on alluvial and colluvial deposits of Pleistocene or younger date. These vary widely in surface condition and in depth of soil; they also vary as to age of soil, and include some of the most fertile and most infertile soils in the Territory.

Low hills and other country of moderate relief are again of very varied origin. Much of this country would be classed as steepland by international standards, with slopes up to 25° and locally steeper. However, in the highland valleys, on some coastal hills and sub-coastal plateaux, and especially on the lower slopes of the numerous volcanic cones, there are wide tracts of land with a general slope no more than 10-15°. In terms of human occupation, these tracts are among the most important in the country. The balance of the Territory includes numerous small tracts of land of only moderate relief, too small to be mapped at this scale, but mainly dominated by steep slopes between 30° and 45°. These slopes are maintained chiefly by landslipping rather than by normal wash and stream erosion, and slopes are frequently scarred by landslides, especially in the earthquake zone which occupies all the northern part of the country, and the Bismarck Archipelago. Weathering extends tens and even scores of feet deep. Also included within this zone on Fig. 3 are some areas of quite gentle relief but at high altitudes, on the crest of the Owen Stanley, Bismarck, and other ranges: here at altitudes far above the limits of human occupation are tracts of gentle almost level terrain, the product of erosion at a much earlier stage of mountain building.

Lithology (surface rocks). Geologically, New Guinea is of recent formation. Except for one small outcrop west of Daru in Western Papua, ancient undisturbed shield rocks such as occur over large

parts of Australia do not exist at the surface, though they underlie
the southern part of the plain of Western Papua at no great depth.
In the central cordillera, and especially in the Owen Stanley Range,
are large tracts of igneous and metamorphic rocks of varied ages,
thrown up in the cores of upfolds and exposed by erosion. These
apart, only very limited areas have rocks at the surface that are
older than the Tertiary era of geological time—that is to say as old
as almost all the formations encountered in the eastern highland
belt of Australia.

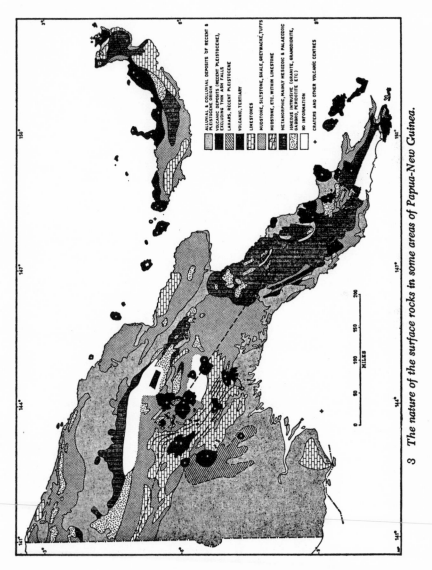

3   The nature of the surface rocks in some areas of Papua-New Guinea.

Most of the sedimentary rocks of New Guinea were laid down between the Cretaceous and Miocene periods of geological time, in a great subsiding trough north of the Australian landmass. The Owen Stanley Range was formed by folding in the early Tertiary, while the main folding in central New Guinea took place in the Miocene, and in northern New Guinea only at the end of the Tertiary and even in the Pleistocene. There is evidence that mountain building continued well into the Pleistocene. In the course of this history there have been several periods of great volcanic activity, and many older sedimentary rocks, especially of the Cretaceous and Eocene, include quantities of redeposited volcanic material. At other times the whole trough lay deep under the sea, and during these periods great thicknesses of limestone were laid down. When the seas were shallower, muds and sands were deposited, to form the present mudstones, shales, sandstones, and greywackes. Since the main period of mountain building, troughs on either side of the new ranges have been filled with great depths of detrital material from the mountains. During the Pleistocene, the period of the Great Ice Age, there was a renewed outburst of volcanic activity that has continued to the present time.

Distinct landform characteristics and soil-forming conditions are associated with each of the main lithological groups whose generalized distribution is within the areas that have been mapped as shown on Fig. 3. The metamorphic rocks everywhere tend to form steep and rugged mountains, resistant to erosion. Intrusive igneous rocks are of two kinds—the granites, some of which weather very readily, giving rise either to basins or to areas particularly liable to landslips, and the basic and ultra-basic rocks, the latter of which have possible significance as sources of nickel. The mudstone-shale-sandstone-greywacke areas give rise to a varied terrain, with impressive escarpments on the more resistant sandstones and broad valleys etched out in the unresistant mudstones and shales. The limestones everywhere produce their highly distinctive landscape. Being porous, they tend to be eroded largely by ground and underground water. In isolation, they stand up as sharp bare ridges, but wide areas of limestone give rise to characteristic karst formations, with sink-holes, pits and hollows, honeycombed rock outcrops and, locally, the kegelkarst of innumerable small, steep hills separated by discontinuous narrow depressions—a landscape resembling nothing so much as an inverted egg-box. The accounts of explorers who penetrated to the Central Highlands from the Papuan side—especially that of Hides (1936)—give a clear picture of immense difficulty of movement in the karst.

Volcanic deposits vary. Some of the older outpourings flowed from fissures, giving rise to tablelands such as the Sogeri Plateau behind Port Moresby. Most of the Pleistocene and Recent volcanics have poured or been blown from central vents, building up some great cones thousands of feet high around central craters. Sometimes the centres of such cones have either foundered or been blown out in paroxysmal explosions, leaving great hollows of which the most striking example is Simpson Harbour, on which Rabaul stands. Eruptions have been of several types. Some have emitted lava which has built up long, smooth cones; where mixed with water and mud the lavas form lahars, which spread widely and thinly far down on to the adjacent lowlands. Some vents, by contrast, have thrown out only boulders, building up no cone; others have, in recent eruptions, emitted mainly ash which builds narrow steep-sided cones and casts a fine deposit of wind-borne ash all over the countryside in the lee of the volcano. Thus the whole of the northern Gazelle Peninsula in New Britain is blanketed by ash falls from the successive eruptions of the Rabaul volcanoes. Still others erupt deadly clouds of burning gas—*nuées ardentes*—which sweep downslope destroying everything in their path. One such, blown out of Mt Lamington in 1951, destroyed the government station at Higaturu and killed over 3,000 people in a few minutes. Mt Lamington was thought to be extinct before this eruption; a classification of volcanoes into active and extinct is by no means always easy. Thus all the volcanoes in the central cordillera are 'extinct', but there are widespread native stories of extensive ash-falls in the Western and Southern Highlands some time between forty and a hundred years ago.

Climate. All Papua-New Guinea lies within the tropics, but its climate is far from uniform. Though at the coast there is no cold season anywhere, in southern Papua there is a difference of some 10° between the mean temperature of the warmest and coolest months, and a difference of about 15° in night temperatures at places a little inland from the shore. Average temperatures fall with altitude at a steady rate, and the diurnal range becomes greater with altitude, so that at 5,000 feet midday temperatures are some 10° below coastal temperatures while night temperatures may be 20° cooler than on the coast. Seasonal variations also become more marked. Night frosts become a hazard in farming at elevations that vary from as low as 5,500 feet to as high as 8,000 feet, depending on terrain in relation to the drainage or collection of cold air. Humidity is high in the lowlands both by day and by night, but relative humidity falls to around 60 per cent at midday at 5,000 feet, and to much less at high altitudes. Persistent heavy cloud lies on the mountains above altitudes ranging from as low as 2,500 feet near the coast to as high as 9,000 or 10,000 feet in sheltered locations within the ranges.

Though contrasts in temperature and humidity are not simply functions of altitude, but bear closer study, the most significant and marked contrasts between places and seasons in New Guinea

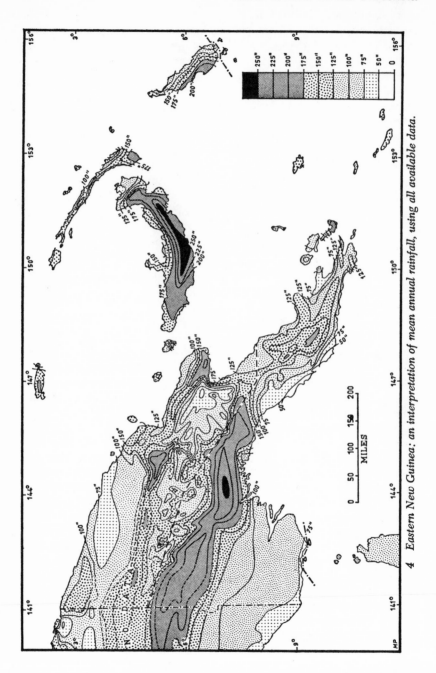

4　*Eastern New Guinea: an interpretation of mean annual rainfall, using all available data.*

are in rainfall conditions. Four new maps of rainfall, the first products of a much larger study of the climate of the Melanesian area, are presented with this chapter. Mean annual rainfall (Fig. 4) varies from over 250 inches to as little as 39 inches, the latter at Port Moresby. There is a belt of over-wet conditions, with rainfalls exceeding 175 inches annually, all along the southern face of the central cordillera, the foothills, and the northern edge of the plains to the south: it does not extend into the valleys of the highlands themselves, which are much drier, especially in the east. This belt is broken across the northern end of the Owen Stanley Range, but resumes around the head of Huon Gulf and achieves maximum intensity in southern New Britain, continuing through the southern tip of New Ireland and along the south coast of Bougainville. Other areas of high rainfall are found in eastern Papua, along the northern face of the cordillera, and in the ocean areas west from Manus. Relatively dry conditions are found in the Sepik valley, at Rabaul, at a few points on the coasts of New Ireland, in the eastern valleys of the central cordillera, and in the Markham, Snake, and Bulolo valleys in the Morobe District, in central and south-western Papua, and especially along the coast on either side of Port Moresby. This pattern may be interpreted in terms of seasons.

During the months from December to March, and for rather longer in the north and north-west of the Territory, the dominant airstream is a weak flow of very moist, unstable air, derived from the equatorial regions to the west and periodically reinforced by Australian weather systems which draw moist tropical air far to the south. These are months of heavy precipitation almost throughout New Guinea, except in the lee of New Britain and the Huon Peninsula: rain is very general, and the effect of relief is at a minimum. Rain is not continuous: dry spells occur and in 1963 they were prolonged over much of the Territory, but the mean February conditions represented in Fig. 5A show clearly the general pattern. By contrast, the months from May to October, and for rather longer in the far south, are characterized by a much more stable easterly and south-easterly airstream, which flows very strongly across southern New Guinea and up to the Bismarcks, but rather more weakly in the north-western quadrant, where westerly winds may be experienced even in the middle of this period. This Trade Wind stream is moist, especially in its northern branch, but gives rise to little precipitation along coasts which lie parallel to the prevailing wind. Where land lies across the path of the winds, however, or where the airstream is constricted by its approach to or passage between high mountains and mountainous islands, the lifting and convergence of the air produces cooling which releases great quantities of rainfall. Once these obstacles are passed, descent and divergence of the air restores stability, and rainfall is low. There are marked changes of weather at this season, corresponding with

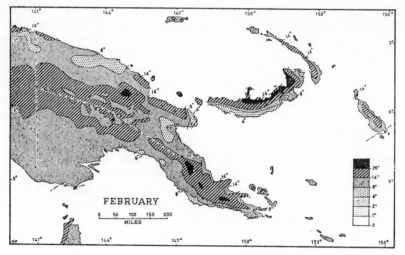

5   *Above: mean February rainfall.*

Below: mean July rainfall.

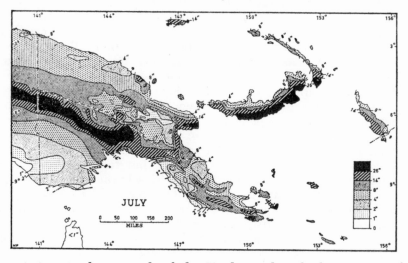

variations in the strength of the Trades and with the passage of
depressions in mid-latitudes from Australia across the south
Pacific. The July rainfall map (Fig. 5B) is representative of conditions at the height of this season. This is the season of very heavy
rainfall along the whole of the over-wet belt noted above, and in
south-eastern Papua, but of prolonged droughts in central Papua,
south-western Papua, and the eastern valleys of the central cordillera, which lie directly in the lee of the long ridge of the Owen
Stanleys. It is also the dry period in northern New Britain and to a
lesser extent in the Sepik valley, though the Trades are not nearly

so dominant in the weather of this north-western quadrant. Were they as dominant as they are in Papua, this area in the lee of the mountains and the whole landmass would be very dry at this season. There are some very sharp rainfall gradients, especially across New Britain, on the rise of land behind the Lakekamu depression in central Papua and along the adjacent coast, and between the Morobe coast and the valleys immediately inland. Localities fifteen miles up the Markham valley from Lae receive less than one-quarter of the rainfall received at Lae. The seasonal reversal of rainfall across New Britain and the Huon Peninsula is very marked on these two maps, and a similar but much weaker reversal may be seen between the northern and southern sides of the central cordillera and between the northern and southern inter-montane valleys.

Despite a location close to the equator, then, some areas of Papua-New Guinea have a fairly well-marked dry season, during which there is a definite liability to quite prolonged droughts, without significant rainfall for several weeks. Other areas, by contrast, are so wet either throughout the year or at one or the other season that all forms of agricultural activity are severely handicapped. Between the two extremes are a number of areas, including most of the valleys of the central cordillera, the Rabaul area and parts of the New Ireland coast, northern Papua, parts of central-western Papua, and most of the north-western quadrant, in which there are only short periods of either over-dry or over-wet conditions, and which experience favourable conditions for the growth of most trees and crops throughout the greater part of most years.

It is possible to go further than this, and to describe the climate of the Territory in terms of the occurrence of wet and dry months in the total rainfall record, following the system of Schmidt and Ferguson, based in turn on that of Mohr, and applied initially to Indonesia (Schmidt and Ferguson 1952). The basis of this system is a series of observations made at Bogor in Java, leading to the conclusion that during a month which receives more than 100mm. (3·94 in.) of rain the soil remains continually moist, while during a month receiving less than 60mm. (2·36 in.) there is a strong tendency to drying out. Months with over 3·94 in. are classed as 'wet', while months with under 2·36 in. are classed as 'dry'. Months with intermediate totals are 'moist'. The method is then to total all 'dry' and 'wet' months ever occurring in the rainfall records for each station, to obtain average values per year, and then to divide the 'dry' months by the 'wet', expressing the result as a percentage, Q. The result is a reasonable approximation, valid for tropical areas, of the mutual relation between precipitation and evaporation. Clearly a long record is desirable: Schmidt and Ferguson limited themselves to stations with over ten years, and in general it would be

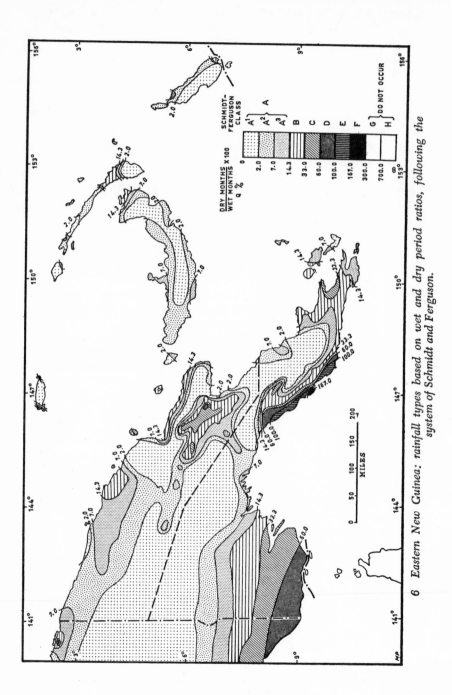

6 *Eastern New Guinea: rainfall types based on wet and dry period ratios, following the system of Schmidt and Ferguson.*

desirable to restrict application to stations with records for at least seven years. However, because of the paucity of such stations in most parts of New Guinea, some supplementary stations with records for as few as three years have been employed in this reconnaissance exercise. Schmidt and Ferguson divide the values of Q into eight classes, as shown on Fig. 6. Class A has no dry periods, class B includes areas with a weak dry season, class C with a moderate dry season, class D with a well-developed dry season, and classes E and F with increasingly long periods of severe drought occupying several months of each year. It seemed desirable to subdivide class A to distinguish those areas in which one or more dry months may occur in some years (A^3), those areas with occasional dry months in the record (A^2), and those areas in which dry months are either of very rare occurrence or are totally absent (A^1). These divisions are, like all climatic classifications, arbitrary, and the lines bounding classes should, except where very sharp gradients occur, be regarded merely as guide lines showing the direction of a *continuum*.

Three areas stand out as having well-marked liability to drought conditions: the Port Moresby coastal strip, where class F occurs at Port Moresby itself, the southern part of the plain of western Papua, and the valleys lying inland of the Huon Gulf and extending as far west as the Goroka valley in the Eastern Highlands District. There are a few other areas characterized by a significant occurrence of dry months, of which the most noteworthy is the northern Gazelle Peninsula of New Britain. Fairly wide areas in the Sepik and Madang Districts, in New Ireland, Bougainville, and eastern Papua and, despite its high rainfall, on both sides of New Britain, have occasional dry months, though these are not of frequent or very regular occurrence. The highland valleys west of Goroka also fall into this class, but not the valleys of the Southern Highlands District which share with the much wetter belt lying immediately to the south a near-total absence of dry months in the record. The area of country without dry periods is, indeed, considerably more extensive than the area with very heavy rain as shown on the map of mean annual rainfall (Fig. 4). There are some extremely sharp gradients, especially inland of Huon Gulf, but none quite as sharp as that between Sukarnapura (Hollandia) and Lake Sentani, just over the border in West Irian.

This map as a whole supplements the rainfall maps by emphasizing certain regional differences that the latter reveal, by providing the basis for further separation of three distinct groups within the valleys of the central cordillera, and by helping to subdivide those areas with a moderate total rainfall into tracts having a well-distributed precipitation without either drought or (by inference) excess and those in which the moderate total fall is in fact produced by sharp seasonal contrasts between rainy and dry periods.

Soil. Soil is the product of climate acting upon the surface rocks. The nature of a soil thus depends on three main factors: the climate, the nature of the surface rocks, and the length of time during which weathering has been active on the site. In the tropical lowlands, soil-forming processes are at maximum intensity; they diminish in rate and intensity from the equator toward the poles, and with rising altitude from sea level. Areas of flat or gently sloping land that are not subject to erosion, and have so remained during very long periods of time, have much older soils than steeplands from which the surface weathered matter is constantly removed by erosion. In New Guinea, therefore, young soils—in which the influence of the parent surface rock material is dominant—are very widespread, while old soils are in the main confined to the elevated plains, in areas which suffer little erosion and receive no deposition of either alluvial or volcanic material.

'Zonal' characteristics of soils thus depend mainly on climate. The zonal influences vary with temperature, rainfall, and evaporation; different influences operate in areas where the temperature is uniform at all times, and in areas at high altitude where there is very marked variation between day and night temperatures on the ground. Areas with a pronounced dry season experience periods when water moves upward in the soil by capillary action, while continuously moist areas are dominated throughout by downward movement of soil water. Site conditions, which control the soil water table, vegetation and geological conditions, which determine the chemical constitution of the weathered *regolith* from which soil is derived, exert modifications even in the oldest soils. In true 'zonal' soils, which have been developing over many thousands of years, these geological influences are, however, at a minimum. In tropical lowland areas with continuously moist conditions the true zonal soil is the latosol, derived from greatly weathered parent materials, depleted of silica and bases to a great depth, and without any strong textural profiles (Cline *et al.* 1955:69). The latosol is a 'soil order'—the highest order of classification: it is subdivided into three 'great soil groups'—low humic, humic, and hydrol—according to increasing rainfall. A fourth 'great soil group'—humic ferruginous latosols—probably represents the end product of the long weathering process, characterized by a massive crust and extreme infertility. In arid areas the zonal soils are light in colour, while in semi-arid to sub-humid areas are found dark-coloured soils, rich in organic matter in the upper horizons, and with a high base status throughout. Where zonal soils are not fully developed, we find intrazonal soils, reflecting the dominant influence of local factors of terrain and lithology. Among these is the brown forest soil group, widespread in New Guinea, which seems to be progressing toward acid latosols but which retains a high base status and a rich supply of organic matter. Also widespread in areas of poor drainage and waterlogging are hydromorphic soils, characterized by mottling and a high soil water table. There are also special soils such as the rendzina group, developed by deep weathering on limestones. Finally there are young azonal soils, classed into regosols mainly on new deposits such as alluvium, volcanic ash, and coral sands, and lithosols found on young slopes of weathered or unweathered rock.

Haantjens and van Royen have in preparation a tentative soil map of the whole island of New Guinea, a draft of which they have kindly made available. They map on the basis of associations, within which they find comparatively few zonal members. They find latosols on the older deposits of the southern plain, and also in the Ramu-Sepik valley and in some other depressions. Brown forest soils and regosolic brown forest soils are general throughout the mountains, though in the Western and Southern Highlands a fine blanketing of volcanic ash is in fact the dominant parent material of what are in fact young regosolic soils.

The soil pattern of New Guinea is infinitely complex. In addition to the innumerable natural variations, soil has been and is being constantly modified by cultivation. Shifting cultivation affects both the content and the structure of soils, and those areas that have become grasslands have a different soil climate, a different balance of nutrient supply and withdrawal, and a different structure from soils still under forest. In classifying soils from the point of view of their usefulness, different considerations come into play in different areas. Thus the permeability of soils developed on volcanic ash makes the disposition of the water table of great importance and raises greatly the limits of precipitation that would give rise to over-wet conditions. In mountain areas, liability to landslipping may be a more important consideration than the innate fertility of the soil. The depth of soil is very often an overriding consideration in determining usefulness and ability to withstand drought. Drainage conditions, or stoniness, are limiting or permissible conditions on a wide variety of soils. Frequency and weight of ash falls in volcanic areas may be a rejuvenating influence on the soil, but also a hazard that can lead to crop failure and worse.

THE DISTRIBUTION OF POPULATION

Before proceeding to a synthesis of the land resources of New Guinea, in the light of the material presented above, some discussion of population distribution is first necessary. This is because no assessment is possible except in relation to the people who will use the land resources. Fig. 7 represents the crude distribution of population by census divisions, the boundaries and areas of which are from a map prepared by the Department of Native Affairs. Their map is amended from a compilation of census division maps which I initially made from records in the Department in 1958:

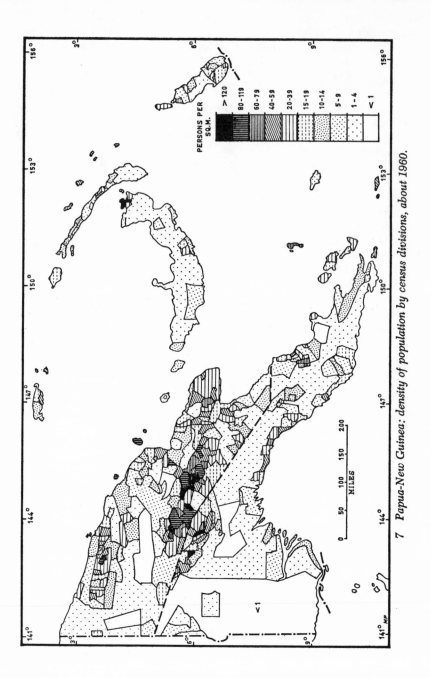

7 *Papua-New Guinea: density of population by census divisions, about 1960.*

both boundaries and areas are still unreliable, and nothing much better will be possible until it becomes the practice in New Guinea to map such sub-units as sub-districts, census divisions, and electoral divisions on topographical maps where available, or otherwise on photo-mosaics. Except along the West Irian border most boundaries are sketched on inaccurate maps that lack topographical detail, by officers unskilled in mapping, and without ground control. Fig. 7 is therefore an approximation, as are the electoral maps of the Territory, the census division maps, and even the sub-district maps, all of which are prepared on the same base.

While little or nothing can be said of distribution in detail, then, much can be said about the broad pattern. About half the whole population of Papua-New Guinea lies in a restricted and sharply bounded belt astride the sixth parallel south, between the Southern Highlands District and the Huon Peninsula. Within this there are a number of nodes of greatest concentration, especially the Chimbu area, the Mt Hagen-Wabag areas, the valleys around Mendi and Tari in the Southern Highlands, and the hills north of Lae in the Huon Peninsula. In central Chimbu as a whole densities below the tree line average over 200 per square mile, and locally exceed 500 per square mile within group territories mapped by Paula Brown and myself. Of all this concentration along the sixth parallel south, all but a small percentage live more than 4,000 feet above sea level.

A second belt of marked concentration lies along the southern foothills of the Prince Alexander Range in the Sepik District: here densities within measured group territories locally attain nearly 400 per square mile. Similar high rural densities are found in the northern Gazelle Peninsula, around Rabaul. Other areas of concentration lie around Madang, in the islands north-east of Papua, along the central Papuan coast, in a small area in northern Papua lying north-west of Mt Lamington, and in southern Bougainville. By contrast, most of the remainder of the country is very sparsely occupied indeed, and wide tracts of country in Western Papua and the southern part of the Sepik District carry less than one person per square mile.

To interpret this map we need to know first how far it is likely to reflect an appreciation of the quality of land resources on the part of the indigenous people. Certainly, in densely peopled tracts such as Chimbu and Enga, there is a detailed comprehension of both local and regional differences, and the selection of land is influenced by this comprehension. From other parts of the Territory the evidence is as yet less clear. However, in the Western and Southern Highlands the work of the CSIRO team has shown a good correspondence between the intensity of use, as measured by extent of land shown as cultivated on air photographs and land capability as evaluated by the Klingebiel-Montgomery system discussed above. Tracts in which 80 per cent or more of the land is in regular use lie without exception in land systems of moderate to high capability: population densities over 200 per square mile occur in only two of the four land systems falling mainly within Klingebiel-Montgomery classes I to III. Similarly in the Buna-Kokoda area of northern Papua the greatest concentration of population, rising locally to 60 per square mile, lies on the best land in the area—the little-dissected footslopes of Mt Lamington, where smooth topography is combined with fertile soils and good drainage. However, other areas of good land are but sparsely occupied, while high densities are found in many areas of quite low capability. On the Territory-wide scale, we note the importance of the country of moderate relief, which carries more population than the plains. Areas of young volcanic formation also stand out: except in central Papua and in northern New Britain, these are areas of generally higher density. The two exceptions are interesting: the volcanoes of central Papua lie in the heart of the belt of highest annual rainfall that is sparsely occupied almost throughout. Other factors are of importance in New Britain and elsewhere. Malaria is absent from many areas above 5,000 feet, and incidence is only light in some lower areas where conditions are unsuitable for the breeding of the *Anopheles* mosquito. In the northern Gazelle Peninsula a relatively light and well-distributed rainfall combines with highly permeable soils to create an absence of swamplands. This stands in sharp contrast to the north coast of New Britain, which has soils of similar origin but a very heavy seasonal rainfall and large tracts of swamp: this area is highly malarious.

Seasonality of rainfall is perhaps as important as total quantity. Thus the only two areas in the main cordillera lying outside the valley system of the Central Highlands that carry notable concentrations are the Kukukuku country south-west of Bulolo and the Goilala area directly north of Port Moresby. The Kukukuku country has moderate rainfall, distinctly seasonal; the Goilala area has a heavy rainfall but a marked dry season, and is the only area in the east-Papuan mountains with this characteristic. A dry season is perhaps important in soil formation, but the most significant factors are the greater ease of clearing by use of fire and also—especially in a mountain region—the reduced incidence of heavy cloud.

Discussion of population distribution could be prolonged, but each area shows up possible correlations with different factors, and consideration of each thus poses a whole set of new questions that can be answered only by reference to crops, agricultural techniques, and agricultural cycles. There are also demographic factors discussed elsewhere by Norma McArthur. It is time, then, to turn back to the question of assessing resources, and, with the distribution of the human population in mind, to try to reach some basis for a comprehensive evaluation.

A SYNTHESIS OF LAND RESOURCES

It will be apparent that certain conditions stand out both as limiting and as favouring the productive occupance of land. Certain tracts of land are totally excluded for agriculture: those above heights ranging locally from as low as 6,500 feet to as high as 9,000 feet that are liable to severe frost, those permanently or semi-permanently waterlogged and either incapable of drainage or of such low natural fertility as not to be worth the large expense involved, those of such unstable soil that any occupation would lead to landslipping and erosion, those of such difficult terrain—for example the worst of the limestone karstlands—that only insignificant pockets of land could be brought into use. In addition to these there are much wider areas where only sparse occupation of the land is possible. These include most of the remaining limestone karstlands, almost all areas receiving over about 175 inches of rain a year except where soils are unusually permeable, most areas liable to severe and prolonged drought during several months of the year, many more waterlogged areas that could only be reclaimed at high cost, and most areas of old soils where the processes of deep weathering have reduced the surface soil to a very low level of fertility. Steep slopes are by themselves far less of a limitation: the soils are generally young, they are easier to clear than flat land by the methods of shifting cultivation, and it is possible to reduce erosion and landslipping by simple protective devices of various kinds.

To attempt to map favourable and unfavourable areas is a dangerous exercise, fraught with possibilities of subjective error. Two highly generalized and tentative maps have been prepared, the one classifying the types of limitation to land use, the other isolating a number of larger areas of relatively favourable conditions. In Fig. 8 emphasis is placed first on the occurrence of over-wet conditions, accompanied by reduced insolation, soggy waterlogged soils in level sites, and severe erosion and landslipping on slopes. Areas with over 175 inches annually are excluded first, and then areas which receive very heavy rain of the order of over about 15 inches a month during some major part of the year, but not throughout the whole year. Some of these latter areas carry significant populations, but most are sparsely occupied and have little potential for development. Next the remaining rugged and mountainous areas and the large tracts of perennial or seasonal swamp are eliminated. Areas with a severe dry season, distinguished as those falling into the Schmidt-Ferguson classes E and F, are also excluded, though some of these are irrigable. Areas of known severe soil limitations, principally those with old and deeply weathered latosols, are further excluded. There remain quite wide tracts, in some of which a marked but not severe dry season is a seasonal limitation—

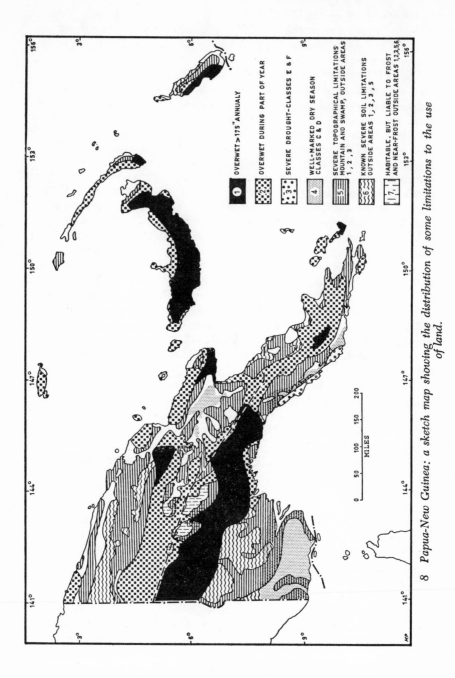

8 *Papua-New Guinea: a sketch map showing the distribution of some limitations to the use of land.*

also a circumstance which has facilitated the replacement of forest by grass and savanna. These latter, and also some areas in which low night temperatures and some ground frosts can occur even at relatively low altitudes, are finally noted on Fig. 8.

These limitations are of varying degree, and many areas thus marked out are in fact occupied, some quite thickly. Some attempt is made, however, to suggest the degree of limitation visually on the map. To some, this map will suggest a far too gloomy view of the resources of the Territory. Yet comparison of this map with the map of population distribution will reveal that the more negative tracts are very sparsely occupied. A more positive view is presented in a matching map (Fig. 9), in which some attempt is made to distinguish areas with more favourable conditions. Emphasis is placed first on terrain and soil in relation to climatic conditions, and thus on these areas of relatively gentle relief with soils derived from recent volcanic outpourings and ash falls or from recent alluvial and colluvial deposits. Among these, areas affected by moderate periodic drought, or by seasonal over-wet conditions, or by low temperatures are separately distinguished by sub-classification. Since slope is not the limiting condition in New Guinea that it is in countries with more mechanized agriculture, and further since many steepland soils are superior in fertility to flatland soils, areas of moderate relief without severe climatic or other limitations are also represented in a third class. Quite large tracts of more favourable conditions emerge, especially along the belt astride the sixth parallel south, along the north coast of New Guinea, and on both sides of the eastern peninsula of Papua. The very limited, but important, areas of moderate to high capability in the Gazelle Peninsula, the Popondetta area of the Northern District of Papua, south-east Bougainville, and in valleys lying inland from Lae and Madang all stand out clearly. The area of relatively dry country south of the Fly River in Western Papua, which has been under examination for several years as potential beef-cattle country, is also noted.

Comparison of this map with the map of population distribution reveals much unevenness. Areas along the sixth parallel south, in the Gazelle Peninsula and in the northern Sepik District, are well occupied, but areas in eastern Papua, Bougainville, and around Madang, and especially the north coast of New Britain, are only sparsely occupied. This maldistribution in relation to resources is well known and has prompted suggestions of resettlement programmes for many years. Recently a large-scale study has been made of the potential of the north coast of New Britain, with a view to settling at least 50,000 people in this area over a period of years. It is remarkable—perhaps incredible to those who do not know the ways of New Guinea—that this survey had to be made on the basis of most inadequate field data and even inadequate air photographs, for while the CSIRO survey teams have surveyed

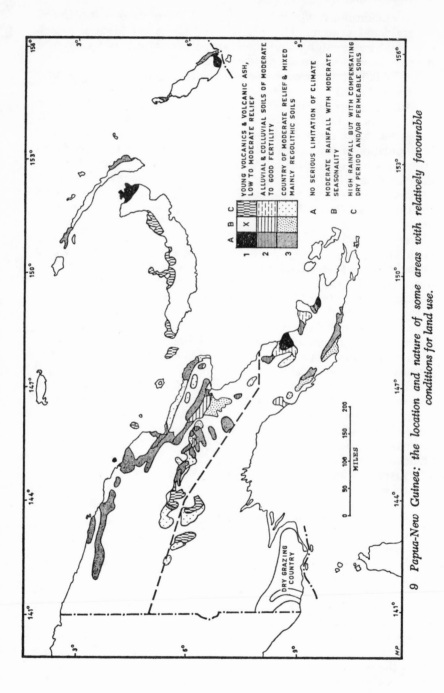

9 *Papua-New Guinea: the location and nature of some areas with relatively favourable conditions for land use.*

large tracts of the Territory at the request of the Administration, the north coast of New Britain is not among them. It cannot be said that the feasibility of agricultural settlement in northern New Britain has been fully established: the effect of the very heavy December-March rains, which total upwards of twenty-five inches in each month at a number of stations, has not been studied at all; its effect on soil water tables alone could, however, well be critical both for tree and field crops.

At the risk of seeming tedious, a caveat must be entered on the use of this map more than of any other map. There are certainly areas of good potential, both large and small, which are not represented here, mainly for want of the data on which to base a determination. Furthermore, some lowland areas that are excluded are capable of reclamation. Within the areas shown are some that are already seriously degraded by erosion, especially in the area inland of Lae and in the Sepik District. But the data are lacking on which to base something better. Even the CSIRO surveys only describe land potential by reference to land systems: they do not undertake a detailed mapping. There are dangers in land-potential maps such as those produced for the whole of Fiji by Wright and Twyford and now being used there as the basis for a land development programme, but there is nonetheless no doubt that land-potential mapping of New Guinea is desirable. Much could be done by simply reworking the CSIRO material, together with material prepared by the Territory soil survey over the limited areas within which they have worked. While there are good and sound reasons why the scientists concerned do not and would not wish to commit themselves to such a map, in the almost certain knowledge that their cautions and qualifications would be ignored by many administrators, it is clear that many worse mistakes are going to be made in the absence of a land-potential map. The preparation of such a map is now a prime need for the fuller development of the Territory's land resources.

The economic aspect of land potential must be mentioned here, but only briefly, as it is dealt with elsewhere in this book. The present food-crop economy of the Territory is based on root crops, and its cash economy mainly on tree crops. But among the tree crops there seems to be far greater potential in the world market for the two main lowland crops—coconuts and cocoa—than for the main highland crop, coffee. Thus the lowland areas should, under present circumstances, be weighted in land assessment, and particular weight should be given to those areas without a cooler season and without either excessive rain or more than a slight risk of drought, which are suited for cocoa production. Changes in the world market or the successful introduction of new crops such as tea and pyrethrum in the highland areas might change this pattern. Radical revision would also be needed if rice were to become established as a major food crop, for potential padi soils are almost totally excluded from this assessment. European potatoes and green vegetables also demand conditions rather cooler than those included as 'favourable' here. Rather different conditions are also required for successful livestock rearing, but in the near future the main potential for livestock is probably on the coconut plantations. Hence it is important that true land-potential mapping should be based on intrinsic conditions, so that selection among these intrinsic conditions can be made in surveying the potential for any particular crop or group of crops.

FOREST RESOURCES

There is one important group of resources, widely distributed over the land, that has so far been excluded from discussion. By far the greater part of New Guinea is closely forested, with a mixed tropical rain forest in the lowlands and foothills and a montane forest of rather different structure and composition in the mountains. While much of this forest is of such mixed composition as to render exploitation uneconomic at present, there are large areas within which development is practicable and, indeed, New Guinea and the Solomons are now being viewed as a major source of hardwood timber. Pre-war exploitation of timber resources was everywhere on a very small scale: essentially similar in scope is the production of pit-sawn timber for local constructional work by numerous small native groups throughout the country. At the end of the war there were only two sawmills working in the Territory. Starting in 1950, however, large-scale exploitation has increased. The initial site was at Bulolo, inland of Huon Gulf, where there are valuable stands of *Araucaria* ('Hoop' and 'Klinki' pine). They emerge through the forest canopy over a wide tract between 2,000 and 5,000 feet above sea level with a strongly seasonal rainfall. The existence of a road to Bulolo, and of a town built to serve the moribund gold-dredging industry, prompted the establishment of a plywood mill here—an initial investment of two million pounds. The company produces some 10,000 tons of plywood a year, exporting it through Lae: road haulage represents some 15 per cent of the total production cost. From 1957 onward the company found it worthwhile to establish a subsidiary mill at Lae to prepare veneers from coastal hardwoods to incorporate in the plywood at Bulolo. At that time only a limited market in the United States had been found to supplement the slender Australian market, but since 1960 there has been a rapid expansion in the demand for timber from Japan, where by 1963 went nearly 70 per cent of New Guinea timber exports. The main supplying region is the north coast of New Britain, where are very large stands of kamerere (*Eucalyptus deglupta*) and other hardwoods, both on dry land and in the swamp forests. The trade has now become sufficiently secure for the Japanese importers to provide specially designed vessels to operate in the shallow waters of the New Britain coast. Other rich areas in Bougainville and in the Gogol valley behind Madang have recently been opened up, and, with an eye to the future, a teak planting programme has recently been commenced in the foothills behind Port Moresby and elsewhere. Production now exceeds 80 million super feet a year, from seventy sawmills, and it is hoped that output will more than double within three to five years.

The exploitation of its rich resources in hardwood timber offers to New Guinea its strongest present hope of building up a non-agricultural export. But since most of the timber areas are in sparsely populated country, remote from services, fresh problems are created in the deployment of labour resources and also in investment in roads and harbours. It seems that it is the wealth of northern New Britain in merchantable timber that has prompted the rural resettlement study referred to above. There are also questions of conservation that have received little serious study. Allied problems arise on the frontiers of economics with politics: the timber industry demands heavy capitalization and careful resource management. Since there is only a small resident native population in the timber areas, it is tempting to neglect the possibilities of infusing native capital into the industry by the reservation of shares for indigenous investors. Yet there is an obvious outlet here for the surplus capital that has accumulated as the result of the successful native cocoa industry in the northern Gazelle Peninsula of New Britain and in other parts of the country. These problems arise even more keenly in considering the other non-agricultural resources of the Territory.

MINERAL, POWER, AND INDUSTRIAL RESOURCES

The immense value of mineral exploitation in accelerating all forms of economic development has been amply demonstrated in a number of tropical countries, outstandingly in central Africa and Venezuela. Closer to home, in New Caledonia, exploitation of a rich mineral resource has led to a great improvement in the living standards of the whole population, though the resulting high wages have led to the destruction of some other aspects of the economy. In Papua-New Guinea the small scale of mineral development to date has not triggered off any significant changes in other fields of activity, though the gold incomes of the Mandated Territory provided an important budget support during the parlous days of the depression, and, as we have seen, the provision of services in the mining area facilitated the subsequent establishment of a more permanent timber industry. There have been small gold-rushes at a number of points in Papua and New Guinea since the third quarter of the nineteenth century, but none has led to solid development. Gold is now a waning resource, and there are few prospects of

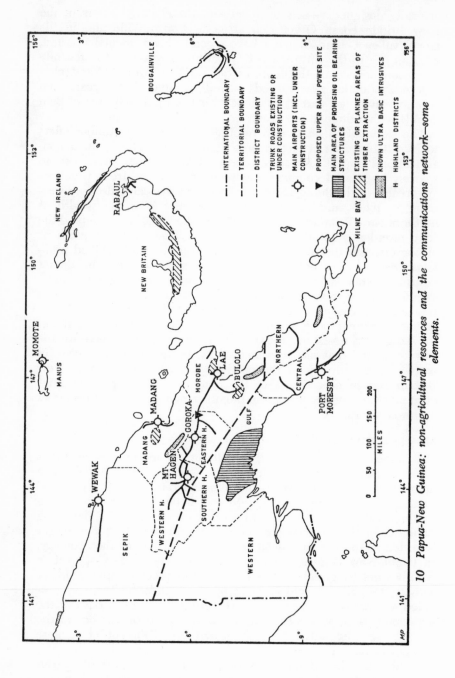

10 *Papua-New Guinea: non-agricultural resources and the communications network—some elements.*

large-scale new discoveries. Copper was worked near Port Moresby for some years earlier in the century, but the deposit is small.

The expansion of geological survey work in recent years has not yet, however, reached a scale at which it can be claimed that the rocks of the Territory are being fully prospected. Certainly, there is nothing comparable to what is going on in the neighbouring British Solomon Islands. In recent years attention has been focused on a series of early Tertiary ultra-basic intrusive formations that occur all along the northern face of the Owen Stanley Range and also on the northern face of the Bismarck Range in the south of the Madang District. Laterization of comparable ultra-basic rocks in New Caledonia has led to the concentration there of rich bodies of nickel ore that are among the world's largest reserves of this mineral. Nickel has been located in economic concentration on the Cyclops Mountains and on Waigeo Island in West Irian, and so far three localities in Papua-New Guinea are known to have nickel, but the grade is doubtful and the possibilities of economic exploitation as yet undetermined.

To date, expenditure on the search for minerals has been concentrated very heavily on oil exploration. Since the early 1920s some £30 million have been spent, initially in a number of widely scattered areas but since about 1950 mainly in the region around the head of the Gulf of Papua, where the folded structures south of the faulted zone of the Central Highlands curve southward toward and into the Coral Sea. A number of excellent structures have been located, mapped, and drilled. Oil has been found not once but several times, but no large-scale pool has yet been tapped, and it remains questionable whether a field large enough to justify exploitation can be established. However, it has been established beyond doubt that there are large reserves of natural gas, a potential industrial resource of great value. The problem is, indeed, to find a market to which the gas can be economically piped. At one stage it was tentatively proposed to pipe the gas under the shallow waters of Torres Strait for use in smelting the Cape York bauxites. However, other plans for aluminium extraction have been adopted, and in any case it might not be politically wise to tap a New Guinea resource to aid development in a nearby metropolitan country that does not freely admit New Guineans.

It seems unlikely that a market for New Guinea gas that is sufficient to justify the large expenditure on workings, pipelines, and communications facilities can be developed, the more so as Papua-New Guinea is extremely rich in more flexible sources of power. High rainfall, large catchments, and steep falls from the mountains to the lowlands combine to create a large number of sites suitable for hydro-electric power generation on every scale from the small local plant to the giant undertaking yielding several hundred megawatts. Some years ago there was discussion of a site in the Purari gorge, which collects the drainage from a large area of the central cordillera: the site suggested proved unsuitable because of fissures in the limestone that would drain away water, but there are other sites. Recently a firm proposal has been adopted to develop power at the point where the Ramu falls 3,000 feet from the plateau around Kainantu to the Markham-Ramu valley, a site that alone could provide far more power than all New Guinea can consume for many years to come, and is very centrally located to the whole Territory. There are certainly other large-scale possibilities on the Lai, the Sepik, the Waria, and at a number of points on the huge Purari system. Total power resources cannot be estimated, but generation of 2,000 megawatts seems well within the range of possibility, enough to sustain the demands of a wealthy industrial country of several million people. Further, there are potential sources of hydrothermal power in the volcanic areas: these have been subjected to a careful investigation at Rabaul.

The very large extent of limestone in the Territory (Fig. 3), some of it of high purity, constitutes a further industrial resource. However, the present demand for cement in the whole country is insufficient to warrant the construction of even one plant of economic size: furthermore, even were a plant to be erected at any specific point, the greater part of New Guinea could import cement more cheaply from overseas than obtain it from the local works. It has been proposed, realistically, that these resources should instead be used to obtain lime in a large number of relatively small kilns: lime could serve many of the functions of cement, including the stabilization of earth to make building materials and surface roads. It could also be used in agricultural fertilizers. Timber, both as planks and as pulp, and pulp derived from other vegetable fibres could also be used to manufacture building and other constructional materials. Other industries that could readily be established include clothing and food-processing: brewing and cigarette manufacture are already established in the Territory.

PROBLEMS OF INDUSTRIAL DEVELOPMENT

It is apparent that New Guinea is not poor in the resources that could serve an industrial economy. However, whereas agricultural and even timber resources are to some extent already developed, there is virtually no utilization of power and industrial resources at all. A few small hydro-electric plants supplying the towns utilize sites of only low potential. Development is impeded by external factors—the overwhelming economic control exercised by a few large Australian trading firms, and the reluctance of these and other companies to invest in a territory whose political future is uncertain. There are, however, more fundamental limitations of local origin. These are the lack of skilled and semi-skilled labour, the small size of the market and the low purchasing power of the bulk of the population, the absence of town populations of any size, and the primitive condition of the communications system which effectively compartments New Guinea into a large number of small hinterlands —both of seaports and airports—most of which can import from outside more readily than they can trade with one another.

Education and training programmes are remedying the shortage of skilled and semi-skilled labour, though slowly and with insufficient emphasis on training for management and responsibility. Purchasing power is growing as a result of successful cash cropping, though the total absence of any energetic attempt by the large trading companies to expand and diversify retail trade outside the principal centres is providing a serious brake on the use of this growing purchasing power. Some small entrepreneurs are showing more enterprise, but they lack the capital to achieve dramatic results. More seriously, though, the absence of central places and the primitive nature of the communications system are linked impediments that will not readily be removed without the mounting of a major programme of capital works and a fundamental change of policy.

It is argued by some that a number of base-points should be established at ports and major airports, each with a radial road system but without much inter-hinterland linkage except by sea and air: it is proposed, that is, to treat the Territory as a sort of archipelago rather than a single large island with a few outlying islands. But an archipelago such as the Philippines or Indonesia has the advantage of cheap and flexible inter-island transport by sea, and these archipelagos include populous and large islands—Luzon and Java—which have highly developed internal road and rail systems. Air transport as a means of linking islands must remain in the hands of aliens for many years to come, and in the absence of an integrated road system there is only limited range for the kind of native enterprise which has built up an immense range of bus and trucking companies in Luzon as a means of intra-island transport. There is scope for a much wider integrated road system than at present exists.

In particular, there is a crying and obvious need for well-graded, hard-surfaced, two-lane highways from Lae and Madang into the Eastern and Western Highlands, through the Markham-Ramu valley, to Finschhafen and Sattelberg, Bulolo and Wau, Chimbu, Mendi, and Tari. Such a road system, with gravelled side-roads and cross-roads in all directions, would integrate the whole populated region along the sixth parallel south, about half the population of the country. The cost would run to several tens of million pounds; the return would be greatly accelerated development and wider diffusion of development. There is also a need for a similar but smaller road system in the northern Sepik District, using the new defence road from Wewak to Lumi as its axis, and also along

the Papuan coast between at least Kerema and Abau, from Rabaul
along the north coast of New Britain, and—with the greatest engineering problems of all—across Papua to link the Popondetta region,
Garaina, Wau, and Lae to the southern coast of Papua. The effect
of such a system of good roads would be to permit the concentration
of development at nodal points, outstandingly Port Moresby,
Madang, and Lae, to facilitate the growth of towns and their supply
with food and raw materials, and to make possible the establishment of industrial plants serving more than purely local hinterlands. The cost would be enormous, but chiefly because of the
failure to build up any sound foundation for such a road system in
the past. Trucking is carried on between Lae and Mt Hagen, but
along a road that is in truth fit only for four-wheel drive vehicles,
and over hand-built bridges quite unsuited for heavy loads.

There are also untapped possibilities of using the Fly and Sepik
rivers—especially the latter—for the carriage of heavy goods. At
the same time greatly improved port facilities are required at the
major central places: there is no place in the Territory where ships
do not require to use their own derricks to handle cargo. Having
regard to the potentialities of the site, the present port facilities at
Lae, in particular, are deplorable. Far better facilities for small
coastal ships need to be established both at central collecting points
on the islands and remoter coasts and also in the main ports. Finally,
facilities for cargo handling at most airports need to be modernized
beyond the present level—which consists too frequently of a 'line of
boys'.

THE NEED FOR INTEGRATED PLANNING

An enormous gulf divides a population that could utilize a power
capacity of several hundred megawatts from the population of the
highland valley discussed at the outset. A territory whose educational system is at the stage described elsewhere in this volume by
Spate, whose people include very many who experience the kind of
'hopeless envy' of the wealth of the Europeans described by Paula
Brown, presents a development problem of alarming scale. It would
be easy to despair were not the immense progress achieved in
many African territories in the course of half a century not before
us as encouragement. But a measure of co-ordinated planning is
essential if any rapid and consistent progress is to be achieved.

If examination of natural resources shows anything of value, it is
that optimal development of these resources requires a major redeployment of population in which a large element must be urbanization. In pre-contact times most of the people of New Guinea
found the resources available to them in their own locality adequate
for the maintenance of life at the standards they then desired;
where local pressures arose, these were relieved either by short-
distance migration or by the evolution of techniques which made

possible the fuller utilization of resources. The introduction of a cash economy has created a wholly new set of values, so that some areas now seem far richer than others, and many people are almost totally without resources that can be converted into cash in their present habitat. The pattern of labour migration described elsewhere (Brookfield 1960) is in part a response to this changed situation. The fuller utilization of those resources that are in rich supply in New Guinea must demand an assessment that is different again.

While the problems of each region and locality need to be considered separately, it is also necessary to develop a national view, to evolve an integrated plan at the centre, and to assess its implications area by area, and locality by locality. It is useless to attempt to develop everywhere; little can be done for people who dispose only of sago swamp and very poor soil, of steep and rugged mountain sides remote from the trunk roads, of tiny islands accessible only to cutters and canoes. It is not necessary to contemplate forced migrations: active development in the favoured areas, and encouragement of free migration, will draw the young and adventurous off from these naturally poor areas fast enough.

What we see at present in New Guinea is a society in the early stages of a rather painful readjustment to the conditions of its natural environment, in response to new wants, new means of achieving them, and the acquisition of a range of new skills. At the present time we may be on the verge at last of significant large-scale developments, arising from timber extraction, rural resettlement, and the possible utilization of power resources. At this time more than ever before it is essential to consider the evolving new pattern as a whole, in all its implications. The people of New Guinea will need much help to effect the continuing and accelerating process of adjustment, both financial help and technical help. It is by no means certain that Australians, who lack experience in other tropical environments, and whose capital resources for overseas grants are slender, are best qualified to provide this aid. Practical advice could perhaps be obtained from among populations whose recent experience is more directly relevant, including for example Malayans, Africans, and the European administrators who have guided the process of change with some success in other parts of the tropics. For finance, there are certainly untapped sources outside Australia. In this, as in other aspects of New Guinea development, it is of no benefit to New Guinea for Australia to continue to 'go it alone'.

The Sources of Data on Natural Resources

CSIRO REPORTS

Four final reports have been published:

Lands of the Buna-Kokoda Area, Territory of Papua and New Guinea, Land Research Series No. 10, Melbourne, 1964.

Lands of the Wanigela-Cape Vogel Area, Territory of Papua and New Guinea, Land Research Series No. 12, Melbourne, 1964.

Lands of the Port Moresby-Kairuku Area, Territory of Papua and New Guinea, Land Research Series No. 14, Melbourne, 1965.

Lands of the Wabag-Tari Area, Territory of Papua and New Guinea, Land Research Series No. 15, Melbourne, 1965.

Interim reports have been prepared covering the following areas:

Gogol-Upper Ramu (Divisional Report 57/2, August 1957; and Technical Memorandum 60/3, May 1960).

Goroka-Mount Hagen (Divisional Report 58/1, October 1958; and Technical Memorandum 60/2, April 1960).

Lower Ramu-Atitau (Divisional Report 59/1, October 1959).

Wewak-Lower Sepik (Divisional Report 61/2, March 1961).

Final reports are in preparation on these areas, and also on a number of other areas which have not been the subject of interim reports.

The Australian Land Research method is discussed in detail, with a full bibliography, in Christian and Stewart (1964).

TERRAIN

This is derived in part from CSIRO reports listed above, from geological reports, topographical maps (especially the U.S. 1:250,000 Aeronautical Series), and photo-mosaics. The wartime *Terrain Studies* prepared for the Southwest Pacific Command have also been employed.

LITHOLOGY

This map (Fig. 3) is prepared from the reports of geological surveys carried out by the Australasian Petroleum Company (Western Papua as a whole), Rickwood, and McMillan and Malone (Central Highlands), Glaessner (central Papua), Fisher (Morobe), Green (eastern Papua), from CSIRO reports, and from general compilations by Stanley, David and Browne, Klein, and Montgomery, Osborne, and Glaessner.

CLIMATE

The survey by Hounam (1951) is now outdated, and this statement, together with the accompanying maps, is based on records of monthly rainfall for all available dates obtained from the Commonwealth Bureau of Meteorology (Melbourne) and held there on punch cards. Data for some additional stations have been collected by CSIRO. Most of the basic work of processing the data has been done by my research assistant, Mrs D. Hart. The account presented here is preliminary: a larger-scale work on the climate of the whole Melanesian region is in progress.

SOIL

Present reconnaissance knowledge of the soils of the Territory depends largely on the work of the CSIRO teams, and especially on that of Haantjens and Rutherford. Haantjens and van Royen have in preparation a soil map of the whole island. However, the broad classification described here is based on the work of Cline *et al.* (1955) in Hawaii, which provides the best basis available for the discussion of zonal characteristics in tropical soils. Some useful local studies have been carried out by the soil survey officers of the Territory Department of Agriculture, among which particular mention should be made of a recent survey of Bougainville by van Wijk (1962-3).

LITERATURE CITED

In an essay of this nature a detailed bibliography would be inappropriate, and only the comprehensive CSIRO reports, which contain regional bibliographies, are here listed in detail. The Bureau of Mineral Resources has in hand a compilation of the geological material available, Haantjens and van Royen are surveying the available material on soils, and material on climate is reviewed in H. C. Brookfield and Doreen Hart, *Rainfall in the Tropical Southwest Pacific*, Research School of Pacific Studies, Department of Geography Publication G/3, Canberra, 1966. It would be pointless to provide incomplete bibliographies on these aspects here.

4

Trade Prospects for the Rural Sector

R. T. SHAND

DEVELOPMENT prospects in the rural sector of the economy, broadly defined to include not only agricultural and livestock enterprises but also timber and fishing industries, are the main considerations in this chapter.

The 1963 World Bank Mission to the Territory is likely to have a marked influence on trade prospects; however, as a concluding part of this chapter shows, the impact of economic measures advocated by the Mission would, if implemented, be felt mainly in the long term. There would be a comparatively small effect between 1964-5 and 1968-9.

The chapter is therefore divided into two parts, the first of which deals with prospects in the normal course of events, particularly up to 1968-9. The analysis focuses on the outlook for individual commodities, both those important now and those with some potential. For each of these commodities the likely market developments and the short-term and long-term supply potential of the Territory are considered. In this section the aggregate short-term effects of individual commodity prospects on the economy as a whole are also examined, with particular attention to the changes that can be expected in the balance of trade (imports exceeded exports by £15 million in 1963-4) and also in the level of imports of goods of rural origin, which in 1963-4 comprised a sizeable proportion of total imports.

The second part of the chapter reviews the Mission's recommendations and calculates the prospects if the commodity targets suggested by the Mission were attained.

COCONUT INDUSTRY

The coconut industry has traditionally been the sheet anchor of the rural sector in Papua-New Guinea. After World War II it provided as much as 67 per cent of annual export income, though in recent years its relative importance has declined as a result of the more rapid expansion of other commodities such as coffee and cocoa. Nevertheless in 1962-3 it was still by far the biggest export earner and provided 41 per cent of export income.

The industry is large by Territory standards but small in terms of the total world market. It is therefore at the mercy of movements in world prices, so a brief review of market prospects for the industry will be helpful.[1] The most profitable way of making this review is to concentrate on the market for coconut oil, the chief end-product of processing; there are other end-products, such as coconut cake, desiccated coconut, and coir and coir products, but these are of comparatively minor importance.

The end-uses of coconut oil fall into three categories: food products (margarine and shortening, bakery and confectionery products), soap, and various products of other non-food industries such as synthetic rubber, hydraulic brake fluid for aircraft, plasticizers, resins, and insecticides. Most of the properties found in coconut oil are also to be found in other fats and oils, but it does gain an advantage with lauric acid as one constituent (palm kernel oil is the only other commodity with a substantial lauric acid content). This acid has distinctive lathering properties, useful for soaps and plasticizers. Further, coconut oil melts at mouth temperature, so it is popular for bakery and confectionery products.

The main markets for coconut oil are in North America, Western Europe, Japan, and Australia. These countries vary considerably in the proportions they use in the various end-uses (F.A.O. 1959-63: No. 8 (1962)): the United States, for instance, in 1961 utilized only 30 per cent in food (mainly bakery and confectionery) while 70 per cent went in non-food uses (21 per cent in soap manufacture and 49 per cent in other uses—mainly in the chemical industries). In contrast, 75 per cent of the Western Europe imports were used for food (mainly margarine). The demand pattern in Japan, Canada, and Australia resembles that of the U.S.A. On the world market as a whole, consumption is fairly evenly divided between food and non-food uses, but, from the viewpoint of market growth in the higher income countries it is the non-food category that is important.

In food uses, coconut oil faces stiff competition. Butter competes with margarine on the consumer's table, and to some extent in cooking, in the higher income countries. There are also a number of oils which are close substitutes for coconut oil in the production of margarine. In the U.S.A. they are cottonseed and soybean oils, while in Western Europe there are more, for example whale and fish oils, palm kernel, soybean and cottonseed oils. Its relative price is the main determinant of the percentage of coconut oil in margarine.

Competition from substitutes is also a factor in non-food uses, though the degree of interchangeability is not quite so high. Demand

[1] This section draws upon a number of statistical sources, particularly F.A.O. 1962a, 1958-63, 1959-63, 1963a, 1963b, 1963c.

elasticity is probably highest in soap manufacture. Tallow, for example, has proved an effective substitute for coconut oil. In the U.S.A. the relative cheapness of tallow has reduced the coconut oil (lauric acid) content of soap to about 15 per cent, a minimum for good lathering. In addition, soap has lost ground to synthetic detergents. In other non-food uses there appears to be less pressure from substitutes at present.

Various segments of the market have changed considerably during the last decade. Demand for soaps has increased in some parts of the world, but has declined in the U.S.A. and Western Europe, whereas U.S. demand for confectionery and bakery products and particularly in chemical industries has risen. However, the data on exports for the period 1953-62 give 'strong *prima facie* evidence that these conflicting trends . . . offset each other during that period, to produce a remarkable stability in the strength of total demand' (F.A.O. 1963c:14). The price variations which have occurred appear to have been primarily due to supply variations.

Prices in the early sixties have been low due to pressure of supplies. It remains now to foresee whether this position might change. It has been suggested (F.A.O. 1962a:p. II-26) that commercial trade in fats and oils will not expand greatly to 1970. Of the large traditional markets, consumption is close to saturation point in the U.S.A., and there will probably be a rise in net exportable supplies of oils. Sales to Western Europe will probably rise only slowly because of progressive saturation of consumption and the increasing competition from synthetics. Most of the increase in demand is likely to come from growth in population and *per capita* incomes in the less developed countries, in some of which, particularly those close to being net importers, a gap between local demand and domestic production could develop. If these countries were free of foreign exchange problems, they would probably import to cover their needs and world trade would then expand. It is highly likely, however, that foreign exchange would be in short supply for many of these countries and their governments would prefer to adopt measures to stimulate local production. In this case world trade would not be greatly influenced by this demand expansion.

The supplies of all fats and oils, with the possible exception of whale oil, are expected to expand in the sixties. Production of animal fats is expected to increase as an indirect result of the expanding market for meat, especially beef. Fish oils appear to have good production possibilities, and may outstrip the others in expansion. One projection expects that, apart from marine oils (whale and fish), all fats and oils will show rates of increase similar to those of the fifties (F.A.O. 1962a:p. II-22).

The market for coconut oil seems unlikely to expand faster than the gradual pace expected for fats and oils as a group. Growth faster than this could probably only be gained through further reductions in the already depressed price level. Substantial and sustained upward price movements also seem unlikely, partly because the general market for fats and oils will be kept fairly well in balance by changes in stocks and varying production levels of annually grown oil-crops, and partly because there is such a high degree of substitutability between fats and oils in most uses.

Prospects for Papua-New Guinea.[2] The potential levels of coconut production in Papua-New Guinea for the years up till 1970 have largely been determined already. Since the coconut palm takes about eight years to come into bearing, production will largely be governed by the planting activity over the past decade. Palms currently being planted will affect production only in the longer-term future. Actual levels of production will be affected by factors such as climate and, particularly among smallholders, the level of prices received.

Whether or not past plantings will expand total production in the Territory in the next few years also depends on the age distribution of trees in the industry. Production will expand in the next decade only if the rate of planting has exceeded the rate of replacement required to maintain past output levels.

The coconut industry comprises both estates and smallholders. In terms of numbers of mature trees they are of roughly equal import-ance, with 9·6 and 10·7 million trees respectively in 1961-2 (T.P.N.G. 1959-63 and 1963e:No. 4, p. 106), though in terms of marketed production the estates dominate—in 1962-3 they contri-buted 73 per cent of the total. The productive capacity of small-holders is not reflected in marketed production, since part of output is consumed by the producers themselves and part, for lack of adequate incentive, is left unharvested beneath the trees. Estate trees are, on average, at an advanced age. In 1961-2 only 18 per cent were immature and quite a large proportion of those in bearing were past their prime. By contrast, smallholder trees are much younger; in 1961-2, 56 per cent were immature (T.P.N.G. 1963e).

Since World War II total marketed output has risen slowly and has not greatly exceeded the pre-1939 peak of production. The rate of estate planting has only barely exceeded the relatively high rate of replacement needed as a result of the advanced age of so many trees and the destruction wrought by the war (B.A.E. 1951; T.P.N.G. 1959-63).

Over the next few years a continuation of the gradual rise in marketed output can be expected, a large proportion of it coming from the smallholders, since they have been planting more actively

[2] This section and equivalent sections for other commodities which follow use a number of statistical sources and reports, particularly T.P.N.G. 1956-63, 1959-63, 1963a, 1963c.

than estates and have a larger proportion of immature trees. The Department of Agriculture, Stock and Fisheries, Port Moresby, in 1964 estimated that production in 1967-8 may be about 7,000-8,000 tons of copra more than 1962-3, when it was 110,000 tons of copra equivalent.

Longer-term supply prospects depend on whether the rate of planting can be accelerated in the coming years. From the estate viewpoint, the currently depressed price level and the unimpressive market outlook for the future is hardly encouraging. In the absence of precise information it is difficult to say how profitable production is at present. Established plantations may find it profitable to maintain and even expand their investment, but it is doubtful whether many new investors, with the choice of product open to them, would select the copra industry, particularly, too, since there is such a long time-lag before returns begin.

For smallholders the rate of planting and the enthusiasm for harvesting are contingent upon the degree of incentive. This depends in turn on such factors as the returns per unit of labour and on the contact producers have with the advanced sector. Characteristically, coconut smallholders are spread along the narrow coastal foreshores of the mainland and islands in Papua-New Guinea. Their outside contacts are occasional and usually fleeting. The remoteness of the villages and the small scale of production result in high transport costs, which reduce the effective level of the prices received and also make consumer goods more expensive. These factors tend to inhibit economic activity. On the other hand copra production is technically simple and is familiar, since it plays an important role in subsistence production. Provided the problem of creating incentive can be successfully tackled there do seem to be long-term possibilities for smallholder expansion in the industry.

COCOA

Cocoa is now the second most important agricultural product in the Territory. As with other export crops, the extent to which the production potential for cocoa will be exploited in the Territory will depend on trends in the world market.[3]

The post-war years have been marked first by a state of shortage and more recently by a tendency towards oversupply in the world market. The reopening of the European market, together with rising population and income in the main consuming countries, led to a fast rise in demand after World War II. Production, on the other hand, responded sluggishly and prices rose. High prices, which reached a peak in 1954, stimulated plantings especially in African countries. These began to make an impact on world supplies in 1959, and from then on prices fell to such an extent that

[3] This section on the world cocoa market draws mainly on F.A.O. 1962a, 1958-63, 1961a, 1962b, 1963a, 1963d.

producers began to fear the development of a market glut. This led
to an unsuccessful attempt in 1962-3 to conclude an international
agreement which would stabilize prices and provide producers
with a reasonable rate of return. In 1962 the price level flattened out.
It showed a tendency to rise a little in 1963 and it remained relatively stable in 1964, but in the first six months of 1965 it plunged
dramatically to its lowest since 1946, due to a record world harvest
in 1964-5.

Data on planting statistics in producing countries are too scarce
to permit accurate predictions of future supplies. Indications early
in the 1960s led to expectations that increases in production would
continue towards 1970 (F.A.O. 1962a, 1961a). The experience of
the 1964-5 crop has now made it clear that production capacity has
exceeded these early forecasts. Whether supply will continue at or
near the record 1964-5 level will depend largely on climate and on
the short-term reactions of producers to the severe fall in the price
level.

Projections of demand, based on assumption concerning population and income levels, suggest that there will be a gradual
growth towards 1970. Reactions to the sudden fall in price in 1964-5
will undoubtedly raise consumption further and can be expected
to bring about a partial restoration of the price level towards pre-
1964-5 levels. It seems likely, however, that, barring future climatic
hazards, the price level will remain considerably below the 1963-4
level. At worst, a continuing fast growth of supplies could result
in very depressed prices, together with an accumulation of stocks,
for many years to come.

Two other factors could influence the picture. One is competition
from substitutes, and the other is the future level of import demand
in the Soviet bloc.

The cocoa bean is usually broken down into two parts during
processing. One is cocoa powder, a flavouring agent, the other is
cocoa butter, the fat content of the bean. High prices in the fifties
encouraged research into cheaper fat substitutes, and results have
been at least partially successful. In some uses there has been
complete replacement of cocoa butter and in others a mixture is now
used. Although substitutes have not yet substantially reduced the
market for cocoa butter, there are signs that the demand is becoming
more price sensitive. However, a continuation of the recent price
level for cocoa will reduce the danger of this encroachment in the
market.

Soviet-bloc imports of cocoa are small at present but have been
rising in recent years. The scope for further increases is considerable, since *per capita* consumption is still low—it is only one-quarter
of the level in north-west Europe. Policy decisions to increase
imports substantially could be important in strengthening the
market; particularly now that prices are so low.

Prospects for Papua-New Guinea. Cocoa production in the Territory is in a highly expansionary phase. The total area planted has
risen from 7,000 acres in 1950-1 to well over 120,000 acres in 1962-3.
Plantations have been primarily responsible for this progress
(106,000 acres in 1962-3), but smallholders are also making an
important and rising contribution with 23,000 acres in 1961-2
(T.P.N.G. 1963e). In terms of output, acreages in bearing yielded
about 14,000 tons in 1962-3, of which 3,400 tons were produced by
smallholders. Export earnings from this crop totalled nearly £3
million, 16 per cent of total earnings for the Territory.

Mainly as a result of past plantings, this fast pace of growth
seems likely to continue at least up till 1970, providing problems of
climate, pests, and disease do not seriously intervene.[4] Only one-
half the total estate area of cocoa is in bearing; in addition,
increasing yields are likely as trees in bearing reach their productive
capacity. Probably no more than one-third of the trees have actually
reached their potential.

Lack of data on the age distribution of trees precludes an
accurate projection of future production, but one estimate (by the
Department of Agriculture, Stock and Fisheries) predicts an annual
increase in output of about 4,000 tons for some years to come. This
rate of increase would bring production to 34,000 tons by 1967-8.
At £150 per ton, this could add £0·6 million per year to export
proceeds, and by 1967-8 total cocoa earnings could be £5 million.
Papua-New Guinea would then be among the leading small producers in the trade.

From a longer-run point of view it is questionable now whether
this present rate of expansion can be sustained. As we have seen,
world price levels were not unfavourable up to 1964 but the recent
price collapse and its supply implications will introduce a new
element of uncertainty and may discourage new plantings.

The Territory has been in a somewhat advantageous position
within the market because of the type of cocoa it produces. There
are three main varieties in commercial production. One is the
'forastero' type, which makes up the bulk grades and a majority of
the world trade. The second is the 'criollo' variety, with a lower
yield but a finer quality, used in blends with bulk grades in choco-
late manufacture. The third is a hybrid of the first two, the 'trini-
tario' variety, which produces the so-called 'flavour' cocoa. Most
of the Territory's production is of the last kind. In the world market
it is only the bulk grades which are in heavy supply; the production
of flavour cocoa has been more or less steady. The insulation which
it receives, however, only operates for a comparatively narrow price
range. Major market fluctuations such as the 1964-5 supply surplus
and price fall are felt by all cocoa producers.

[4] Some losses are being experienced from the disease 'die-back', which, if it
spreads, could check the rate of expansion.

COFFEE

The world cocoa and coffee markets have displayed similar movements since World War II, though for coffee they have been somewhat more exaggerated.[5] After the war, demand recovered while supply showed little change and consequently prices soared. The prospect of high profits led to new plantings of high-yielding varieties particularly in Brazil and Africa but, because of the time-lag before the trees began bearing, they had little effect on world supplies until the late 1950s. From 1957 onwards prices began to fall rapidly, until in 1963 they were lower than at any time since 1949.

Prices would have fallen further but for the success of a series of annual agreements between exporters to limit the flow of coffee on to the market. However, the agreements inevitably led to the accumulation of stocks and by 1960 these had reached a level equivalent to more than total world demand for a year. The agreements were therefore only stop-gap measures and in no way solved the basic dilemma of excess productive capacity among producers. One calculation (F.A.O. 1961b) showed that over the period 1959-60 to 1961-2 world coffee production had already passed all projections of consumption for 1970 and further price falls could not hope to stimulate demand sufficiently to bridge the gap.

The situation drove producers to find ways of correcting the imbalance. In 1962 the producing and consuming countries drew up an International Coffee Agreement (U.N. 1963), which was designed to restrict the amount of coffee coming on to the market by means of export quotas in much the same way as annual producer agreements had done. Producers had the additional responsibility of bringing production into line with these quotas, for example through tree eradication and agricultural diversification. Ways and means of expanding world consumption were also to be investigated. In May 1965 the U.S.A. finally passed the legislation which would authorize her membership in the Agreement. Previously there had been co-operation among the rest of the signatories which helped to stabilize the market. U.S. participation can be expected to add a further stabilizing influence.

Prospects for Papua-New Guinea. This essentially is the situation which has brought the growth of a promising infant industry in the Territory almost to a halt. As in other producing countries, the high coffee prices in the early fifties stimulated plantings, mainly of Arabica coffee in the Highlands, both on an estate and on a smallholder basis. Coffee has in fact become the most important money-earner for the indigenous Highland population. From a

[5] Material used in this section is derived from F.A.O. 1952- , 1961b, 1962a, 1963a, U.N. 1963, and Wickizer 1964.

beginning around 1950, post-war planting rose to over 10,000 acres by June 1963. Production followed a four to five year time-lag while trees matured, and by 1962-3 it had reached 5,000 tons, worth £2 million in export income, or about 11 per cent of total export income. Indigenous smallholders contributed almost half of the output.

Once again statistics are inadequate to allow production forecasts of any great reliability, but it is clear that there will be a considerable expansion in coffee production in the next few years because of the earlier plantings. Immature trees comprise 40 per cent of estate plantings and a large proportion in bearing have not yet reached their full productive capacity. The Department of Agriculture, Stock and Fisheries estimates that production could reach 11,500 tons by 1967-8. Further increases will probably be registered beyond this point, but aside from these effects of past plantings the future for the industry appears rather gloomy at present.

Under the International Coffee Agreement Papua-New Guinea is classed with Australia; as long as the two combined remain a net importer, no export quota is applied. By 1967-8 production will have probably closed the gap and will make the two combined a net exporter. It will then become necessary to apply for a quota and, if there is no great improvement in the world supply-demand balance, it may be difficult for the Territory to obtain a substantial allocation. Meanwhile the prospect of becoming a net exporter has necessitated a policy of discouragement of further plantings, in accordance with the Agreement. The Administration has ceased to encourage smallholder plantings in the Highlands and no further areas of land are being released to planters for coffee growing.

Barring a radical change in the market outlook, the only likely long-term growth will be a slow expansion on the coastal lowlands of Robusta coffee production for the Australian market.

Before writing off this industry it is worth noting that the most recent events in world production suggest that some reassessment of the market situation may be needed. The world-wide production increases expected for the sixties as a result of planting in the fifties have not yet materialized. Furthermore, trees in Brazil have suffered severe damage recently from frost, drought, and fire. Production in Brazil was greatly reduced in 1963 and 1964 and may continue below her annual export quota for a few years yet. The country will be forced to use a considerable proportion of her stocks to make up the deficit in her annual quota. Large numbers of trees will apparently not recover at all, and this, together with the programme of tree eradication and agricultural diversification, will contribute substantially towards restoring balance in the international market.

RUBBER

Rubber is the fifth most important export industry in Papua-New Guinea. Production comes almost exclusively from a small number of estates. Since World War II these estates have shown a moderate rate of expansion, raising production from 1,290 tons in 1955-6 to 4,760 tons in 1962-3. Much of the effect of increased plantings is yet to be felt, as about 30 per cent of all trees were immature in 1962-3. According to the Department of Agriculture, Stock and Fisheries, production is expected to reach 11,000 tons by 1967-8. Indigenous producers have some stands of immature trees and a small area of trees in bearing which yielded 20 tons of rubber in 1962-3. The Administration plans to encourage greater smallholder participation in the industry in the future.

Territory rubber has the advantages of an assured market and preferential tariff treatment in Australia. All production is given duty-free access, while imports from other sources are subject to a duty of 2d. per lb., waived only when all Territory rubber has been absorbed (Australia 1957 and 1963b).

There appears to be no shortage of land suitable for rubber in Papua-New Guinea. The key factors for exploitation are the market outlook and the competitive abilities of Territory producers.

The total rubber market[6] (including the market for synthetic rubber) should continue to expand in the non-Soviet section, mainly because of increased demand in the industrial countries of North America, Japan, the United Kingdom, and the European Economic Community. The pace of increasing demand will be governed by the rate of increase in national incomes, increases in motorization, and the relative demands for new and replacement tyres.

The outlook for natural rubber within the total market is not particularly promising, due mainly to the increasing competition from synthetics. The main competitor at present is SBR. It is not a perfect substitute for natural rubber but it has cut deeply into its market. It is estimated that, in the U.S.A., SBR is preferred for 40 per cent of the total rubber market, natural rubber in 25 per cent, while in 35 per cent of the market the choice is governed primarily by the relative prices of the two types.

Competition with synthetics does not end here. New and more perfect substitutes, the 'stereo-regular' rubbers, give promise of a serious threat to natural rubber. Unit costs are still high and production is still relatively low, but progress towards lower and more competitive prices could be made within a few years. If this occurs the demand for natural rubber will become much more price elastic.

The future strength of demand for natural rubber will also

[6] This survey of the rubber market draws mainly on the following sources: the International Rubber Study Group, 1947- , 1962; F.A.O. 1962a, 1963a, and Corden 1963.

depend on quantities imported by Soviet-bloc countries and mainland China. The intention of the Soviet government, the biggest
importer of the group, is to replace imports completely with home-
produced synthetics, but up to 1964 the programme has not
proceeded far towards this goal. The volume of imports for these
countries as a group rose to a peak of over half a million tons in
1961, due largely to the record level of imports by the U.S.S.R. The
latter's imports have since fallen but were still at a high level in
1964. Other countries in the group have imported more since 1961
and have collectively almost counterbalanced the reduction in
U.S.S.R. imports. This suggests that even if the U.S.S.R. does
successfully implement her import replacement programme, the
group as a whole might continue to be a strengthening influence in
the market.

The supply of natural rubber is expected to increase in the short
term, though it is difficult to estimate by how much. Extensive
replanting with high-yielding material is likely to substantially raise
Malayan production. The prospects are obscure in Indonesia, but if
increases do occur they seem unlikely to be on any important scale.
Small increases are expected in other Asian countries and in Africa.

One supply factor which cannot be ignored is the huge U.S.
stockpile of one million tons (March 1962), of which only 13 per
cent is now considered to be essential. The U.S. government has
endeavoured to minimize the depressing effects of disposals of
stocks by setting a minimum price below which undeteriorated
stock cannot be sold. It is, however, permissible to sell deteriorating
stocks or those in danger of deterioration at prices below this minimum level, and recently supplementary arrangements have been
announced which allow further disposals under foreign aid and
defence programmes. Sizeable reductions in these stocks will certainly have a depressing effect on prices.

To sum up prospects for 1970 in more quantitative fashion (see
Corden 1963), non-Soviet demand for rubber might be around 5·3
million tons. If the share of the world market held by natural rubber
is reduced slightly and no important change in the relative prices
of natural and SBR occurs, the demand for natural and stereo-
regulars could be about 2·3 million tons. If sales of stereo-regulars
are around 0·3 million tons and the demand in the Soviet bloc and
mainland China is a conservative 0·2 million tons, the consumption
of natural rubber may be about 2·2 million tons. Since production
is expected to be about 2·7 million tons, a surplus of 0·5 million
tons could occur, arising partly from a reduction in demand from
the Soviet bloc and partly from the intrusion of stereo-regulars. If
this situation develops, the price of natural rubber could fall, to
bring the market into balance. If on the other hand there is no
diminution of demand from Communist countries, such a fall may
be averted.

Despite the possibility of declining prices there are some reasons for believing that rubber production can profitably expand further in Papua-New Guinea. Physical conditions appear to be most suitable, and weed control is, apparently, not as great a problem as in other major producing countries. Furthermore, growers have access to an increasing supply of high-yielding plant material.

OTHER CROPS

Two other categories of crops deserve some mention in relation to future prospects. One includes those crops which at present make a minor contribution to the output of the sector, namely peanuts, passionfruit, tobacco, and various truck crops. The other comprises those which appear to have worthwhile potential but which are not yet grown on a commercial scale, such as tea, pyrethrum, and sugar.

Peanuts. Peanut exports from the Territory have been stable for some years at around 2,000 tons per annum. This production comes almost exclusively from a small number of European farmers; native farmers produce a quantity for their own use and have, in the past, made a small contribution to exports, but they have generally been discouraged from producing for the market by low and fluctuating prices.

Owing to difficulties in competing with low cost suppliers in other markets, all exports have been sold in Australia, where they enjoy duty-free access (Australia 1963a). The 2,000 tons do not appear to have appreciably depressed the Australian market; however, any significant increase could substantially reduce prices. Such expansion seems rather unlikely, since at prevailing prices the profit margin is apparently low.

Passionfruit. This is grown as a sideline cash crop by indigenous Highland farmers. From 1957-8 to 1961-2 output averaged nearly 40,000 gallons per annum of juice equivalent. This has been wholly absorbed by Australia, where up to 60,000 gallons are now permitted duty-free access (Australia 1964). The Australian market is quite small (100,000 gallons of juice equivalent in 1961-2), and the duty-free quota for Papua-New Guinea is probably a fair indication of the volume which can be absorbed at this stage without causing sharp downward movements in price. For any substantial expansion in production, the Territory would probably have to locate new markets.

Limitations on expansion are probably more important on the production side. The crop is at present harvested from vines dispersed through forest country, and although production could be gradually expanded in this manner any substantial development of the industry would require more intensive cultural methods. For this to occur, problems of pest and disease build-up will first have to be overcome. In the short run it is unlikely that production in the Territory will exceed the present duty-free quota of 60,000 gallons.

Truck crops. A steady, if undramatic, expansion is likely in the production of truck crops for sale within the Territory. In 1960-1 these were valued at a little more than £800,000 (derived from White 1964). Production mainly meets the needs of the urban indigenous population. Further urban growth, together with some development of agricultural specialization, can be expected to expand demand in the future. It should be noted that the expansion of sales will mainly signify a greater inclusion of production in the monetary sector rather than an increase in total output. There appear to be no immediate prospects for the replacement of the large annual imports of fresh fruit and vegetables for European consumers.

Tobacco. A policy of import replacement in tobacco production is being pursued by the Administration. At present only a small proportion of demand is being met locally, but as a first step towards self-sufficiency the manufacture of cigarettes has commenced in the Territory. Expanded leaf production is also planned, to meet internal needs. If successful the import bill for tobacco will be gradually reduced.

Tea. The most promising new agricultural crop for the Territory is tea. A rapid expansion of the tea industry is planned following the successful establishment of a pilot tea plantation by the Administration (Graham *et al.* 1963). This experiment indicated that high yields could be obtained under Territory conditions; it showed that a high quality product was possible and that New Guinea labour could quickly learn the arts of efficient plucking. Investigations have also shown that large areas in the Highlands are suitable for tea production. It is likely that, under Highland conditions, bushes will come into bearing a year earlier than in other major producing areas in the world, and, furthermore, that the even distribution of rainfall over large areas of the Highlands will result in a year-round harvest, affording some cost advantages in the use of factory facilities.

The world market is in reasonable balance at present and prospects are sound.[7] Production increases are expected in some countries, notably in India, and to a lesser extent in Japan, Pakistan, Africa, Latin America, and Taiwan. Economic difficulties in Indonesia and policy in China and the Soviet bloc make their respective influences hard to assess. Growth in demand may produce some

[7] References used for this section include F.A.O. 1952- , vol. 11 (1962): 7-9, 1960, 1962a, 1963a.

changes in the market. Consumption will probably be slow growing in high income countries, depending more on social habits and changes in tastes than on income changes. A faster rate of growth is expected in less developed countries producing tea and this will probably absorb most of the increased output from these countries and keep the market firm in the face of restricted expansion in world import demand. Most output increase will occur in countries producing plainer teas, and any weakening of the market will probably affect mainly these types. The quality tea market, which Papua-New Guinea intends to enter, should remain firm, or may even improve.

The Administration envisages plantings of 20,000 acres within a few years. If this proceeds as planned, tea will soon make a considerable contribution to export earnings. Assuming a yield of 1,000 lb. of made tea per mature acre, and that 20,000 acres are planted by 1970, when the acreage is in full production by 1977 output will be around 20 million lb. or almost 9,000 tons. At an average price of 4s. 3d. per lb., this would earn the Territory just over £4 million. If 60,000 acres were established in ten years time, full production would bring export income to £12 million per annum.

Pyrethrum. Attempts are being made to establish a small pyrethrum industry in areas of the Highlands above 6,000 feet, as a means of introducing a cash crop to people who have had little or no opportunity up till now to produce for the market. The short-term aim is to establish about 1,000 acres, sufficient for the operation of a locally-sited processing factory. This could provide export income in the vicinity of £50,000 within a few years. Longer-term prospects depend partly on securing firm marketing arrangements in the closed world market for pyrethrum and partly on how the end-product, pyrethrin, fares in competition with synthetic substitutes. At present the competition from synthetics appears to be principally limited by toxicity problems associated with the chemicals employed.

Sugar. Physical conditions are thought to be suitable for the cultivation of sugar in Papua-New Guinea, though the programme for the development of a sugar industry has not yet advanced beyond the exploratory stages. Field trials are currently being carried out to gauge the production potentialities of sugar for the Territory. If these are successful it is likely that efforts will be made to establish a small mill within a decade. One inhibiting factor has been the small size of the internal market, which is still well below the capacity of the smallest economic mill unit. However, a small industry could be established if an export market could be found for the supply in excess of home requirements, at least until internal demand caught up with supply.

Timber. Sizeable additions to export income in the short term are likely to come from expanding timber sales. In 1962-3 the total log harvest was around 76 million super feet: about one-half was absorbed by the local market, and the other half was exported. Production has been marketed in the form of logs, sawn timber, and as plywood and veneers. Exports in that year were valued at £1·3 million, making timber the fourth-largest export earner in the Territory. Over half the value of exports was obtained from plywood sales, mostly to Australia. Logs and lumber each earned about £300,000. In recent years export sales of plywood and sawn timber have made no important gains, indeed there has been some decline in the exports of plywood. The important feature has been the sharp rise in exports of logs, principally to Japan. Between 1958-9 and 1962-3 the volume exported rose from less than one million to nearly fifteen million super feet. The rise in value, to £319,000, counterbalanced the decline in earnings from plywood.

The Territory has extensive forest resources of marketable value. The Department of Forests (T.P.N.G. 1963d) has estimated total forested land at roughly 90 million acres. About 36·6 million acres are classified as accessible, of which about 20-30 million acres have commercial promise. Most of the stands contain a proportion of useful timber but there are few pure stands of any species (beyond the small area of plantations being established). At present only a little more than a million acres are being exploited. Until recently the mixed nature of the timber stands discouraged their exploitation, but Japanese millers have found uses for a wide variety of Territory timbers, in plywoods, veneers, etc., and have adapted their equipment to handle the mixed consignments. This technical ingenuity, together with the rapid rate of expansion of the Japanese market, has opened the way for fast exploitation in the Territory.

A five-year plan formulated by the Department of Forests envisages that the log harvest will be increased from around 80 million super feet in 1962-3 to 180 million super feet by 1968-9. Sawn timber production will show a moderate rise of 4 million super feet. Plywood output may fall. The value of total output will be doubled over the six years, reaching £6 million by 1968-9. Export income from timber will increase, mainly through higher log exports which may rise to a value of £2 million (an increase of £1·7 million over 1962-3), bringing total export income from timber to about £3 million.

Livestock industries. The main efforts in livestock are centred on the development of a beef cattle industry. The Administration also encourages poultry and pig industries but these have not shown much commercial growth so far. Experiments with sheep have met with little success.

The initial objective for beef is self-sufficiency in the Territory (Anderson 1963). Total consumption is the equivalent of about 35,000 carcases, of which imports supply around 33,000 (27,000 equivalent in canned meat imports and 6,000 in imported frozen meat) and local production accounts for the rest. The local kill represents a 10 per cent takeoff from total herd numbers of 30,000. Present policy is to build up numbers to 50,000 head by 1966, which would give an annual turnoff at present rates of killing of around 5,000 carcases. This increase of 2,000 carcases would mean a saving in imports of £245,000,[8] but would be only a small step towards self-sufficiency. Long-term prospects seem bright in view of the extensive areas of grasslands suitable for grazing and the lack of serious diseases in the Territory.

Fisheries. Investigations of the fishing potential of Papua-New Guinea have been proceeding for some years. For the long term, possibilities seem promising (van der Meulen 1962; T.P.N.G. 1963a), for example barramundi in the Gulf waters and crayfish, prawns, and tuna east of Rabaul. More research is needed on possible and known fishing grounds before production is undertaken on a commercial scale, but it is hoped that eventually local waters will supply the Territory's needs and will contribute to export earnings. The need for preliminary investigations means, however, that rapid progress towards self-sufficiency in the near future is unlikely.

AGGREGATE SHORT-TERM PROSPECTS

The next few years should witness a fast rate of expansion in production in the rural sector. Most of this will contribute towards higher exports, so that total value of exports could rise to £29 million by 1967-8, at an average increase of about £1·8 million per annum (see Table 4.1).

Export income from coffee, timber, and rubber and possibly cocoa should at least double in the period to 1967-8, the main increase coming from the cocoa and coffee industries. By that year cocoa and coffee will probably begin to challenge the coconut industry as the leading export earner. Minor expansion can also be expected in passionfruit and pyrethrum.

It is unlikely that expansion of production of commodities to replace imports of rural origin will make much progress in this period. Livestock output will rise gradually, but the rate of expansion currently expected may do little other than cover the rising internal demand. There are, on the other hand, longer-term prospects for the replacement of imports of fish, meat, and dairy products, of fruit and vegetables, tobacco and sugar.

[8] Assuming a 500 lb. carcase dresses out at 350 lb. and sells at 7s. per lb.

Table 4.1   Territory of Papua and New Guinea
Projection of Export Income

Commodity	1962-3		1967-8*		Increase over 1962-3 £m.
	£m.	% of Total	£m.	% of Total	
Coconut products	7·38	41	7·89	29	0·51
Cocoa	3·00	17	5·10	19	2·10
Coffee	2·01	11	5·15	19	3·14
Rubber	1·16	6	2·77	10	1·61
Timber	1·34	7	2·70	10	1·36
Other†	3·25	18	3·38	13	0·13
Total	18·14	100	26·99	100	11·37

*1962-3 price level is assumed for all products in 1967-8, except cocoa, for which a considerably lower price of £A150 per ton is used. It is possible that the price of rubber could fall by 1967-8. A 10 per cent reduction, for example, would lower export income by £227,000 in that year.

†It is assumed that all sources of export income in this category other than passion-fruit and pyrethrum remain at 1962-3 levels.

Between 1950-1 and 1962-3 imports almost trebled, with an average annual growth of £1·5 million. In recent years the rate of growth accelerated slightly (from 1957-8 to 1962-3 the annual average was about £1·6 million). Export income, on the other hand, has been increasing at the slower average rate of £0·8 million per annum. The annual increase of £1·8 million per year projected for exports over the next five years thus constitutes a sharp acceleration over this period. Nevertheless it may only just cover the annual increase in imports if these continue to grow at current rates, and will do little to bridge the large deficit in the balance of trade.

WORLD BANK MISSION

One most important influence on the future economic development of the Territory will be the effect of the recent World Bank Mission (I.B.R.D. 1965).

The Mission sees the development of the rural sector as the chief means of generating economic development. Within the sector, it generally advocates an acceleration of present rates of development and sets targets over the next ten years for most commodities. Set against the pattern of development now evolving and now favoured by the Administration, there are no changes in the range of commodities to be encouraged, but there are changes in the priorities assigned to particular commodities. Among the major products, a continued emphasis for the cocoa and the rubber industries is advocated, but a significantly greater priority is given to expanding the coconut, beef cattle, and timber industries. No targets are set for coffee because of restrictions imposed by the International Coffee Council.

The Bank envisages participation both by indigenous and European farmers in this programme. Overall, the greater part of the increase is to come from the Europeans, particularly in the short run, though there is some variation according to the commodity. The Bank recommends that the expansion in timber should be organized by attracting large-scale European commercial units. The higher rubber output would be through further plantings by estates, with a gradual expansion in smallholder activity. Half the additional plantings of cocoa would be estate-grown over the ten-year period, towards the end of which the rate of planting by smallholders would build up to twice that of the estates. Estates are to establish almost half the additional coconuts planned. The planned expansion of the beef industry is to be based initially on the multiplication of herds, mainly under the control of European ranchers; distribution would eventually provide indigenous farmers with a half-share in the industry in terms of stock numbers.

Some appreciation of the scale of the expansion envisaged can be obtained from the planting programmes recommended for individual products. The annual rate of cocoa plantings would be quadrupled and coconut plantings almost doubled over the ten years. The rate of establishment of estate rubber would be quadrupled and that of smallholder rubber gradually expanded. In total, the average annual rate of rubber planting would be increased to about six times the present level. Beef cattle numbers would be enlarged ten times within ten years, with a higher annual rate of takeoff. The Mission also advocates raising the current five-year plan for the annual log cut in the timber industry by two-thirds, mainly to expand the export sales of logs. There is also a modest plan to develop the tea industry, along with more minor suggestions for the pyrethrum and passionfruit industries, and there are recommendations for research into other crops.

The programme would, if implemented, have relatively little impact on production and income in the short term, that is to 1968-9. Most of the major suggestions are for crops which take four or more years to come into bearing, so that augmented plantings from 1964-5 would not affect production until 1968-9 and later. The two exceptions, which could have an appreciable influence within the next few years, are the suggestions for accelerating the annual log cut in the timber industry and, to a lesser extent, the suggestions for expanding beef cattle numbers and production. By the Bank's calculations, export income from the timber industry could rise to £7 million per annum by 1968-9, roughly £4 million more than the expansion expected without the Bank's influence. There would also be a total replacement of imports of fresh, chilled, and frozen beef by that year.

The calculations in the preceding section showed that export income might be expected to rise by about £1·8 million per year over the five years from 1962-3 to 1967-8.[9] The Bank's recommendations with our assumptions would add an average of about £600,000 annually to export income over this five-year period. Total export income could therefore be £32·8 million by 1968-9, and the annual addition to export income might be raised to around £2·5 million.[10]

Implementation of World Bank recommendations would mean they would begin to exert their main influence in the seventies. Assuming prices at 1962-3 levels, the achievement of production targets for the four major crops and for tea would realize more than £37 million in export income by 1973-4.[11] The level of total export income then depends on earnings from timber and upon other minor sources of income. Even if timber exports remained at the 1968-9 target level of £7 million per year and other categories remained similarly unchanged at £3·4 million, the total would be about £48 million. This would mean an increase of £12·5 million over the five years, or about £2·5 million per annum. A continued expansion of the timber industry and exports (and a higher proportion of sawn timber in exports) could raise this further. In addition, there would be a partial replacement of canned meat purchases by 1973-4.

In view of the wide margin of error possible in estimating the effects of the Mission programme beyond 1973-4, only the most general extrapolations should be made. On the basis of production increases likely from planting programmes, and provided no radical changes take place in the market situation for the products con-

[9] It can be assumed that by 1968-9 export income will have risen by approximately a further £2 million over 1967-8 to £31·5 million without implementation of the World Bank's recommendations.

[10] One factor which could reduce this figure is a reduction in rubber prices, which appears quite possible from world supply-demand projections. A 10 per cent fall in rubber prices might reduce the 1968-9 total export income by £300,000. The World Bank Mission assumed more conservative price levels for most commodities: £60 per ton for copra, £197 for rubber. For cocoa, however, they assumed a price of £210 per ton, which in the light of 1965 prices appears to be too optimistic. By their calculations, which also included some differences in production of copra and rubber for 1968-9, total export income in that year for the major agricultural crops and timber came to about £30 million. By including an estimate of £3·4 million for other categories, total export income would amount to £33·2 million as against the £32·8 million calculated above.

[11] Using the price levels assumed by the Mission, which include a further fall in the price of rubber by 1973-4, export income from the four main agricultural crops and tea would be £33·8 million, and with similar assumptions for timber and other income sources the total would amount to £44 million. This would mean an average annual increase of £2·2 million over the second five years.

cerned, the annual expansion of production and export income would continue but possibly at a slower rate—that is expansion might be £2 million per annum or less. In this later period (say up to 1982-3), the annual figure for the increase would tend to be raised by the production effects of planting programmes for coconuts, rubber, and tea, but two factors would be working the other way. One is the modest objective of the cocoa planting programme suggested by the World Bank: the rate of planting would actually be slower than the rate recorded in the late 1950s. Thus the annual production increase resulting in the seventies would probably be less than the 4,000 ton annual increase expected in the late sixties. The other, more important, factor is the exclusion by the Bank of coffee planting from recommendations for the sector. A relaxation of planting restrictions on this crop would greatly assist in maintaining the level of annual additions to export income. A further expansion of timber exports would also have the same effect.

In summary, a substantial expansion in export income can be expected up to 1968-9, whether the Bank's recommendations are successfully implemented or not. If they are, this expansion would be accelerated to a limited degree during this period. The major outcome, however, would be that the expansion would be extended for at least five years beyond 1968-9, with roughly the same average annual addition to export income in money terms. In other words, a programme of production targets, on a scale such as the World Bank has outlined, is essential for the rural sector if the progress forecast for the last half of the sixties is to be sustained in the seventies. In the light of these income consequences, the Mission's targets appear quite reasonable and modest.

The success of the Mission programme depends a great deal on increased participation by Europeans. In recent years European investment has been seriously affected by the uncertainty generated by the approach of independence for the Territory. General pessimism has led to a considerable movement of capital out of Papua-New Guinea, reaching a peak in 1959-60. Can Europeans be enticed to remain in the Territory and can new investors be attracted from Australia? In the two to three years preceding 1965 there has been some evidence of a resurgence in business confidence, aided by the successful inauguration of the Legislative House of Assembly and the assurances of continued support from the Australian government. Several of the Mission's recommendations may further assist in this, for example the call for tax concessions, selective tariff policies, a supply of credit on favourable terms, and, if necessary, an investigation of schemes to insure or guarantee investment in the Territory.

Assuming for the moment that capital is attracted for investment, will this flow the way the Mission desires? Investors will tend to favour opportunities with relatively short pay-off periods. For example, investments in timber production might be preferred to agricultural tree crops with lengthy periods between planting and the commencement of yields. Among such crops, cocoa would be preferred to coconuts since it has a shorter gestation period, except where it is advantageous for the two crops to be interplanted.

Another factor is the current price levels and future prospects of the commodities. Here it is questionable whether many investors will be drawn to cocoa, rubber, or coconuts, as present and prospective world prices are not encouraging. Of the three, rubber might prove to be the more attractive. Conditions for production are particularly suitable in the Territory; in addition, rubber producers can take advantage of higher yielding planting material to maintain profits in the face of falling prices. The same technological opportunities do not seem to be available in the coconut industry. Cocoa prices will have to show some recovery from 1965 levels before many new investors are likely to show interest.

In view of the attractiveness of tea as a crop for Papua-New Guinea it is also quite possible, provided the heavy capital requirements do not deter investors, that the rate of development will exceed the rather conservative level indicated in the Mission programme.

In summary there do appear to be grounds for suspecting that investment may diverge from the pattern considered desirable by the Mission, particularly for estates. Timber production might receive its quota of capital: possibly rubber too since most of the investment is expected to be made through extending plantings on established plantations. Tea could well receive more than expected and the coconut and cocoa industry somewhat less. The availability of credit on reasonable terms to these industries may act as a general stimulant to investment, but it would probably not alter this pattern to any extent. The three most important factors retarding the participation of indigenous producers are lack of motivation, problems of land tenure, and limitations on the availability of technical advice and education. The general approach favoured by the Mission is to concentrate on the stimulation of village cash cropping rather than on land settlement schemes, and it is in the village that these three problems occur most prominently.

The degree to which indigenous producers would meet the Mission's targets of planting depends largely on how quickly and successfully these impediments are overcome. The Mission also suggests that the provision of credit could be a strong motivating force in their development. While agreeing that this would fill a need for the few most progressive indigenous entrepreneurs, this writer would not agree that there is any notable urgency for a credit supply amongst the great majority of cash croppers. This will undoubtedly develop, but at present few of them actually purchase inputs, which consist almost exclusively of family labour. The development of a credit system in the near future would probably anticipate, rather than serve or stimulate, the need of the majority of indigenous smallholders.

The development of a desire for change and progress, producing in its train a willingness for economic activity, comes largely from the breakdown of village community isolation and from exposure to new ways of life, for example with better communications, a better transport system, and a greater familiarity with new goods via such means as trade stores. The disincentive stemming from isolation will not affect production of all crops equally. It is likely to be a particularly strong impediment in the programme to encourage indigenous coconut planting, since the coastal producers are spread thinly along a narrow littoral some thousands of miles long and have quite tenuous and infrequent contact with more advanced ways of life. It is unlikely that any measures taken will cause a substantial change in attitudes in as short a time as ten years, even with technical assistance and better transport facilities more readily available.

In some areas, generally the more advanced, the inappropriateness of traditional land tenure systems for modern commercial farming is already impeding the pace of indigenous smallholder development, although where development is at an earlier stage and where the land:population ratio is favourable, expansion appears less obstructed by this system. It is not possible to estimate the extent to which this problem would threaten the Mission's objectives at this stage, but it is true that the need for a change in the tenure system will become increasingly common as the numbers of smallholders and the scale of their enterprises increase.

The third most important factor in meeting the targets for indigenous development is the provision of the necessary technical information at the village level. The Mission's programme calls for a very considerable expansion in advisory personnel within the Administration. The availability of the additional staff will be crucial in determining whether production targets can be reached. Allowing for normal losses, the total number of professionals and sub-professionals is to be more than doubled, mostly within the next six years. The annual rate of intake will have to be around eighty, half of whom should be university graduates and half diplomates. At current rates of graduation in Australia, which will be the major source, this requirement seems prohibitively high. The Mission recognizes that shortage of skilled manpower will be the chief limit on economic progress, but even so it may still be too optimistic about Australia's capacity to supply the expanded needs under the proposed programme of rural development. Thus although the production targets set by the Mission imply a fairly modest rate of progress in the sector their achievement will tax to the limit the supply of technical assistance which Australia can provide.

Although there may be room for argument over the methods of development and the pattern of emphasis suggested by the Mission, nonetheless its investigation has done a valuable service in reinforcing and elaborating the view that the sector has a bright potential for economic development. Although the exceptionally mountainous terrain of Papua-New Guinea limits the economic exploitation of resources, there are nevertheless large areas capable of development. The rugged topography is in one way an advantage, in that it provides a variety of ecological conditions which in turn allow useful diversification in the rural sector. The years since World War II have witnessed the growth of five major rural industries; the next decade or two should witness the development of at least two more, as well as a number of minor industries. The sector has the capacity to make Papua-New Guinea self-sufficient for most of its rural requirements. It also has the physical and economic capacity for extensive growth in production for export.

5

The Demographic Situation

NORMA McARTHUR

THE TOTAL indigenous population of Papua and New Guinea probably numbered about two millions in 1964, 95 per cent of whom had been recorded by name in either a tax register or a village book, and the remainder were the numbers thought to be living in areas difficult of access where no listing of the people had yet been attempted. Because of the practical difficulties involved in enumerating the population in such a territory at a particular moment of time, census-taking there is very different from an enumeration of Australia's population, and the method that has evolved requires periodic 'census patrols' through the contiguous geographic areas into which the Territory has been divided, when the inhabitants of each village or cluster of hamlets in the path of the patrol are asked to assemble on some specified day for the census. The patrol carries with it the tax register (or village book in the few areas where the people do not yet pay taxes) for each such group of people, and when they are assembled the officer conducting the patrol checks through the list of inhabitants, adding the names of children born since the previous patrol and anyone who may have joined the group, and deleting the names of people who had died or had gone elsewhere to live.

When this check is completed, the numbers of males and females, births and deaths, and various other details are summarized, and such totals for each 'census unit' are subsequently aggregated to provide totals for the whole 'census division', and thence for the sub-districts which are the basic administrative units. Not all census divisions are patrolled at the same time, nor is any one census division necessarily patrolled at the same time each year. Hence the interval between successive censuses in a division may range from a few months to nearly two years, and as the population figures published in the annual reports for each Territory incorporate the results of the most recent census in each division, some of these may relate to the population that was there nearly two (and occasionally more) years previously. Given this and the proportion of the total population that is estimated, it would be unwise to be too precise about the number of inhabitants either within the whole Territory or for any part of it.

These two sources of variability also make it difficult to assess the rate at which the population is growing. The proportion of the total that was estimated decreases each year as administrative control is extended, and there are frequently changes in the boundaries between census divisions and sub-districts which prevent the numbers of people recorded in the course of one year being compared with those recorded some years later. In a detailed review of censuses taken before and during the fiscal year 1953/4, (McArthur 1956:pt vii) it seemed that the counts for seven sub-districts were probably fairly reliable, and those of a further six were less reliable but probably satisfactory, whereas the population records for thirty-five sub-districts were either quite unreliable or incomplete, and in nine the population was either unknown or estimated. Only two of the first group of sub-districts could be followed through to 1961/2, although the boundary changes between a further three could be eliminated by combining them into a single unit for each year from 1953/4 to 1961/2. Three of the sub-districts in the second category— probably satisfactory—could also be followed through to 1961/2, although one had a suspected excess of a hundred people in 1953/4 and not all census divisions were checked in 1960/1.

The average annual rates of growth exhibited by these sub-districts ranged from 1·5 per cent to 2·7 per cent, and the average for the five sub-districts where censuses taken during 1953/4 seemed to be reliable was 2 per cent per year from then until 1961/2. In the sub-districts where the 1953/4 counts were less reliable, the average annual rates of increase to 1961/2 ranged from 1·5 to 1·8 per cent. More detailed and more accurate data from smaller groups in both Australian New Guinea and the former Netherlands New Guinea indicate that in some areas at least populations are increasing more rapidly than this, and though some may be increasing more slowly, it is unlikely that any are decreasing consistently. In some years there may be more people dying than there are children born, but even in the population which suffers most from the baffling and fatal disease known as *kuru*, more births than deaths were recorded between June 1961 and January 1964, though for one year of this period there was a net loss of females, but not of males. In the total population of the Territory the increases or decreases in individual areas each year will be smoothed out, but until more is known about the rates at which more sectors of the population are changing, any estimate of the average growth rate for the whole population can only be an uninformed guess.

Nowhere in New Guinea is it particularly easy to compile accurate and complete records of population, but in some areas it is

more difficult than others. Much depends on the topography and
climate of the area, but even more important are the attitudes and
personalities of the people living there. Many patrols must be made
on foot because even where there are vehicular roads, the roads do
not pass through all villages in a census division. Where the
villages are large and either close to one another or separated by
relatively easy terrain, a census patrol may not be particularly
arduous; but if, as so often happens in mountainous areas, the
villages or hamlets are perched on hilltops and separated from their
neighbours by deep valleys, a census patrol can be strenuous. In
sparsely populated areas the patrol may walk for days to reach the
next village, only to find it deserted by all except the few too old
or too sick to join in the hunting or sago-making expeditions which
had begun before news of the patrol got through. A patrol officer
reporting on his travels through a newly contacted part of the
Western Highlands in the early 1950s complained bitterly that all
he saw of the native population during several weeks of patrolling
were their backs as they disappeared over the nearest ridge.

Still more exasperating to census patrols are people such as those
who inhabit part of the delta region near the mouth of the Fly
River on the western side of the Gulf of Papua. Their villages are
built on land—'if land it may be called, composed [as it is] of
fluviatic mud', one patrol officer wrote disgustedly—and the paths
through the villages are precarious board-walks built over the mud.
Travel between villages is by native canoes, some of which are very
fast, but seemingly these were seldom placed at the disposal of the
patrols. As one officer was paddled slowly by 'fatalistic tribesmen'
towards a village, he saw the villagers themselves—commonly
accused of being lazy or inherently lethargic—paddling swiftly
away upstream (T.P.N.G. 1950/1). On another occasion, a census
patrol was sadly mis-timed and 'the tides, when low, were really
low, and several times the canoes were left sitting on the mud
several hundred yards from some villages, and progress from then
on through almost knee-deep mud was, of necessity, slow'. During
this patrol, the officer also learned of the disconcerting habit of
these people not to make their village their 'place of residence', but
to visit friends in other villages in turn, returning to their own
village after an absence of several months only to act as hosts to
similarly nomadic friends. As a result, many were recorded in more
than one village book (T.P.N.G. 1951/2).

By now there are probably few areas where people are so reluctant to meet the patrols, but there is still quite considerable movement of population between villages, either for informal visits or
for special ceremonies or ceremonial exchanges, and migration away
from villages into nearby towns in search of paid employment.
Persons absent from their village at the time of a census are
designated as 'absentees', but are still included in the count of the

village population even though they may be away for years at a time and their whereabouts not always known to the village headman. If they choose to marry and live in a town, they will probably remain in the register for their home village, but unless they return home it is unlikely that any children born since their departure from the village will be recorded anywhere because there are no registers for towns comparable to the village lists. Nor would it be practicable to try to institute them, and if the indigenous populations of urban areas are to be counted, different techniques of census-taking are needed and the system for village populations must be modified to avoid counting some people twice.

The numbers of villagers living in towns are not yet large enough to affect the general pattern of distribution of population throughout Papua-New Guinea (see Fig. 7 of Chapter 3). The most densely populated regions are the three Highlands Districts, which contain 40 per cent of the population in one-eighth of the total land area. The northern mountains between the Sepik River and the coast contain some areas of high population density, as do the Finsch-hafen peninsula and a narrow coastal strip along the eastern edge of the Gulf of Papua. The vast area from the western shores of this gulf through to the West Irian border and northward is very sparsely populated; so too is much of the southern portion of the central mountain range and the island of New Britain, though the north-western tip of New Britain's Gazelle Peninsula is the most densely peopled area in the Territory.

High or low population densities based on the total land area of census divisions do not mean much in a country as heterogeneous as New Guinea, especially as the census divisions range in size from one to more than nine thousand square miles, though almost half of them are less than two hundred square miles in area. If the populations could be related to the cultivable land area of the census divisions rather than the total, the range of densities might be reduced, but much variability would remain. The amount of land available for food cultivation is not the sole determinant of where people live, nor will it necessarily affect the number of children that will be born or the number of people who die. Ultimately both of these depend on the sex and age composition of the population, and, in the absence of migration, the size of a population at any given time depends on the relative numbers of births and deaths that have been occurring each year for many years past; these in turn determine the extent of the changes likely to occur in the future.

The number of children that can be born in any year depends on the number of women who are physiologically capable of bearing them, and this capacity is limited to a span of thirty or thirty-five years from about fifteen years of age. Once a child is born it is continually exposed to the risk of dying, but this risk is not uniform throughout life. High at or soon after birth, the risk diminishes progressively as a child survives through each year of age to a minimum somewhere between the ages of ten and fourteen years. From then on, the risk increases gradually with each additional year lived, and the older people become the greater the chances of their dying. The number of deaths that will occur in a population in a year thus depends on the number of people who have survived from birth to each age, and if one-tenth of a population are at ages where the mortality risk is high, there will be more deaths in a year than there would be if the population contained fewer people at those ages.

Accustomed though we are to the concept of chronological age, it is quite alien to the majority of Papuans and New Guineans. Only those who have had some education are aware of the convention of measuring the passing of time by calendar years, and only those whose parents were similarly educated would be likely to know the date of their own birth. Hence the ages for most adults and many children must still be estimated, either from their physical appearance or by trying to associate their birth with an event of some importance which occurred in some known year. For most primitive populations whose history is unknown, this second method is not particularly helpful, and when the village books were compiled initially the patrol officers, complying with instructions to record sex and approximate year of birth for each individual, relied chiefly on physical appearance.

As there are no absolute standards of how a person of a given age should look, the years of birth recorded for people could only be very rough approximations. More accurate estimates would have required long and tedious questioning and cross-questioning, making comparisons between individuals which are impossible unless both questioner and respondent speak the same language. Some officers declined to assess the years in which people then obviously adult were born, and recorded them simply as either 'adult' or 'aged'. The years of birth for children born since the books were compiled in the post-war years, and particularly those of recent years, are probably reasonably accurate, provided no errors of transcription occur when a dilapidated old book is replaced with a new one and each family group stays in the village in which the post-war children were born. Should they move to another village to live, the years of birth recorded for them in that village's register may differ from the originals.

So far little use has been made of these records of age, and summaries of population by sex and years of birth are available for only a few census divisions. Some of these relate to the populations of the Gazelle Peninsula as they were more than a decade ago (McArthur 1956), and the more recent ones are of two groups of people in the Eastern Highlands, both of which are abnormal

because of the prevalence among them of the fatal disease *kuru*
(McArthur 1964). The village books for these two groups were
compiled initially in 1958, and the dates of birth recorded showed
the patrol officer's preference for such years of birth as 1918, 1928,
1938, 1948 and 1920, 1930, 1940, 1950. Because of the large numbers
assigned these years of birth, the numbers of people allegedly aged
5-9, 15-19, 25-29, etc. years in 1960 were very much smaller than
the numbers aged 10-14, 20-24, 30-34, and so on respectively,
whereas the usual distribution of a population by age is decreasing
numbers in each group as age increases. By laboriously distributing
the numbers with each recorded year of birth over the range of
ages within which the initial estimates might lie, more regular age
distributions were achieved for both populations, and arbitrary
though the procedure was, these probably represent the age
structure better than the original data. To use the data that have
accumulated for all other areas, similar adjustments would be
needed to eliminate the compiler's preferences for certain ages or
years of birth.

Several anthropologists and medical officers have tried to discover
the age composition of the populations amongst whom they were
working. Some have been helped by mission records of baptisms,
though not all missions keep these and many of the pre-war records
were either lost or destroyed during the war years. More often the
ages have been estimated by comparative rankings of members of
the group, using genealogical data and recognized 'age-mate'
groups who played together as children or shared some ceremonial
ritual. Most of the populations studied by such researchers are
necessarily small, and interesting though their demographic data
are against the background of their social organization and economic
activities, their very smallness is a handicap to any broader interpretation.

As a simple illustration, let us imagine a village of fifty households
each of which contains one woman of reproductive age. If the
average interval between successive births is three and a half years,
fourteen babies on the average would be born each year and
because the sex of each child is determined independently, one
would expect any number between four and ten of these babies to
be girls. In exceptional circumstances there may be fewer than four
or more than ten girls in a sample of this size, but as few as four
or as many as ten would be within the normal range of variation
when the chance of each child being a female is one in two. In a
period of five years one would expect the annual variations in the
numbers of each sex born to even out, but they may not and it
could happen that at least forty-five of the seventy children born
in the village over a five-year period were girls.

If three-quarters of these children survive to marriageable ages,
and both males and females marry at about the same age, there

would then be only eighteen young men to become husbands to thirty-four girls, and if the parents of the redundant females wished their daughters to marry, marriages would have to be arranged with men of other villages, the young women then going to live in their husband's village. This would leave only thirty-six people in this particular five-year age group in our village instead of the fifty-two that would be expected had equal numbers of males and females been born. If a census was taken of the village at this time, there would probably be considerably more males and females in the age groups on either side of the one that had been depleted by the out-migration of the young brides.

Knowing nothing of this background, the census-taker might at first sight suspect some error or bias in the estimates of age, for example a tendency to exaggerate the ages of married people and understate the ages of children so that few people were assigned to the intermediate range of ages. If the age estimates appeared to be reasonable on the basis of other evidence, what kind of events may have caused this distortion? Was there perhaps an epidemic of some infectious disease about the time when this small group was very young which caused exceptionally high mortality among infants and young children? Or were people of reproductive age the chief victims of the infection, so that fewer babies were born in the years immediately after the epidemic? Had the villagers perhaps suffered defeat and heavy casualties in a local war, which left many young women widowed and therefore less likely to have children for a few years?

The equal numbers of males and females in the age group in question would lend support to hypotheses of this nature and no doubt, on questioning, it would be found that the villagers had experienced epidemics from time to time, and also that they had engaged in periodic fighting. However, it would probably be difficult if not impossible to construct a precise timetable of such events because, unless one outbreak of disease was in some way exceptional, few people would be able to distinguish between an epidemic which had occurred twenty-five years previously and one of the same disease five or even ten years later. Even if different diseases were concerned, the accuracy of people's recollection would depend partly on their age at the time of the epidemics and partly on the degree of personal suffering or deprivation, so that, with each of several informants giving conflicting versions of the same event, the hypothesis that the distortion in the age distribution was due to, say, a war or an epidemic could not be confirmed or rejected.

If the matter were left there, as it might well be if the investigator was in the village for only a short time or had become discouraged by the apparent fruitlessness of such lines of inquiry, the real cause might never be discovered. The genealogies collected by an anthropologist would contain the relevant information, but the association between population structure and marriage outside the village might not be immediately apparent, especially if only one or two young women had gone to each of several villages and the ages of some of them either could not be, or had not been, estimated. Without genealogies, the only other data likely to provide a clue would be complete histories of each woman's pregnancies, and again the relevance of the absent daughters to the current population structure would be detected only if their estimated or assigned ages were reasonably accurate.

If the peculiar age distribution was eventually discovered to be the result of chance fluctuations in the sex of births, and not the aftermath of war or epidemics, no one would be tempted to infer that this one village was 'typical' or 'representative' of other villages in the area. Had fighting or disease been responsible, some of the surrounding villages might have been similarly affected, but before assuming typicality or representativeness it would be wise to collect comparable data from other villages in the immediate vicinity. Extension of this principle leads inevitably to the folly of assuming, without checking, that one can generalize from just one village, however its population may be distributed with respect to sex and age. The corollary to this is that if the other villages are checked appropriately, it is no longer necessary to rely on just one small population to unravel the demographic situation within some defined area.

The extension to more villages introduces a scale of operation beyond the resources of a lone anthropologist or even a small research team, especially when, to achieve the best results, the villages should be selected by some impartial and statistically valid sampling procedure. The method of selecting the villages, whether the choice is from all villages within an area or whether some areas are chosen and all villages within each are then canvassed, depends on the objectives of the survey and the personnel and financial resources available. If the operation was to be limited to a relatively small area, such as one census division or perhaps two or three adjacent divisions, it would be feasible to select villages within the area which would then be the 'sample villages' whose populations were to be recorded and studied. If information concerning the population inhabiting a much larger area were required, it might be more practical to select 'sample census divisions' from within that area and record the details required about the populations of all villages within these census divisions.

If a sample census of the whole territory was contemplated, the second scheme would have several advantages. Fewer investigators would be needed to cover some pre-determined proportion of the total population if the time spent in travelling between villages was kept as short as possible; and, perhaps more importantly, the quality of the data recorded would probably be higher if an investigator were dealing continually with one relatively homogeneous cultural group, about whom he could be reasonably well briefed in advance, than if he were assigned to several villages, each of which had a distinctive cultural pattern. In addition, the effects of inter-village migrations, especially those of a temporary nature, would be minimized by an 'area sample'; and it would be administratively simpler to enlarge a sample of census divisions over a period of years, to cover the whole territory eventually, rather than to expand gradually a sample of widely scattered villages.

Except that its initial areas were not selected on any statistical basis, a project such as this was started in the former Netherlands New Guinea, and preliminary reports on six areas have now been released (Groenewegen and Van de Kaa 1962-4). Two of the areas censused are the Schouten Islands and Noemfoor in Geelvink Bay; there are three widely separated coastal areas which also include some if not all of the relevant hinterlands, and the sixth is an area in the southern foothills of the central mountain range close to the border with Papua. The total indigenous population included in the censuses of these areas is more than 70,000, but nearly half of this number was contributed by just one area—the Schouten Islands —and the sum of the six populations is therefore no more likely to be a representative sample of the indigenous population of West Irian around 1960 and 1961 than are the various samples collected by individuals in Papua-New Guinea. On the other hand, each sample is relatively large—none comprised fewer than 5,000 people and the four areas on the mainland each contained 8,000 or 9,000—and diverse geographic and climatic conditions are represented, so that the data indicate the range of values for some demographic indices that might also be expected on the other side of the border.

The people of the truly inland area were the only ones with less than 43 per cent of their total number aged less than fifteen years, and they also had the lowest crude birth rate and the smallest average numbers of children born per woman at each age. The crude birth rates ranged from 38 to 53 births per 1,000 population per year, but most were within the range of 45 to 50 births annually per 1,000 population. In four of the six areas the women who had survived to ages 40-44 years had borne an average of more than six children, but in two of these areas as many as one-quarter of the children had died within their first year of life; elsewhere the infant mortality rate was one-fifth or one-sixth of all children born. The two regions where the women nearing the end of their reproductive life had had the fewest children on the average also seem to have experienced the lowest infant mortality rates in former years. Strangely enough, malaria is hyperendemic in one and the other is not highly malarial. These were also the only areas where the infant mortality rate has not declined markedly in recent years,

and the proportions of survivors to age one year amongst the
offspring of women aged approximately 20-24 years in all areas was
within the fairly narrow range of 0·80 to 0·90.

The subsequent fate of children who attained their first birthday
is not disclosed in these preliminary reports, and the Schouten
Islands was the only area for which there were records of the
deaths that had occurred during some specified period. These
indicated a crude death rate of about 14 per 1,000 population in a
year, and as the birth rate there was estimated at about 53 per 1,000
annually, the population of the islands was increasing at about 4
per cent per year. If the crude death rate in each population is
proportional to its infant mortality rate, then two of the populations
are currently increasing at rates of about 1½ per cent a year, two
others at about 2½ per cent per year, and the other island population
at about 3 per cent.

Though this simple relationship between mortality in the first
year of life and mortality at all ages may not be valid, it does seem
to hold for some populations with similar age structures, especially
those where deaths in infancy and early childhood contribute very
largely to the total mortality. But until the appropriate data are
available for populations such as these, any more elaborate assumptions would only convey a spurious accuracy to growth rates which
are probably ephemeral, partly because of the age structure of the
populations, partly because the health measures which were being
or had been instituted in these areas may affect the incidence of
disease and, in turn, the levels of both mortality and fertility. If
mortality falls and the birth rate remains unchanged, growth will
be accelerated, and in some areas at least the present age structure
of the populations is such that current birth rates are likely to
be maintained. The limit to the acceleration of growth is immort-
ality, but the higher the initial level of mortality the faster it is
likely to fall, and the more people who survive through the reproductive period the more babies will be born. Because improved
health may increase the chances of conception and reduce the likeli-
hood of early foetal deaths, the birth rates may even rise and so
enhance the difference between them and the falling death rates.

Both the timing and the magnitude of changes such as these in
any part of the mainland or islands of New Guinea are totally
unpredictable. The only certainty is that neither will be uniform,
nor even particularly regular. Though little is known of the contribution of specific diseases to the total mortality pattern, their
relative incidence will no doubt be found to vary from one locality
to another, even from one year to another, and the extent to which
they can be controlled will likewise be variable. The principal
causes of death listed in the Annual Reports for 1961-2 were
pneumonia, tuberculosis, dysentery, gastro-enteritis, and malaria;
but the cause of death can be ascertained for only very few among

all who die in the course of a year. The native diagnoses recorded by some census patrols are colourful, but seldom specific or particularly informative as to cause rather than symptoms. Even in years when some particular disease assumes epidemic proportions, its incidence throughout the Territory is likely to vary: some sectors of the population may escape infection entirely, others may be protected by the immunity conferred by an earlier attack so that only people born since then may succumb, others may be so remote from the initial source of infection that the infective agent has lost some of its pathogenicity by the time it reaches them. The possible sources of variability are endless, and the only safe assumption to make about the future course of mortality is that it will either remain much the same as now or decline.

Given this and the not dissimilar assumption that the birth rate will not change much within a decade, Papua-New Guinea's population ten years hence is likely to be between two and three millions, though the latter figure is unlikely unless the present population exceeds two millions. Between 40 and 45 per cent of the total will probably be aged less than fifteen years, and as about three-fifths of these would be children of school age, between one-half and three-quarters of a million children may be seeking primary education. There could be the same numbers of adult males in what in other communities are described as the 'economically active' age groups, approximately one-fifth of whom would be aged between forty-five and sixty years and consequently unlikely to be seeking employment outside their villages, though they may well be economically active there.

There is little point in elaborating these figures: a margin of 50 per cent between the lower and upper estimates makes nonsense of attempts to translate them into practical terms such as the numbers of schools and schoolteachers that will be required under varying assumptions about the proportions of the school-age population who should be receiving primary education. On the other hand, expanding the existing staff and facilities by only 50 per cent over the next decade may do no more than maintain the fraction of the population of school age which is now attending schools. If this fraction is to be raised from less than one-third to about one-half over the decade, expansion of the order of at least 100 per cent should be planned.

The only statistics currently compiled for the indigenous labour force relate to persons in wage employment, and their source is the annual return each employer makes to the Department of Labour (Labour and National Service 1964). In March 1963, 75,000 males were receiving wages and 56,000 of these were employed by private enterprise. The number employed by the Administration had increased by 4,000 over the previous year's total, but the net increase in all kinds of employment was only 2,500. These wage-earners would constitute perhaps one-seventh of the total labour force, and as more than half of them were employed in some form of agriculture (one-third in the production of copra and cocoa), the numbers engaged in all other kinds of employment would amount to perhaps one-twelfth or less of the available work force.

No matter what (within reason) happens to this non-agricultural sector over the next decade, by far the greater part of the prospective increase in the work force must be absorbed by agriculture, and the ease with which this can or cannot be done is an inherently local problem. If the structures of the populations inhabiting the different regions are as variable as the sparse data concerning them suggest, the work force component of each will increase in a highly individual fashion. The net gain to the work force over a ten-year period depends primarily on the number of children aged five to fourteen years at the start of the period; and if the initial age structure of the population is as distorted as those of two Tolai settlements in 1960 (Epstein 1962), the work force after ten years could be 55 per cent larger than at the start, whereas the growth during the preceding five years would have barely exceeded 10 per cent. Only by having more adequate and more reliable statistics of the populations can contingencies such as this be foreseen; developmental programmes planned without reference to such vital facts are likely to benefit neither the supposed beneficiaries nor the planners.

III

Social Problems

6

Education and its Problems

O. H. K. SPATE

THE EXPERIENCE on which this paper is based was mainly obtained as a member of the Commission on Higher Education in Papua and New Guinea (1963-4). It seems proper to state that the views here expressed are not necessarily those of the Commission collectively or of any other member of it, although there is no substantial divergence between the Report of the Commission and the conclusions put forward here.

THE MISSION CONTRIBUTION

The three great factors in the Western impact on indigenous society —administrative, economic, and religious—are virtually of an age; in both Papua and New Guinea the first permanent missions and trading stations were established in the 1870s, about a decade before the first administrations. Apart from earlier abortive ventures, the London Missionary Society began work at Port Moresby in 1874, the Methodists in the Duke of York Islands in 1875; on the New Guinea mainland, German Lutherans were active around Finschhafen from 1886. Somewhat later, permanent Roman Catholic missions were founded in Papua under the auspices of the Sacred Heart of Jesus and in New Guinea under the Society of the Divine Word; these orders drew their workers mainly from France and Germany respectively. German expansion was of course stopped by World War I, after which American societies took over previously German missions, although some of the pioneers stayed on. After World War II there was a striking increase in missions run by newer groups, most notably perhaps the Seventh Day Adventists.

The very interesting details of mission history and organization, and of inter-denominational relations, cannot be considered here. On the whole, relations between the older and better-established missions have been reasonably harmonious; and, having themselves learnt much in over 150 years of work in the Pacific, they have usually been more cautious in their approach to tribal custom than the more aggressive newer sects. Even so, their impact on indigenous ways of life has been very far-reaching, both in quantity and quality. In 1963 just about half the population—1,206,000 souls—were ranked as Christians; of these about 483,500 were Roman Catholics and 317,000 (nearly all on the New Guinea side) Lutherans. Making all allowance for the obviously great variations in the degree of informed belief, these are impressive figures.

The qualitative effect of the mission effort has been profound: so far as any one world-view has replaced the congeries of tribally-fragmented sets of beliefs, it has been predominantly a Christian one. Undoubtedly the real beliefs of many nominally Christian indigenes are shot through with animistic survivals; practices such as sorcery are not confined to those who remain pagan; and the role of misunderstandings of the Old Testament and the Apocalypse in the rise of millenarian movements and cargo cults is painfully obvious (Worsley 1957). Yet it would be callously imperceptive to deny that sometimes, and perhaps often, the re-integration of belief has been reasonably complete and coherent (Hogbin 1951).

Missionaries have been pioneers in the introduction of health and welfare measures, and often in a more intimate way than is usually possible for administrators and entrepreneurs; they have made important contributions to cultural studies, especially in linguistics; and their direct economic role, if at times ambivalent (as in plantation ownership), is not inconsiderable. It is in education, however, that their influence has been strongest: of the present generation of indigenous leaders, perhaps none—certainly no more than a handful—of those who have received any formal Western education at all have done so otherwise than in mission schools.

This position will change, but the current validity and significance of the statement above is reflected in the frequent insistence of indigenous leaders that the Papua and New Guinea of the future must be a Christian country, or perhaps indeed a Christian state. This is natural: since European contact, the history of the peoples, as distinct from the history of the Territories, has been very largely a Christian history; and, despite the fact that half the population is still in the strict sense pagan or heathen, and that animistic beliefs still have a hold on many of the other half, the country is quite as much a Christian country as is Australia or Britain or America, and in fact is probably more truly so styled. After all, it is a long time since incipient co-operatives or trade unions in those countries began their proceedings with Christian prayer.

Before World War II, the Administration's direct share in education was slight indeed: one school, for Europeans, in Port Moresby, and in the then Mandated Territory an expenditure which fell from £18,000 in 1923 to £5,000 in 1937 (N.I.D. 1945). The policy was to subsidize mission schools, subject to the maintenance of minimum standards which were sometimes minimal indeed. Numerically, the missions are still dominant: out of a total of 220,000 pupils at all levels in 1963, no fewer than 179,000 (81 per cent) were in mission schools, including 69,000 in 'exempt' schools of standard too low to qualify for Administration subsidy. In post-primary and technical schools the pattern is different: in 1963 Administration schools accounted for 1,640 out of 2,732 secondary pupils and for almost all of those receiving any but the most rudimentary technical training (*P.A.R.* No. 77 (1962/3):250; *N.G.A.R.* 1946-(1963/4):129). In part, as is frankly recognized by the missions, 'This has arisen because the comity agreements . . . have resulted in each mission pressing on with its own separate secondary education. None of these has a school to match the teaching resources of the Administration, which means the contribution to producing an elite is a minor one.' (A.C.C. 1965:23.) Although there are shining exceptions, especially perhaps in seminarian training, standards in mission schools are by and large lower than those in Administration schools, by reason largely of even scarcer resources and of less well-trained teachers. To some extent this is inherent in the natural desire for the expansion of the Gospel, in which education is rather an ancillary than an end in itself.

In one important respect some mission education has had rather a negative effect; this is the preference for teaching in Pidgin[1] or in indigenous languages. Whatever the abstract merits or demerits of teaching in the mother-tongue or in English, there can hardly be an excuse, except one of expediency, for teaching in a vernacular which is *not* the child's mother-tongue. Unfortunately, some missions long persisted in teaching, even in the Highlands, through Pidgin or the languages of coastal areas where they had made their first penetration; this on account of mere tradition or the economy of using already printed educational material. Since 1956-8 the Administration's subsidization policy has strongly favoured schools teaching through English, and so this problem is a receding one.

Much devotion has gone to the building of mission education in Papua and New Guinea, but it is surely no disparagement to suggest that the mission approach, though it will long remain essential in the earlier stages of schooling, has been overtaken by the pressures of the new times. The effort now needed is beyond the resources of voluntary association; the wider secular needs of the people now call for a diversification and intensification of education beyond the essentially evangelistic purpose of the missionary pioneers. Despite serious limitations of scope and method, what the missions have done has been of essential value as a beginning; but it is only as a beginning.

[1] The term 'Pidgin' is used in this book in conformity with general practice in Papua and New Guinea as the name of a structurally Melanesian language that has become widely used as a lingua franca in the area. Some specialists prefer to call it 'Neo-Melanesian', and this is in many ways a preferable term, but it is not as yet in general use.

SOME CULTURAL PROBLEMS

At present most indigenous people in Papua and New Guinea are
basically dependent on subsistence gardening, supplemented by
commercial cropping which in many areas is still a somewhat precarious venture; really solid economic development, certainly by
indigenes, is confined to agriculture and is very patchy in distribution. Something like three-quarters of the population, perhaps more,
lives in small hamlets, often tucked away in difficult terrain,
mountainous, jungly, swampy. Not only are these bush hamlets
difficult to reach, but the developed areas are not readily accessible
to one another: from the port of Lae roads reach the Eastern
Highlands and the Wau-Bulolo area, but these two are not directly
inter-linked, and yet this is in effect the only system of 'trunk'
roads. It is true that air transport is highly developed—so much so
that the Safety First lessons in the primary school syllabus begin
magnificently 'Do not play on the airstrip'; yet air transport in New
Guinea conditions has a friction of its own which is not easily
apprehended by those who do not have to rely on it, and it is
also costly.

The logistics of any sort of Territory-wide development are thus
extremely difficult, and education is certainly not exempt from this
rule. When we add to this the almost complete dependence of the
economy on a very narrow range of primary products (vulnerable
to world market conditions), served by a very limited development
of secondary and tertiary industry (in which the indigenous share is
minimal), and the fact that two-thirds of Territory revenues are
provided by Australian subsidies, it will be recognized that the
material base for an educational programme is indeed slight.

On the cultural side, the difficulties are no less great: the
language problem is perhaps not the greatest, only the most obvious.
It is true that in the Highlands groups of up to say 150,000 people
can inter-communicate in tongues which have little more than dial-
ectal variations, and Pidgin is widespread as a lingua franca, more
particularly in the coastal regions of the Trust Territory. But clearly
neither the Chimbu languages nor Pidgin can well be adapted for
education beyond a very elementary level; there are simply too
many modern ways and devices not dreamt of in their philosophies
but which Papuans and New Guineans must learn to handle if they
are to run their country effectively. Yet Pidgin at least has its
devotees, who perhaps let their indignation at the unwarranted
slur that it is a mere bastard *patois* of English blind them to the fact
that at any serious level of abstract discourse—and the capacity for
abstraction is a vital skill in the modern world—it is by far too
concrete and circumlocutory to be of much use. An excellent
language in which to say 'Take out the spark plug and clean it', it is
of less use in the task of explaining the function of a spark plug as
an electrical component of an internal combustion engine.

Since it is clear, and not least to the indigenous people themselves, that a reasonable command of English is the key to the knowledge so essential to any kind of advance, there seems less than no point in interposing another language, which can relatively rarely be a mother-tongue, as an additional hurdle on a path difficult enough already; and, while there is more to be said for using some of the larger Highlands languages as the medium for the earliest formal instruction, most of them are spoken by so few people that the provision of even primary-level school material in them seems quite uneconomic. There is no possible doubt that, except locally and at a very elementary level, English must remain the chief medium of instruction. The question—and it is a much more difficult question, to which we will return—still remains: *What sort* of English?

There are other aspects of indigenous society, less obvious than language but not unrelated to it, which make the transition to a new way of looking at life exceedingly difficult. The very limited development of counting in some groups; the general absence, natural enough in an agrarian environment where there is little seasonality, of any emphasis on or even understanding of the significance of time; the universal (and again entirely natural) stress on the local, the particular, the concrete; the weight of loyalty to tribe and family, at most to the local region; the survival of super-naturalist explanations even for quite ordinary events—all these inhibit the growth of a generalized and rational approach to the problems inherent in the objective of Papua and New Guinea as a united and independent country.

It seems clear that a traditional approach to the method and content of education will be self-stultifying. External pressures towards independence within a limited term of years are strong, internal pressures are at least incipient, and the introduction of a House of Assembly with an indigenous elected majority is an irrevocable change. Yet, in a couple of decades at most, something like the step from pagan Anglo-Saxon England to a modern state must be taken. The material obstacles to educational advance in Papua and New Guinea are great indeed, but at least they are material and hence tangible: given money, they can be overcome. No such simple solution can cope with the intangible and intractable cultural or social obstacles. Here a truly heroic effort of detailed research and rethinking, for which the *Report of the Commission on Higher Education* is merely an agenda paper, must be faced.

It is obvious to the point of triteness that Papuans and New Guineans must acquire sufficient knowledge and understanding of the world at large to be able to 'know their place' in it (in no depreciatory sense) and to take that place. How is this knowledge to be obtained? It seems clear that in many respects the educational process must be nicely adjusted to the local environment and its needs; for instance, the history of the British and Australian

Commonwealths, in any detail, may be less important than that of a
small backward island, inhabited by savages who paint their faces
and burn, if they do not eat, their prisoners of war, an island lying
just north of a powerful and technologically developed civilized
empire—in short, the history of the change from pre-Roman Britain
to Norman England. It is important that Papuans and New Guineans
should know that other small backward communities have been
subsumed into rich and powerful civilizations, have gone through
the vicissitudes of imperialism, and emerged with their identities not
only preserved but unified and enhanced. Yet of course the political
science of the modern world, as well as its economics, will also be
an essential component.

Again, the existing heavily literary approach to the teaching of
English—as if the road to English were through Shakespeare—seems
wasteful to the point of cruelty; yet we must not be so one-sidedly
utilitarian and functional as to bar the road to Shakespeare through
English: so, once more, *what sort* of English is a vital question.
Science cannot be understood without stress on the local illustrations,
in geology for example; yet these in turn cannot be comprehended
without understanding of the universal rules, and so the dialectic
of teaching goes on.

At every turn we meet this conflict between the local and immediate need, empirical and technical, which because of the vast
difference between New Guinea social and cultural traditions and
our own must bulk large in any programme; and against this need
the converse need for an education which, if Papuans and New
Guineans are ever to stand on their own feet, must be much more
than the mere inculcation of Useful Knowledge. The total education
must not neglect the formation of character responsibility in terms
appropriate to a democratic community; it must include training in
thinking and must instil some understanding of the scientific process
as well as awareness of its end-products; must give at once some
geographical breadth and some historical depth to the world-view of
indigenous leaders, and not only the leaders. This is an ideal,
doubtless, which will never be perfectly attainable; it is indeed very
imperfectly achieved in our own society with all its resources of
communication. Yet something like it must at least be approximated;
and the conflict must be resolved in a context in which communication between the two cultures is exceptionally difficult.

There remain some fundamental questions: do we desire (as
most argument on 'development' seems blandly to assume, without
having the guts to say so) that all mankind should be people like
ourselves, doing the same developed things in much the same way,
only some with black faces—mere 'carbon copies' of Europeans? If
we do desire this, will the people themselves also desire it? Can they
preserve a proper pride in their own achievements—the architecture
of the *haus tambaran* and the *lakatoi*, the dance and the household

arts—when essential economic development has destroyed the social as well as the economic bases of such achievements, when they learn to rely on fertilizers rather than fertility cults?

Short-term, then, the empirical and the technical may seem paramount; long-term, one cannot be so sure; policy in ultimate terms must be as 'open-ended' as is possible. In the nature of the case, this may not be very far. It is futile to say—a truism but a half-truth—that in the long run the people themselves must decide their course. They can only do so in the context decided by previous decisions; whatever they build, and when, foundations must be laid *now*; and these will determine the superstructure in the broad if not in detail. All the more care, therefore, must be taken in laying out the foundations, and it is for this reason that the Commission on Higher Education gave first priority to an Educational Research Unit with wide terms of reference; and it also stressed the urgent need for research into problems of communication and for experiment in the teaching of the two skills basic on any line of development, English and mathematics.

THE CURRENT POSITION AND THE ECONOMIC ASPECT

After World War II the Administration took a much more direct and active part in expanding educational facilities, and the results, quantitatively assessed, have been not unimpressive: expenditure rose from £303,500 in 1950 to £4,150,000 in 1963-4 (1,400 per cent), schools from 61 to 485, teachers from 159 to 1,571, pupils from 3,375 to 61,683. More particularly in the last five or six years, a good deal of effort has been put into research into method and into teacher training, including a crash scheme (the 'E' course) taking in people with a limited (Intermediate) standard of formal education but of some maturity; this seems to have been a marked success.

However, one cannot but feel that in the earlier post-war years this development to some extent sacrificed quality to quantity. The aim seems to have been to spread some—or any—sort of bush schooling as widely as possible. This was in tune with the theory of 'uniform development' and its implicit distrust of *élites*, and might have been acceptable in a context of slow and steady development all round. In response largely to external pressures, however, the political sector has as it were shot ahead, and it is now clear that the responsibilities which are rapidly devolving upon Papuans and New Guineans call urgently for the formation of *élites*, and from this angle the policy of the first decade or so after 1945 seems responsible for a very serious leeway which it will be extremely difficult to make up. A crash programme for post-primary education is now essential.

Until quite recently, then, the policy appears to have been unbalanced, and the policy change has not yet had time to redress

the balance. Apart from the three multi-racial high schools at Port
Moresby, Lae, and Rabaul, the first Administration secondary
schools were set up in 1957, and there are now, in addition to these
three high schools, a new indigenous high school and fifteen junior
high schools run by the Administration, and thirty-seven run by
missions. These go up to Intermediate and may become full high
schools in the future. Yet had there been rather less expansion of
what were virtually bush schools some fifteen years ago, and in its
stead an earlier provision of well-found secondary schools, it is
likely that the Territory would not now be in the paradoxical
position of having taken a considerable step towards indigenous
responsibility in government before there was a single indigenous
university graduate.[2]

On the technical and vocational side, the situation is generally
unsatisfactory. There are a number of teacher training colleges at
various levels, and their work in general is good; though even if
the rate of growth of primary education were to be slackened in
favour of the urgent need for a more rapid expansion of secondary,
technical, and vocational education, there would still remain a need
for a much increased effort in teacher training. The Papuan Medical
College maintains good standards; there may well be some question,
however, of whether these standards are not too much influenced by
the traditional form of medical education in Australia, overlooking
the need for good all-round men for the villages, men who need not
be trained so highly, or at any rate so comprehensively, as the
specialists in base hospitals. The Department of Agriculture has a
variety of training schemes for the lower levels of field workers and
is opening at Vudal, near Rabaul, an agricultural college to turn
out officers at diploma level. At Port Moresby there is a multi-
functional administrative college and the good specialized training
done by the Department of Posts and Telegraphs. The three
technical schools at Port Moresby, Lae, and Rabaul have provided
training to tradesman level, associated with apprenticeship.

Nevertheless a great deal more is needed. There is an almost
total blank at the all-important technician level; many jobs which
could be done by indigenes are done by expatriates (at a time when
there is no surplus of such labour in Australia), and the extra costs
involved may average around £1,000 per person per year. Savings
on this account would go some way to offset the cost of a comprehensive scheme of technical education.

There are many reasons for the existing imbalance and the slight
development of secondary education, among them the fact that

[2] By mid-1965 one indigene had taken a B.Sc. in Agriculture at Sydney and
another had qualified for a pass B.A. in economics at Sydney but was staying
on to do honours, and there were about a dozen Papuan or New Guinean
undergraduates in Australian universities.

the demand for indigenous people with some degree of education for minor clerking and so on led to poaching by administrative departments and private employers, so that bright lads were siphoned off too soon. The result, however, is a tragic waste of potential, especially as the further *ad hoc* in-service training needed may well be given by persons not particularly fitted to be teachers, without continuity, and with duplication of instruction in basic subjects such as English and mathematics. More co-ordination and a great strengthening of secondary education are manifestly urgent needs.

This is apparent not only from any realistic empirical assessment of the Territory's economic and administrative trends and needs, but from more general consideration of the investment aspect of education. An impressive body of opinion is beginning to question the wisdom of over-concentration on mass literacy where resources are so limited that this emphasis would inhibit the training of adequate technical and vocational cadres. The weight to be given to mass literacy and to a general humanistic education ('consumer goods'), and to a more vocational technologically-oriented education (a 'producer good'), must vary with the circumstances of the country concerned. It is no kindness to put the educational clothes of an affluent society on to the famished body of a backward one; not only will they fail to fit, but the load of debt may result in further malnutrition. As the ex-Rector of the University of Rangoon puts it,

> the comforting doctrine that the extension of education in the [consumer] sense will automatically lead to an increase in investment in human capital in the [producer] sense and will therefore promote development . . . turns out to be a dangerously misleading notion (Hla Myint 1962:119).

Where resources are scarce, as they are in New Guinea, 'those who make compulsory primary education their first priority are asking for trouble, and get it' in the form of disproportionate demands for clerical jobs for school-leavers and for a plethora of tertiary institutions (Lewis 1962; cf. Ashby and Harbison 1960). The Territory is a long way from Arthur Lewis's target, for sub-Saharan Africa, of 50 per cent of each appropriate age-cohort in primary schools, 5 per cent in secondary, and 0·5 per cent in universities; the respective figures are more like 30, 0·375, and an infinitesimal.[3] While there is bound to be a political demand for the extension of primary education, in the immediate future its attainment might well depend on some slackening of its own rate, so that a much stronger secondary component may be inserted to supply the necessary teachers, and so that tertiary education (including higher vocational and technical training) may be provided on a scale

[3] To be more exact (in 1963), 0·00015 per cent approximately.

appropriate to the needs of an emerging nation—in short, so that the
present glaring imbalance may be rectified. It is a pity not to be
able to advance equally on all fronts; but so far primary schooling
has made the running, and it is educationally imperative to avoid
any further dilution of education.

There are other important aspects of school education in Papua
and New Guinea which can be only glanced at here. Among them
is the lag in female education (in 1963 only 90,294 girls were receiving instruction against 139,982 boys), which at least in large part is
due to indigenous attitudes natural enough in a tribal society and a
subsistence economy. The length of the school cycle is of peculiar
local significance. In many tribal communities, the male child takes
his first steps from the maternal hearth—into the company of his
father and his uncles—at about five years of age; and to begin
school at six plus would mean a most drastic amputation of what
must be, for that majority of little boys whose life will basically
remain within their own tribe and village, an incalculably significant
phase in the process of growing up. This suggests a later age of entry
to primary school, say seven plus; and this in turn has relevance to
the age of leaving primary for those who do go on to secondary
school. The Territory adheres to the International Labour Office
ruling that the minimum age for taking up paid employment (unless
in training positions) should be sixteen years; if then we start
primary school at five or six plus and give seven years' schooling,
we have a very nasty gap, and it is not in New Guinea alone that the
awkward social consequences of such a gap in village-based societies
are evident; Fiji is a striking example. A later age of primary entry
would at least help.

Another most important problem is that posed by the necessity
of breaking away from syllabuses designed to suit children in
Australia. There are reasonable doubts as to how well Australian
syllabuses are so suited; there can be no shadow of a doubt that
they are unsuitable to the needs of Papuan and New Guinean
children. The Territory Department of Education is alert to this
problem, and has already devised its own primary syllabus—in
which, it may be noted, there is a good deal of emphasis on the
fostering of national rather than tribal or local loyalties; no trace of
'Divide and Rule'. The Department is now tackling the more
difficult task of recasting the secondary curriculum, and in this it
can be materially aided by the establishment in the Territory of an
institution of tertiary academic education, so that education at all
levels can be both integrated and adjusted to the real needs of the
people of Papua and New Guinea, rather than forced into the
mould of an Australian state system. At this point, then, it is
appropriate to consider the findings of the Commission on Higher
Education in Papua and New Guinea.

THE COMMISSION ON HIGHER EDUCATION (1963-4)

The Commission was appointed in February 1963 by the then Minister for Territories, Mr Paul Hasluck, and consisted of Sir George Currie, originally an agricultural scientist but with much experience in academic administration as Vice-Chancellor successively of the Universities of Western Australia and New Zealand; Dr John Gunther, an Assistant Administrator of the Territory noted for an unbureaucratic forcefulness of personality; and the present writer, whose sole claim seems to have been that he was at least a working academic. It was given very wide terms of reference, covering technical as well as academic higher education and also the responsibility for presenting detailed statements for the first triennium of any institutions it might recommend and general ones for the second triennium. Between its first and its final formal meetings, exactly one calendar year elapsed. Its Report, presented in March and published in July 1964, gives much more detail on all the topics treated briefly in this paper, and on others perforce omitted here. It would be unbecoming of the present writer to say that it is a good report, though this disclaimer will deceive nobody, and least of all those who know him; but at least it is comprehensive enough to be regarded as a basic document.

The Commission had cognizance of Mr Hasluck's statement, made in the House of Representatives of the Commonwealth as long ago as 11 October 1962, that there would be some institution of university type started in the Territory by 1966. It took as its major premise that the approach to self-determination is not likely to be slackened; if the general experience and temper of the times are anything to go by, it is much more likely to accelerate. This obviously means that the lag in post-primary education must be overtaken as rapidly as possible by making much more adequate provision on both the academic and the technical sides. The Department of Education's plans envisage an increase of secondary pupils to some 30,000 by 1974; this would be about 7·5 per cent of the total primary enrolment it is hoped to attain by then, and calls for a very much more intensive effort in the training of indigenous teachers. This is necessary on any prognosis, even one which considers the 1974 estimate too optimistic. In the Commission's view, the great bulk of the needed facilities for higher education must be provided within the Territory.

There are several reasons for this. Apart from the debatable question of whether it is better that the first degree should be taken overseas or at home (and there are strong arguments on both sides), it seems likely that the need for tertiary training and the numbers coming forward from the secondary schools will in a few years be so large that to meet the demand in Australian universities would be a matter of some difficulty, except of course in some special fields which could not reasonably be cultivated in a Territory institution. The most important factor of all, however, seems to be the necessity of setting up a system of education for the Territory *integrated at all levels*. It is axiomatic that school education cannot be really adjusted to local needs so long as it must be geared to the needs of school-leavers in New South Wales or Queensland, and that such local adjustment is essential if teaching is to be generally effective. But then, there is no point in a Territory school system which will not take a reasonable proportion of its products on to further education without additional training, and this implies that the system should be completed by the provision of tertiary education within the Territory itself: otherwise school education must continue to be geared to unsuitable outside systems or made top-heavy by a proliferation of uneconomic special courses, or indeed both.

Moreover, the tertiary needs of Papuans and New Guineans demand a different approach from that normal in Australian universities; tertiary education itself must be in some harmonious relation to the local environment, if it is not to be an artificial veneer. There is always risk of alienation in the creation of an *élite*, and this will be much more acute if higher education takes place in an environment or on lines completely divorced from the homeland and its current problems. In method, then, there is a need for experiment to find the best means of bridging the communications gap; in content, much should be omitted, but much should be added. The desire for 'parity of standards' is genuine and valid; but parity is not identical with identity.

With the prime need of integration in mind, it seemed obvious that the whole structure of education in the Territory would have to be examined: in the last analysis, education is indivisible. In this difficult task, the Commission received invaluable support from the Territory Department of Education. It reviewed the school system and put forward suggestions, some of them doubtless controversial, concerning the length of the complete cycle of schooling, the organization of curricula, and the introduction of new methods. Everything considered, it seemed to the Commission that entry to primary school at seven plus, followed by a primary cycle of seven and a secondary of four years, would be a reasonable structure; as will be seen, the normal time between entering a tertiary institution and graduating from it would also be four years instead of the standard three. The suggested school cycle would also be appropriate for those going on to vocational, rather than academic, further study; it would go some way to avoid the difficulty, felt in Australian education, that secondary education is too closely geared to the needs of the minority going on to the university, a minority likely (at least after the initial stages) to be smaller in New Guinea than in Australia. All these matters are bound up with detailed discussion of social needs and scholastic procedures; for instance, the need for new approaches in English and mathematics teaching, and for a much more intensive effort in science teaching.

On the particular question of a university institution, a very specific point in its terms of reference, the Commission decisively favoured the establishment in the Territory of a fully autonomous university, rather than a university college. Here again a main point is the need for a fully integrated system. A university college is after all an institution subordinate to its parent university, and even with a 'special relationship' is likely to be too closely bound to traditional academic philosophies and procedures appropriate to a very different state of society; yet, obviously, a conservative approach would be totally inadequate to the very novel and difficult problems of tertiary education in Papua and New Guinea, and this appears amply confirmed by African and Asian experience. Again, it seems more than likely that staff of the right sort—the sort of people to whom it is more attractive to pioneer an entirely new thing than to walk into an established concern—are not going to be content with an institution subordinate to a base a thousand miles from the front line where they will wish to do their own planning for their own operations.

Staffing is indeed a crucial problem; its difficulties are likely to be most severe in the pure arts and pure sciences (though even here there may well be unsuspected research opportunities), least in those field and social sciences for which New Guinea is itself one vast laboratory. The problem can only be more acute if it is advertised in advance that the institution will be a subordinated one. Even within Australia, even within the same state, the university/university college relation is not too easy to work; how much more difficult when parent and child would live in such utterly different homes!

But while thus insisting on the paramount need for an institution as it were conditioned by and responsible to the Territory environment, the Commission was very conscious of the need to maintain good standards, and to strike the nice balance between the local and the universal, without which there could be a slide into parochialism. At the entry end, a university may be its own judge of the standards it requires; at the exit end, it will be judged by its peers. Internally, the main recommendation of the Commission in this regard is that there should be a preliminary year, taken by all or nearly all students, and devoted on the one hand to further basic training in linguistic and mathematical skills, on the other to studies designed to broaden the cultural horizons of the students. This would make the total course for a pass degree one of four years, thus going some way to offset the lack of background to be expected of nearly all students; it would avoid premature specialization; and it would also form a humane cut-off point for those who could not make the grade. External measures to maintain standards would include fairly heavy direct representation of Australian academics not only on the council of the university, but initially on its professorial board; the use of external examiners (a measure which would be of value in Australian universities); and the formation of an academic advisory committee on the lines found useful for new universities in Britain.

A New Guinea university would have to be basically residential, though with provision for part-time and external studies; and this will call for a liberal scholarships policy. On the vexed question of the site, it seemed to the Commission that the choice really lay between Port Moresby and Goroka—there were of course bids from almost everywhere except Daru (the Commission did not visit Daru . . .). The attraction of Goroka as a site is very readily apparent, but after an exhaustive discussion the Commission felt that technically there was no real alternative to Port Moresby; any other decision would have to be made on political rather than academic grounds. There will be a need for a second university in the not too distant future, say within twenty years, and by then Goroka might well be the logical choice. Another question, more significant in New Guinea than in Australia, concerns the relation of religious bodies to the university; but pending clarification of their position by the missions, it was possible only to welcome their participation—but not their monopoly—in the provision of residential colleges. (Cf. A.C.C. 1965:29-33.) Many other questions of academic and organizational detail are canvassed in the Report.

Technical and vocational education are no less important than academic. On the strictly technical side, the Commission reviewed in some detail the existing arrangements mentioned above and recommended the establishment of an institute of higher technical education, in juxtaposition to the university but not a part of it. This institute would in general work to diploma standard, and in particular a detailed scheme was put forward for an engineering diploma to meet one of the most imminent needs of the Territory— the creation of a cadre of good generalist engineers, especially on the civil engineering side. At the same time, the existing technical schools should be strengthened to the point at which they could be upgraded into technical colleges. While insisting upon equal opportunities for women as a general principle, the Commission drew attention to the scope for some specialized training for young women in such fields as welfare work.

Other higher vocational training presents more complicated problems, in part because we cannot start with nearly so clean a slate as in engineering: teacher training, the Administrative College, and the Papuan Medical College are going concerns, while the Department of Agriculture has already done a good deal of work in connection with Vudal. Although the precise organization must differ for each of these fields, the Commission felt that it is of great importance that they should be in some relation to the university. The objective is to strengthen standards and to enhance the repute of these avocations, and so to avoid the 'arts-law' fallacy which has so often led, as for example in India, to over-production of an ill-equipped semi-intelligentsia. This is in full accord with indigenous feeling, which has a sharply realist attitude to priorities —teachers, doctors, diddymen (agriculturalists), engineers—these are the felt priorities. It is, however, necessary to guard against the danger that this natural, and to a point entirely correct, attitude might run away with things and end in the dilution of the university into a super-polytechnic and nothing more. Oxbridge and ivory towers are out; the real issues for New Guinea are in the market-place; but this does not mean that the university should be tied down to a meanly utilitarian approach.

The Commission gave a high priority to teacher training, so much so as to recommend that the first *teaching* faculties should be education and arts, and the first graduates would most likely be Bachelors of Education. A science faculty should follow as soon as possible, while at an early stage deans should be appointed for *planning* faculties in agriculture, medicine, and law; for the last of these, the Commission followed the findings of an independent inquiry by the Law Council of Australia. The detailed recommend-ations for these professional subjects are too complicated to be summarized here, but it may be said that, as the Commission envi-saged the scheme of things, teacher training would be carried out by colleges of the university as part of a school of education. A faculty of law would be an integral part of the normal university structure; the existing medical college should in due course become the medical school of the university; and eventually the Admini-strative College should become an institute of administration within the university. The agricultural college should be affiliated rather than completely integrated.

This scheme is complex; so are the problems.

CONCLUSION: THE PROSPECT

The expansion of education is certainly one of the gravest issues confronting New Guinea today, ranking with those of economic viability and political stability; and of course all three are closely bound together. It must be admitted that when the degree of indigenous political responsibility already attained is put alongside the degree of indigenous intellectual advancement (in modern terms), the discrepancy is alarming: on the one hand, an elected majority in the House of Assembly; on the other, a dozen *under*-graduates and only some scores, hardly hundreds, in a population of two millions, who have even completed a full secondary course.

Unredressed, such an imbalance could lead straight to a Congolese situation.

There is nothing at all to suggest that the proportion of adequate intellectual capacity among Papuans and New Guineans is less than the human norm; but it lies fallow, and the vastness of the cultural gap is strikingly obvious. The lack of background familiarity with the modern world, the narrowness of horizons, the prevalence of particularisms, the survival of superstitions—all these must be overcome, or be on the way to being overcome, before the people can stand on their own feet. To enable them to overcome these things calls for an intense effort on the part of the Australian people who, will they nill they, are responsible and cannot decently shirk their responsibility—though they might consider sharing it with some of those who are more prodigal of ideological nagging than of practical aid.

Were all its proposals fully implemented, the Commission on Higher Education estimated the total capital costs of the university and the institute of higher technical education, spread over the first two triennia, as about £5,343,000. This is a large sum; but—admitting there are many other demands—it may be put into an interesting perspective by pointing out that it amounts to just about the price of half a packet of cigarettes each year for six years for each inhabitant of Australia in 1964.

There seems no real reason why assistance should not be sought from agencies such as UNESCO and some American foundations, at least for specific projects and installations. It is clear enough, however, that much the greater share of the cost will fall to the lot of the Australian taxpayer. If he is unwilling to meet this bill, it might well be that more awkward ones will be presented, in the form of political developments offering openings for interventions which could really imperil Australia's security. The balance of economic advantage might well be in favour of meeting the educational demand note.

It may well become evident that the easy antithesis of economic development and educational growth, as priorities, is a false one. Any solid economic development will call for very much larger and better-educated trained cadres, in all fields, than are now available; any solid educational advance will need a better-balanced economic development. And political stability depends on both, and affects both.

Setting this aside, there are of course many unresolved problems, many hazards, in such a large-scale educational programme. The dangers of forming an *élite* divorced from the realities of its local environment (whence the necessity of adjusting education to that environment); the dangers of over-raising expectations, so that education becomes 'the greatest of the cargo cults'; the difficulties of staffing so great a project and of maintaining momentum—all these should not be ignored. Yet it can be said with confidence that, on any view of the future of Papua and New Guinea and its relations with Australia, these can only be worse, not better, if there is not to be a sufficient number of indigenous people sufficiently well educated to cope realistically with the manifold problems and activities of a modern state, however modest its scale of operations. And, whatever may be thought on details, this quantum of trained intelligence can only be obtained by a programme at once comprehensive, co-ordinated, and not run on the cheap.

The leeway to be made up is very great; but opportunities are not lacking. There is now a wealth of experience, both positive as well as negative, to draw upon, particularly in Africa; and to some extent there is the advantage of the clean slate. Any advance will need imagination and daring as well as money, and very much of all three. Yet the refusal to take up this challenge can only lay up greater difficulties, greater troubles, for Australia, as social, economic, and political developments in New Guinea become even more lop-sided. In all probability, an educational policy boldly conceived and resolutely carried out is the only thing which can prevent a slide into a messy, anarchic, and quite possibly literally bloody waste of factionalism; a second Congo, and on Australia's very doorstep.

The Currie Commission's recommendation for an Institute of Higher Technical Education was accepted by the government almost at once, but it was not until March 1965, a year after the presentation of the report, that the Minister for Territories announced the acceptance of the university. There was some debate in the New Guinea House of Assembly, mainly concerned with the question of site, but Port Moresby was accepted. The long delay in dealing with this central recommendation of the Commission had produced criticism; but a more serious matter has not received a great deal of attention. This is the failure of the government to accept the Currie Commission's recommendation that at least for the first two triennia 'the moneys needed for the development of the University and associated institutions should be in the form of earmarked grants from the Commonwealth Government'.

This means that perhaps the most vitally important single institution in Papua and New Guinea, apart from the House of Assembly, must simply take its place in the queue for the annual departmental struggle for allocations. The objection to this is not only that it is likely to lead to a university run on the cheap, a type of 'economy' which can be ill afforded; much more serious, it is a very likely way of ensuring the premature politicizing of the university, so that instead of becoming a unifying factor it might become the object of factional struggle. If the history of universities in developing countries shows anything, it shows the social and political dangers of making the university dependent on local politics. It is lamentable that a government which spontaneously added £10,000,000 a year for five years to the expenditures proposed by the World Bank Mission should show itself so penny-wise and short-sighted as regards the much smaller investment needed to give the Territory a really well-found university.

7

Language and Literacy

S. A. WURM

THE New Guinea area, of which the Territory of Papua and New Guinea forms a large part, is one of the most complex regions of the world linguistically. The number of distinct languages is tremendous: at the present state of New Guinea linguistics, estimates of around seven hundred different languages in the entire New Guinea area[1] do not seem exaggerated. Of these, nearly five hundred may be located in the Australian part, much of which is as yet linguistically unknown or only little known, though extensive work carried out under the auspices of the Australian National University and the Summer Institute of Linguistics, New Guinea Branch, during the last few years has greatly expanded our knowledge of the language situation there (Wurm 1964). It is quite possible that further research will enable us to reduce this estimate somewhat, but the number is certainly very considerable.

One fact revealed by recent research has fundamentally affected the linguistic picture of New Guinea: the discovery of some very large groups of more or less closely interrelated languages. It had been believed until quite recently that the hundreds of languages in New Guinea were either completely unrelated to each other or that there were only small groups of interrelated languages, each comprising not more than a few languages (Wurm 1960).

Apart from the large number of the languages in the New Guinea area, many of them rank amongst the linguistically most complex of the world.

This forbidding language picture is somewhat brightened

(a) by the presence of two widespread kinds of lingua franca, Pidgin (or Neo-Melanesian) and Police Motu. These are spoken and understood over wide parts of Australian New Guinea, and the number of speakers of Pidgin is increasing rapidly;

[1] The Indonesian and Australian parts of New Guinea, including the Islands of New Britain, New Ireland, Bougainville, Manus and lesser adjacent islands.

(b) by the existence of eight or so major regional forms of lingua franca; and

(c) by the prevalence of bilingualism and multilingualism. For practical purposes multilingualism reduces the number of languages necessary for communication in Australian New Guinea to between one-half or one-third of the actual number of different languages spoken. Many speakers of small languages are equally at home in a neighbouring large language or languages, whilst many speakers of large languages also speak at least one other large language.

The number of Papuans and New Guineans, especially children and young people, who have a working knowledge of English is steadily increasing, but is still small.

Although the number of distinct languages spoken in Australian New Guinea is about five hundred, two facts, in addition to the prevalence of multilingualism, simplify the picture considerably from a practical angle:

(a) Of these approximately five hundred languages, thirty-seven are spoken by groups of more than 10,000 people, and between them number over 760,000 speakers, or more than one-third of the total population of the Territory.

(b) Thirty-four of these thirty-seven widely spoken languages can be arranged into three groups of more or less closely interrelated languages.

It is an interesting fact that in the New Guinea area large languages, i.e. languages with a considerable number of speakers, tend to be interrelated. These form groups of languages with very large numbers of speakers, whereas small languages show a much greater tendency to be isolated, i.e. unrelated to each other, though some can be shown to link with some larger languages. The general impression given by the linguistic picture of the New Guinea area is one of geographically and numerically extensive groups of predominantly large interrelated languages (mostly situated in the inland, and especially in the mountain areas), each of which is surrounded by a very large number of small unrelated languages each spoken by only a few hundred people. However, many of the speakers of such small languages are fully at home in the adjacent large language or languages, and from a practical point of view can be treated as additional speakers of these large languages. On the other hand there are some areas, especially near the coast, in which there are no large languages at all and, though multilingualism is present, the general means of intercommunication beyond the immediate neighbourhood is only Pidgin or Police Motu.

One important linguistic aspect of native education is the

possibility of using the various local languages for literacy work and for elementary education. Linguists have long recognized that basic education, and especially literacy work, in their mother-tongue has the advantage of very considerably accelerating the natives' absorption of education. Progress is much slower when they first have to familiarize themselves with a foreign, in particular European, language, especially when this foreign language, as it usually does, constitutes the reference system of a culture and complex of concepts totally alien to them. In addition, experiments have shown that natives who were made literate in their own language first, received their elementary education in it, and then gradually switched to English for the purpose of more advanced education, by far outstripped other natives of similar age and background who received their entire education in English from the start (UNESCO 1953:123-31). The members of the first group outmatched the second not only in their general performance and educational achievements but also in their ultimate proficiency in English.

It seems, therefore, that for proficiency and speed of basic education in New Guinea the best linguistic choice would be to use the individual local languages for literacy work and for elementary education for, say, one year or more, with a gradual switch to English after this period. This would provide the most favourable educational background for the natives' thorough mastery of English and for their absorption of more advanced education through the medium of English.

While this is undoubtedly the best choice in theory, the practical difficulties it presents are quite staggering.

The most serious problem is that the majority of the New Guinea languages are either not known at all or not sufficiently known. It is true that many of these little-known languages are spoken in uncontrolled or only recently contacted parts of New Guinea in which native education is not of immediate concern, but quite a few of them are located in areas in which native education is a matter for the present. The most important prerequisite for using a language for elementary education, and in particular for literacy purposes, is that its phonology, i.e. its sound system, must be well enough known in terms of modern linguistics for a consistent, simple orthography to be devised in which each symbol corresponds to one significant sound unit. With such an othography, natives can be made literate in their language in a very short time. Once the sound system of a language has been sufficiently well studied for this purpose, and a competent linguist has created an orthography, then native informants under the supervision of the linguist can prepare primers and teaching materials. For this the linguist need not be familiar with the language to such an extent that he could prepare such materials himself.

Our knowledge of the sound systems of New Guinea languages and of the structures of the languages themselves has been rapidly improving during recent years. This improvement has resulted mainly from the efforts of the members of the Summer Institute of Linguistics, New Guinea Branch, and of linguists of the Australian National University. Primers and other teaching materials have been prepared in a number of New Guinea languages, and their number is growing rapidly.

However, it must be borne in mind that to establish the nature of the sound system of a previously unstudied language well enough for a reliable orthography to be devised for the language takes at least several months' study by a competent linguist. In view of the large number of languages not yet treated on these lines in New Guinea, the time factor involved, and the scarcity of trained linguists in Australia, it would be unrealistic to suggest that the optimum solution would be to try to carry out this gigantic task immediately, particularly as compromise solutions, which will be discussed below, are available.

One argument often levelled against vernacular education is that the production of primers and teaching materials in a multiplicity of languages is impracticable and prohibitively expensive. These difficulties are, as a rule, greatly overrated: once orthographies suitable for an ordinary typewriter have been created, such materials can be duplicated by one of the modern, cheap offset processes. Native informants who are to be trained as the elementary teachers (see below) can in a very short time be taught to type efficiently in their own language,[2] and are the obvious persons to type such materials. A single duplicating machine prints a very large number of sheets in a day's run, and a modern, low-cost collating machine, requiring very little skill for its operation, makes collation a quick and easy task. Moreover, the total number of primers and other elementary teaching materials required in New Guinea remains the same irrespective of whether they are all in one language or in a multiplicity of languages.

Another difficulty commonly raised is the provision of suitable teachers for literacy work and elementary education in the vernaculars. For obvious reasons, Europeans are only in rare instances (e.g. some missionaries and members of the Summer Institute of Linguistics) capable of carrying out this work, and local native teachers have to be used. The informants who are to help the linguists to devise the orthographies, and who are to prepare the primers, literacy materials, and other elementary teaching materials under

[2] Members of the Summer Institute of Linguistics, Australian Branch, trained uneducated Australian aborigines to touch-type in their own languages. After a few weeks' training, these aborigines were able to touch-type extensive text materials in their languages (oral communication from W. Oates, Director, Summer Institute of Linguistics, Australian Branch).

the supervision of the linguists, are also the best persons to be trained for the purpose of literacy work and elementary teaching. Such training could well be given by the linguists supervising the preparatory work, for their knowledge of the vernaculars should be sufficient for this and for the supervision of the teaching at several schools, even if their active command of the languages is insufficient for them to carry out the teaching themselves.

As has been pointed out, this linguistic choice, while being the optimum solution in theory, is practicable only where the necessary linguistic work has already been carried out or is in the process of being finished. In such cases, it provides the best way to rapid literacy and the quick assimilation of some elements of basic education and—this is most important—the most advantageous background to literacy in, and mastery of, the English language. It must be made quite clear in this connection that education in New Guinea beyond the elementary stage must be in English. This alone can give the natives the key to the knowledge of the civilized world and enable them to proceed to the secondary and tertiary education which they have to absorb in much greater numbers if their country is to undergo the development it needs. In this, however, the important question is how the natives can best be prepared for their education in English, with a view to speeding up this education and to making its results more far-reaching and satisfactory. It appears that prior literacy in the vernacular, and some basic education in it as outlined above, is the best, if the requirements for such vernacular education are already available or can relatively easily be obtained. This does not mean, of course, that the study of further languages for the provision of such basic requirements should be discouraged, but it will often not be practicable to wait for the results of such studies before undertaking education work in a given area.

There is, however, one kind of situation in which it seems justifiable to advocate the vernacular-first approach, even if the necessary linguistic work has not yet been carried out. This is where the language is one spoken by several thousand people in an area in which education is to be introduced. Under these conditions it would be better to try the vernacular approach rather than the compromise solutions reviewed below. In actual fact, there are only a few large languages left in Australian New Guinea whose phonologies and structures have not been studied sufficiently for the purposes discussed, and it does not seem very likely, to judge by our present state of knowledge of New Guinea linguistics, that further unknown large languages will be discovered.

It will be noticed that in suggesting that the vernaculars be used for basic education no distinction has been made between large and small languages where sufficient knowledge about them is at hand. There is no linguistic reason for not using a small language just because of the limited number of its speakers; nor are the practical difficulties overwhelming. The one instance in which a distinction ought to be made is in the case of vernaculars not yet properly studied: as has been pointed out, large languages deserve priority over small ones in such study.

Before proceeding to the alternative solutions, a word or two may be said about the elementary introduction to mathematics, which is one of the most important subjects of basic education. Many New Guinea languages lack higher numerals, and even if they possess numerals going up to ten and beyond they are mostly very clumsy and unwieldy and sometimes lack precision. Clearly, these languages are unsuitable for teaching mathematics beyond an absolutely primitive level. At the same time, the teaching of mathematics in English brings the natives face to face with a formidable problem: they are to absorb a thinking process largely alien to them (i.e. mathematical principles) which utilizes alien concepts (i.e. higher numerals), and all of this is explained to them in a foreign language which they often understand only rudimentarily and which is the vehicle and reference system of a culture alien to them. Natives who know Pidgin or Police Motu (as most do) will be in a better position in at least being familiar with the notion of higher numerals. However, when the vernacular is used for first literacy work and elementary education, it seems most appropriate to use the English numerals as the basic symbol-words from the start, and to give the explanations of the numerals, the numerical system, and the basic mathematical operations in the vernacular. This is perfectly possible, and it leads to far better understanding on the natives' part, and in a much shorter time, than when English alone is employed.

Therefore, wherever sufficient information is available on a vernacular, the most satisfactory and speedy results will be achieved if the vernacular is used for literacy work and elementary education before the switch to English is made.

There remain, however, many native languages on which the information is inadequate or non-existent, and of which the number of speakers is too small to warrant special study on the lines already indicated. For these there are several possible approaches.

As already mentioned, the prevalence of bilingualism and multilingualism reduces the number of distinct languages necessary for communication. In theory, this ought to simplify the situation quite considerably, because for the purpose of literacy work and elementary education a second language mastered by such speakers as proficiently as their own language is just as satisfactory as their own vernacular. In practice, however, the general benefit derived from the presence of bilingualism and multilingualism in New Guinea for vernacular teaching is much less than might be expected, because this phenomenon is generally confined to males above school age, and can therefore not be relied on for the education of children in the vernacular. Only in relatively few instances, in particular in very small speech communities with a local vernacular of their own adjoining a large speech community speaking a different language, will all or most members of the former community, including the children, be found to be bilingual. In these special cases the second large idiom can be utilized for vernacular education just as effectively as if it were the native language, but in most cases this will not be so.

The next possibility is offered by the existence of about eight major local varieties of lingua franca. Most of these have been spread through the activities of various missions, i.e. Kâte, Yabêm, and Graged[3] by the Lutherans, Wedau (in the Milne Bay District) by the Anglicans, Dobu (also in the Milne Bay District) by the Methodists, Kuanua (in New Britain and New Ireland) by the Roman Catholics and the Methodists, Toaripi by the Anglicans and the Roman Catholics, and Kiwai (in the Fly Delta area) by the Anglicans. The result is that, while the number of natives understanding and speaking one variety of lingua franca in addition to their own vernacular is quite considerable (in the case of Kâte over 40,000), the great majority of these natives have already received some education through the missions in the course of which they were familiarized with the lingua franca. These varieties of lingua franca can therefore not well be considered for the basic literacy work and elementary education under discussion. However, in some of the areas in which such varieties of lingua franca are used, a number of natives are familiar with them without having undergone any formal education or literacy training, and this applies not only to adults but also to children. This is particularly so in the areas in which Toaripi and Kuanua are used. For such children (and young adults, if adult education is envisaged) a lingua franca could well be employed for literacy work and elementary education instead of the various vernaculars encountered in the area, with the practical advantage that there would probably be available a sufficient number of native teachers, and also of European teachers with a fair command of the lingua franca, to make such a task feasible from the start.

This leads to the often debated question of the merits or demerits of using, for literacy work and basic education, a native language other than that with which the natives to be educated are familiar at the time when their education is to begin. Such another language could either be an established native lingua franca or a large local language which is artificially extended beyond its natural boundaries for educational and other purposes. In other words, natives to be educated would receive their introduction to literacy and their

[3] The first two in the Morobe District, with Kâte also used in the Highlands Districts, the latter in the Madang District.

elementary education in a native language which they themselves
would have to learn first.

The main argument usually levelled against such a procedure is
that it is wasteful of time and effort; if the natives to be educated
have to learn a foreign language to receive their literacy training
and basic education, such a foreign language might just as well be
English in the first place.

This argument overlooks the fact that, for a New Guinea native,
it is totally unrealistic to place the learning of English and the
achievement of literacy in it on the same level as the acquisition of
a working knowledge of another native language and of becoming
literate in that. New Guinea natives experience relatively little
difficulty, and need only little time, to become quite proficient in
another New Guinea language, particularly if the latter is typologi-
cally similar to their own language. Its sound system and grammatical structure are not fundamentally divergent from those of
their own language, even if the vocabulary may be different. It
serves as the reference system and vehicle of communication of a
culture quite comparable to their own, and does not abound in totally
alien concepts. At the same time the orthography of such another
native language is simple and consistent, so that achieving literacy
in it is a relatively easier task for natives to whom being made
literate is a novel experience. By way of contrast, the sound system
and grammatical structure of English are totally and fundamentally
dissimilar from those of any New Guinea language, the language
constitutes a reference system to a culture whose very essence is
completely alien to the natives, and it abounds in concepts which
they cannot even begin to understand on first being confronted
with them. In consequence, the mastery of English is a very hard
task indeed for the natives, especially for those who have had no
previous education of any sort, and the achievement of literacy in
English, with its highly complex and inconsistent orthography, is
a long and difficult process.

The argument that the natives might as well be taught English
from the start, if their education and their becoming literate are
to involve their learning another language anyway, is therefore not
soundly based. On the contrary, being made literate and receiving
some basic education in another native language greatly facilitates
their prospects of absorbing literacy in English and of achieving a
good command of it.

At first sight, therefore, there seems to be every reason to suggest
that in New Guinea, when vernacular education is impractical, the
local lingua franca should be used for the purpose of making natives
literate and of conveying some basic education to them, before they
are taught and made literate in English. However, conditions in
New Guinea usually present a simpler and easier practical approach
to the problem. There is only one situation in which utilizing a

kind of local lingua franca may perhaps be preferable to the suggestions made below: if a large language is found to consist of a number of divergent dialects, it may be possible to select one of these dialects and use it as the standard form throughout the entire language area for the purpose of literacy work and basic education. It will be of advantage if the dialect chosen has some prestige value amongst the natives (for instance because it may be spoken in the area in which a ceremonial ground or a patrol post or mission station is located), because this will help overcome the resistance which speakers of other dialects may offer to it. Linguistically, speakers of other dialects should have only very little difficulty in becoming accomplished in the standard dialect.

In all other instances in which the vernacular cannot be used, and in which the natives would have to learn another language first, it seems most plausible to resort instead to a language which the majority of the natives already know, and which is perfectly suited for this purpose: a lingua franca already in general use over wide areas of Papua and New Guinea: Pidgin or Police Motu.

The attacks which have been made upon the former on a variety of grounds are very largely emotionally based or are attempts to rationalize emotional attitudes. It is indeed unfortunate that Pidgin happens to be spoken in an area in which the European population speaks English and finds its ears insulted by the form of a number of Pidgin words which resemble uncouth English words, though their meanings are in fact quite different and harmless. The suggestion that Pidgin is clumsy, ambiguous, and a very inadequate vehicle for communication is largely unjustified, and stems from the fact that the number of Europeans in New Guinea who have a really proficient command of the language is astonishingly small. The suggestion that Pidgin is a debased language invented by the Europeans for the purpose of keeping the natives in their place is contradicted by the fact that Pidgin is essentially a native creation, is structurally a Melanesian, i.e. a native, language, is spreading amongst the native population without active participation of the Europeans, and is not really well known by more than a small portion of the European population in New Guinea.

The fact that Police Motu, which is just as much, if not more, a 'pidginized' language as Pidgin itself, is rarely the target of comparable attacks, demonstrates quite clearly that the attacks on Pidgin have their root mainly in the emotional, and rationalized emotional, attitudes of English speakers. To them Pidgin sounds unpleasantly familiar, whereas Police Motu sounds as alien as any other native language; and they think they can easily 'pick up' Pidgin (mostly with disastrous results), but that Police Motu calls for more serious study.

Whatever the reasons for attacking Pidgin may be, be it in New Guinea itself, in Australia, or at the United Nations, it appears

highly unrealistic and wasteful not to utilize a language well known
by a large portion of the native population, including children, for
the purpose of literacy work and elementary education. Provided
it is realized that a good command of Pidgin requires a certain
amount of concentrated study, Pidgin has the great advantage that
European teachers can relatively easily be trained in it. Also,
literacy and basic teaching materials can be produced in it more
readily than in vernaculars for which native informants have to be
trained first, and the number of users of the same materials is very
great. Much the same, with little more complication, holds true for
Police Motu, which is a well-known and fairly simple language.

One argument frequently heard against the use of Pidgin in
literacy work and for elementary education is that it is likely to
prejudice the chances of the natives to learn good, i.e. 'correct',
English afterwards. This argument is based on the erroneous
assumption, held by most Europeans in the Territory, that Pidgin is
in fact only 'incorrect', or 'corrupt' English. This may well be true of
the 'Pidgin' spoken by many Europeans in New Guinea, but is
certainly wrong with regard to correct Pidgin, which is very much
a native language. One other important factor which such critics
persistently overlook is the fact that the natives to be educated are
usually quite fluent in Pidgin already, even before receiving any
instruction, and its use for literacy work and elementary education
therefore does not introduce an additional factor which may ad-
versely influence their subsequent learning of English. On the
contrary, being made literate in an orthographically simple and
consistent language like Pidgin, which they already know well, and
receiving some systematic training in organized thinking through
basic education with Pidgin as a medium of instruction, will have a
beneficial influence upon their ability to learn English properly
afterwards and to become literate in it.

What has been said of Pidgin applies equally to Police Motu as
the medium of elementary instruction and first literacy work, except
that no comparable fears and criticisms are, as a rule, voiced
concerning its use.

At this point the obvious question arises of whether, because of
the comparative ease and simplicity of their application in practice,
Pidgin and Police Motu may not be more appropriate for first
literacy work and elementary education in all instances in New
Guinea than vernacular education in those areas in which this is
feasible. The answer is that in all instances vernacular education
constitutes the optimum means for achieving literacy and conveying
elementary education prior to the switch to English. The reason:
Pidgin and Police Motu, while completely native in their basic sound
systems and grammatical structures, and familiar to the natives in
constituting reference systems of essentially native cultures, reflect

the phonologies of local vernaculars in the finer details of their sound systems in given areas. In consequence, it is not advisable to assume that the pronunciation of Pidgin as spoken by the natives of a given area will exactly correspond to the Pidgin phonology underlying its orthography, so the teachers, or the linguists assigned to undertake this task, must observe the local peculiarities in pronunciation carefully and must take them into account in literacy work. This is exactly the same problem which faces teachers in elementary schools in English dialect areas, especially in the British Isles, in which regional pronunciations of English require special attention for literacy work. This problem is therefore nothing unusual or additional to ordinary elementary teaching activities, and teachers in New Guinea would require only a little additional training to cope with it. An example may illustrate the problem in Pidgin: in several areas of New Guinea, speakers of Pidgin do not differentiate between *l* and *r* sounds, but use only one, e.g. *r*. This reflects the phonology of the vernaculars spoken by these natives, and is not a fault of Pidgin. In making these natives literate, the teachers must give special attention to their learning to distinguish, in pronunciation, between *l* and *r*, which they are taught to keep separate in writing. If this is not done, they will carry over their failure to distinguish between these two sounds into English, but *not* because they were first made literate in Pidgin; the trouble they have in separating the two sounds is due to the nature of their vernacular. If they were made literate in their vernacular first, they would become acquainted with only one of the two symbols in writing, e.g. with *r*, and recognize it as representing an *r*-sound. When switching to English, they would be familiarized with the written symbol *l* as something new, and would associate it readily with one of the new alien sounds of the English language, i.e. the *l*-sound. A good parallel example from European languages is the difficulty which some German speakers have in distinguishing between *f* and *v* when learning English: both these symbols are associated with the *f*-sound in the German orthography (as both the letters *l* and *r* are associated with an *r*-sound in Pidgin in some areas), and German students of English tend to associate both the letters *f* and *v* with the pronunciation of *f*.[4] At the same time, they will have less difficulty with the English *th*-sound which is alien to them, and which they associate readily with the equally strange and new written symbol *th* (as natives having become literate in the vernacular and knowing only the *r*-symbol readily associate the new symbol *l* with the alien *l*-sound when learning English).

The last, and at present officially adhered to, linguistic solution to make New Guinea natives literate, and to introduce them to

[4] They are of course in a more favourable position than the Pidgin speakers referred to, because the *v*-sound exists in German, whereas the *l*-sound is absent from the regional types of Pidgin under discussion.

elementary education, is to utilize English from the start. This has a number of obvious advantages: one set of literacy and elementary teaching materials can be used for the whole of New Guinea, teachers can be trained relatively easily, can be of lower proficiency than those needed for supervising vernacular or some other native language teaching or even than those required for teaching in Pidgin and Police Motu, and are therefore more easily available and in more plentiful supply, and there is no need for a switch of the language of instruction as the education progresses beyond the basic elementary level. On the debit side there is the fact that the natives face the extremely difficult task of having to learn a totally strange language serving a culture utterly alien to them, to be made literate in its highly complex and inconsistent orthography, and to cope with the problems of the incompatibility of the sound systems of their vernaculars with those of English (like those described above with reference to *l* and *r* in Pidgin) at the same time. These difficulties have already been discussed above, and there is no need to repeat them. Suffice it to say that the overall difficulties confronting the natives in this situation are of a much higher order than those of the other approaches discussed. Results would be more speedily achieved by one of the alternative methods in the long run, and would be of a much better quality than those produced by the utilization of English from the start, even if the oral method of teaching English is used first and literacy work in it left for later.

It remains to look at a situation in which none of the possibilities discussed so far apply, i.e. in which the vernacular has not been studied and the natives to receive education are not familiar with another known vernacular or a local lingua franca, or with Pidgin or Police Motu. Such situations are not likely to be encountered frequently in areas in which native education is to be introduced, but they are a possibility to be reckoned with. In such a case one of the following two courses of action seems likely to yield the most satisfactory results in the long run:

(a) Every effort should be made to have the local vernacular studied by a competent linguist sufficiently well for vernacular education to be initiated. This may, however, prove to be a lengthy task if the bilingual approach to linguistic study cannot be applied, i.e. if the native and the linguist have no language in common, so that the linguist has to use the slow monolingual approach. This method would, however, be impracticable where a number of different small vernaculars are encountered in the area in which native education is to be introduced, with no single one of them spoken by a sufficient number of bilingual or multilingual speakers of the other vernaculars to make feasible its use as the language of first education. In such instances, approach (b) should be resorted to.

(b) An assessment of the language situation should be made to establish which known language or existing lingua franca is likely to spread shortly into the given area in the near future— one of them certainly will if the area is brought sufficiently under government and/or missionary influence for the introduction of native education to be seriously considered for it. Once the nature of the wider language has been established, its introduction and spread should be encouraged, the language actively taught if necessary, and it should be made the vehicle of the natives' literacy work and basic elementary education before they are introduced to English. As has been pointed out above, the introduction of English from the start is not likely to yield results comparable in the long run in speed or quality with those achieved if the suggested approach is followed, and they would be particularly unsatisfactory in a situation such as this because of the natives' total inexperience with European culture and the complete absence of a means of communication between them and the English-speaking teachers.

As this chapter has stressed, one of the most important first goals of native education in New Guinea is to make the natives literate and proficient in English in large numbers in order to enable them to progress towards higher, and eventually tertiary, education. The teaching of English must be done as quickly, thoroughly, and proficiently as possible, for which it is of great importance that the surest and most efficient ways be found. What has been demonstrated in this chapter constitutes the author's opinion of the linguistic methods most suited to arrive at this goal. In summary, they are:

(1) Natives should first be made literate and should receive some elementary basic education in a language with which they are already familiar before their formal education begins.

(2) This language should be the local vernacular whenever possible, i.e. whenever the vernacular has been sufficiently well studied for a linguistically correct, consistent orthography to be devised for it.

(3) If a given vernacular is insufficiently known, compromise solutions are suggested because the study of unknown vernaculars is a very slow process the results of which may be too slow for the purpose of native education. The compromises suggested are:

    (a) making use of the phenomenon of bilingualism and multilingualism in using a well-known vernacular; or

    (b) employing a local lingua franca already known to the natives to be educated; or

    (c) using Pidgin or Police Motu, if the natives to be educated are already familiar with either.

(4) If in a given area none of the compromise solutions mentioned under (3) is applicable, and the local vernacular is insufficiently known, either:

(a) the vernacular should be studied and utilized, or if this is impracticable,

(b) the introduction or spread into the area of that large vernacular or lingua franca which is likely to be introduced or to spread into the area in the near future should be actively encouraged and it should be employed for native education.

(5) The use of English for literacy and basic education from the start produces difficulties for the natives which are greater than those they encounter if one of the methods mentioned above is first employed and the education is subsequently switched to English.

The very important educational goal of making the natives of New Guinea literate and highly proficient in English is likely to be achieved sooner, and with more satisfactory results, if one of the methods referred to above under (1)-(4) is followed, than if English is used from the start for native education.

8

Social Change and Social Movements

PAULA BROWN

SOCIAL and cultural change is continuous in all societies. The changes which take place in an isolated non-literate community are largely inaccessible to scholars; archaeology and the analysis of traditions provide limited information, but this work has hardly begun in New Guinea. For the most part, we discuss social change as it occurs in communities which are in contact with vastly different societies or are in transitional periods of revolutionary or especially rapid change. But the description of change we might attempt for an isolated community has to be concerned with somewhat different problems, problems like population growth and decline, adaptation to environmental variations, diffusion of the relatively small stock of ideas taken from other communities, and the acceptance of internal discoveries and inventions.

Our lack of knowledge about social change in pre-contact New Guinea cannot be remedied. Even if we were to discover and study a hitherto isolated community, our very presence there would be a source of change. Many cultural descriptions by anthropologists assume that a relatively static situation preceded discovery and contact with Western society. The ethnographic description is of a timeless pre-contact way of life. When we talk about social change, we talk about those changes which have occurred since discovery by Europeans, and sometimes that which has taken place during some specified period. Changes which follow contact between greatly different societies and cultures are of a more traumatic kind than those which take place either within an isolated community or within a complex Western society. These changes can be viewed in the context of colonization, and for our purposes we can contrast two broad types, without attempting to include all possible colonial situations.

1. Colonists occupy the land and the aboriginal population becomes a dwindling minority with a decreasing proportion of full-bloods, as has been the case in North America and Australia.

Such colonies develop from the standard of the immigrants, and rapidly become economically advanced and politically independent.

2. Where the area has a dense indigenous population and/or is unattractive to the colonists they enter in small numbers and establish a few settlements, plantations, etc. They assume political control and introduce Western techniques, economic forms, religion, and culture. The aboriginal inhabitants mostly remain in their own communities. They become the objects of educational, medical, and administrative activities and religious missions. Often large-scale changes are introduced, such as economic development programmes to raise the standard of living. This has been the form of colonization in most of Africa, southern Asia, and the Pacific. Many of the former colonies of this type have now achieved independence with an economic and cultural standard far different from that before their discovery and colonization. But most of them have higher birth, mortality, and illiteracy rates, lower incomes and standards of living than Europe or former colonies of the first type.

The Territory of Papua and New Guinea is one of the second type, a dependent country; it is one of the backward parts of the world, largely undeveloped and primitive. There are still a few New Guineans who have never seen a white man. I shall not examine the historical, political, or economic reasons for this backwardness. But I shall ask whether there are any special characteristics of the people of New Guinea and their communities which help to account for it. My principal interest is in social movements as organized efforts to change social conditions. Cargo cults will be discussed as a form of social movement, and I shall suggest some reasons why they occur in New Guinea and the conditions under which they may disappear.

NEW GUINEA SOCIETIES

Many writers have remarked upon the very large number—many hundreds—of distinct languages in Papua-New Guinea (see Chapter 7). The exact number may never be known, since some will have become extinct before they can be recorded, and linguists will disagree about the distinction between language and dialect. However, the counting of languages and differentiation of language families is a side issue; what is significant is the separateness of native communities. Melanesia is notable for the small scale of indigenous political organization, the absence of any central authority or formal legal procedures within a tribe or even a village, the constant intertribal and intratribal warfare. These conditions prevailed even in areas where tens of thousands of people spoke the same language and shared the same culture. In the highlands of New Guinea the largest language and cultural groups of Melanesia are found, but even there the largest unified group which restricted internal warfare and joined together in occasional ceremony was a tribe of a few thousand people. And in these no central authority could prevent internal conflict and fighting.

The small local community, rarely more than a few hundred people, was normally the largest effective political unit. Beyond this, most people had relatives and partners in trade and ceremonial exchange. Outsiders were on the whole regarded with suspicion; one did not travel among strangers. Intervillage and intertribal raids and attacks might occur at any time.

There were no great differences in forms of political organization between New Guinea communities; none was differently armed, more productive, or stratified so as to achieve domination over another group; there were no states, no slaves, no rulers or ruled. However, there were some differences in the size and area of community and in the number of people who combined to fight or to hold a ceremony.

Colonial administrations in Africa and Asia have had to overcome established systems of local authority and privilege to form a Western style of administration on the large scale necessary for a modern nation. They have had to meet organized conservative resistance to innovation, and have had to substitute other selective procedures for hereditary privilege. In New Guinea these problems do not exist. There were no centralized states, no hereditary positions of political authority, no competing organized systems of government. Some local leaders in a few parts of Papua-New Guinea were called 'chief', and there was a 'Paramount Chief' in the Trobriand Islands, but these did not have officially established power nor any important legislative, judicial, or executive functions.

Such absence of indigenous political structures has given the colonial power no foundation on which to build modern government; but it has also relieved it of the necessity, so common elsewhere, of breaking down the old hereditary system and transforming it into a modern one (Brown 1963). Once tribal warfare is stopped, larger associations can be introduced. It does appear that regional alignments may precede a national one, but there does not seem to be resistance to the idea of a central government.

There is, in some respects, a kind of sameness about these small and separate New Guinea communities. Before the Europeans arrived all these communities were technologically at more or less the same level, using stone, wood, and occasionally bone or shell for tools, making pottery in only a few places, working vegetable fibres into clothing, belts, and containers, cultivating tubers, bananas, sugarcane, and vegetables, raising pigs, building houses of wood, reeds, leaves, and grass, and using bow and arrow, spears, and occasionally clubs and shields to fight. However, there are striking regional differences: the advanced agricultural techniques of the highlanders as compared to shifting cultivation in the lowlands and sago gathering in the coastal swamps; specialization and trade in food or other products between coastal fishing and inland gardening communities; large villages in the Eastern Highlands and dispersed houses in the Western; and arts, cosmological beliefs, myths, rituals, and magic were distinctive in different areas. The people were generally disinterested in tradition, myth, genealogy, and other ways of preserving the past. Thus in some places cults were adopted, spread, and abandoned as soon as new cults were introduced (Ryan 1961; Williams 1930).

Subsistence did not fully occupy the time and energies of the people; they had leisure to fight, to trade, and to celebrate. A dominant interest throughout New Guinea is material wealth—not only in the possession of it but in its use for exchange. In the absence of fixed hereditary positions of authority or the accumulation of heritable property, prestige is gained by participating in the exchange system. Essentially, a man gains prestige by his application and shrewdness in exchange relations; he arranges marriages and ceremonial distributions, takes a leading part in group activities, adopts younger men who become his dependants and supporters, takes several wives, who produce food and raise pigs for distribution, and enters into exchange relations with his wives' brothers and his sisters' husbands.

Leadership fluctuates as men's fortunes and activities wax and wane. A young man has not the productive resources, the accumulation of exchange partnerships and credit, to be a leader; an old man has no longer the energy to keep up his obligations. Achievement is the result of hard work and intelligent investment. Native ideas of power and wealth are concerned with gaining supporters and dependants within the local community to help the leader hold a successful ceremony or win a single battle. There is no permanent accumulation of power or wealth, no inheritance of privilege. The valuable goods—shells, stone axes, bird of paradise feathers, etc.— circulate within and between communities through a complex exchange system based upon personal ties of kinship and marriage.

REACTIONS TO CONTACT

New Guinea was discovered early in Pacific exploration, but until the late eighteenth century there were no European settlements. Explorers, missionaries, and commercial companies preceded administration in many places. Only in the late nineteenth century was administration at all regularized, and this was restricted to the coastal fringe and smaller islands. Administration changed from British to Australian in Papua and from German to Australian in New Guinea long before the interior was visited and patrol posts were established.

Interior New Guinea was explored in the present century, with a more advanced technology than in the exploration of Africa, Asia, or America. The first view of Europeans that most inhabitants had was of a well-equipped patrol composed of one or two Australian officers, a native police force, and a line of native carriers. Many such patrols carried radios and cleared areas for aeroplane landings or airdrops of supplies. The dominance of the European, his wealth, and his material possessions have been evident from first sight. The Australian differs enormously from the Melanesian in power and wealth. The unschooled native knows nothing of the history of Western technological, political, and economic development. He sees the European in possession of material goods, but he sees no mine or factory; he may only know that these goods arrive from outside in ships or aeroplanes. In remote government stations nowadays several planes arrive daily, carrying passengers, mail, and a great range of goods, from frozen foods to power equipment, for the station officers. Native prisoners unload the planes and crowds gather. The plane then departs for unknown places to reload and bring further supplies. The European does no menial labour to obtain these things; he sits in an office and sends messages by letter or wireless.

The goods and power of the European (and of the natives associated with him as assistants, police, etc.) are very attractive to New Guineans. Cloth and metal are eagerly sought, and, while they are very rare, confer prestige on their possessors. They are often incorporated into the system of valuables used for prestige-giving exchanges. Money becomes a valuable, a vital part of ceremonial payments; European goods such as knives and axes replace native manufactures in ceremonial exchange at marriage and death. But European manufactures are also a coveted part of a rising standard of living—clothing, tools, and domestic hardware are quickly incorporated into daily life.

New Guineans can obtain none of these things as easily as the Europeans seem to get them. Only small quantities come through hard work, often as a plantation worker far from home, or by trade. Not only does the white man own many of these things, but he sets the terms of trade and the wages whereby the natives can get them. Only occasionally does he introduce a cash crop or other source of cash income, and these incomes are often pitifully small. A high value is attached to European goods, and people want them. At first they may be just novelties, but later they are incorporated into daily life as luxuries or even as necessities.

Social Movements

Movements, cults, and protests have been reported in many parts of Melanesia. Only a few of these have been reported in any detail by scholars who have remained in the communities long enough to

gain the confidence of leaders and participants and compile a
description, history, and analysis of beliefs and actions. Several
writers have attempted to state the general characteristics of cults.
Here I draw upon some accounts of social movements, my own
experience in New Guinea, and the general discussions, to determine the place of movements in general, cargo cults, and protests
in the changes now occurring in Papua-New Guinea.

The feelings of the indigenous people towards Europeans have
been aptly described as 'hopeless envy' (Mair 1948:67). The people
are not always content to wait for the ordinary processes of education and economic advancement to reach them through the slow
expansion of services by the Administration. In a number of places,
at different times since the 1890s (Hogbin 1958:207), native-led
social movements have had as their goal the quick acquisition of
European goods, and often also of power. I consider cargo cults
to be a kind of social movement.[1]

A great deal of attention and concern has focused upon 'cargo
cults' in New Guinea, and this shows no sign of abating. Jarvie
(1964) devotes a book to the problem of explaining the cults, and a
number of studies have appeared in recent years (Schwartz 1962;
Burridge 1960; Worsley 1957; Lawrence 1964). Most of these have
emphasized the bizarre nature of the beliefs and the behaviour of
the adherents—destruction of property, trembling, credulity. They
are often regarded as phenomena quite apart from social developments, retrogressive, fantastic, hysterical, led by insane or pretendant
prophets. Some writers have directed attention to the political and
economic factors and the problems of the people undergoing change
in Melanesia (Stanner 1953; Worsley 1957; Hogbin 1958): their
tensions, crises, and their poor and apparently hopeless plight in
comparison with Europeans. The general situation is comprehen-
sible, but the appearance of a cult at a particular place and time is
more difficult to explain (Inglis 1957). It depends upon certain
common conditions as well as upon the presence of an outstanding
leader who may have visions and the gift of prophecy. It also
requires acceptance by the community.

Stanner (1953:63-4) lists six common characteristics of cargo
movements:

1. Leadership—the initiative of distinctive personalities.

2. Contact with the spirit world; visions, swoons, etc.

3. Orders, charters; systematic instruction of followers. These
   vary and may include positive or negative exhortations and
   the abandonment of old ways.

[1] King (1956:27) presents an appropriate definition of social movement: 'A
group venture extending beyond a local community or a single event and
involving a systematic effort to inaugurate changes in thought, behaviour, and
social relationships'.

4. Prophecies: the arrival of a ship or plane sent by the spirits with a cargo of non-traditional wealth for the natives.

5. Mass demonstrations, often hysterical or eccentric.

6. Symbolic Europeanism in articles and forms of organization.

Of these characteristics all but the second occur in social movements which are not cargo cults.

Many movements with goals similar to those of cargo cults have occurred in Papua-New Guinea. They have a number of characteristics in common with cargo cults: a leader, moral reforms with orders and charters, co-operative community effort, expectations of wealth, mass demonstrations, symbols of Europeans in the form of books and papers, and quasi-military discipline. They often bring together members of a number of communities, former enemy villages and tribes, and sometimes several language groups. A common feature is the re-siting and re-building of villages with new architectural styles.

An example of this, the Tommy Kabu movement in the Purari Delta of Papua, has been well reported (Maher 1958, 1961). Tommy Kabu returned from wartime work with Australians in 1946 and began a programme of change. 'The aim of the movement was to establish the Purari economy on a co-operative tribal basis so far as productive effort and its returns were concerned, but what was produced was to be sold for cash on European or native markets in Port Moresby' (Maher 1961:58). The economic programme 'was only part of what was planned and attempted. The already tottering ceremonial system was swept away . . . Christianity was held up, at least in name, as the proper religion for the new order' (ibid.:59). 'Villages formed their own police force, raised a flag and copied military ceremonies some of the people had seen in Port Moresby' (ibid.). 'Wherever he established a more or less permanent headquarters, he had an "office" set up with tables, chairs, and official-looking papers which he had gathered from various places' (ibid.: 60).

> Given the strong and common desire for change, the negative aspects of the program were rather easily accomplished . . . the rejection of the old, both real and symbolic, could be done, or at least appear to be done, with desire and a moment's action, but the construction of the new required continuing activity and a knowledge of specific techniques which were also essentially new (ibid.:61).

New village sites and new architectural styles replaced the old. The Kompani, with contributions from the people, purchased a boat in which produce of the Purari Delta was to be transported to market. The scheme foundered because the specific knowledge and techniques were lacking, the boat was lost in a fire, account books were not kept, the distribution centre in Port Moresby was inefficient and expensive, and the business was badly run. The movement brought together in one organization for the first time a number of Purari tribes, but it did not obtain help from the Administration, and the necessary management skills were not acquired. Although the Kompani continued, it had much reduced support and few achievements. 'As failure became apparent, disillusionment with the Kompani spread but the Purari's interest in "doing business" remained strong' (ibid.:73). Tommy began a much more modest business venture in 1955, but except for this there was no further organized effort.

Maher suggested that the failure of the movement might be followed by apathy and stagnation, or by a cargo cult for which some ideas were present (1958, 1961). The second alternative has not been reported, but it has been a later phase of other movements in New Guinea. Paliau and Yali began as leaders like Tommy Kabu; their early efforts for practical programmes were quickly re-directed into cargo cults. Guiart (1952a) describes a 'borderline type of cargo cult' in Malekula, in the New Hebrides.

In order for people to join any movement for social change, their wish for a different life must be strongly held. Their wishes can vary greatly in content. They can wish to return to the golden age of the past (as in the American Indian Ghost Dance); they can wish for a somewhat better standard of living in the present (a labour movement); or they can have millennial dreams of a perfect age and salvation. In its common Melanesian form the wish is for the achievement of European wealth and power. These feelings are often linked with resentment at the native's present position. 'The white man shall go' is a common, though not universal, element; nationalism is often involved as well (Guiart 1951).

There have been many types of movement in other parts of Melanesia (Kouwenhoven n.d.; Allan 1951; Guiart 1951, 1952a), and indeed in undeveloped territories everywhere. Movements and cargo cults are not restricted to Melanesia, although some of their features may be distinctive. Goals other than European goods may be sought (for example in North America, the religious movements of Handsome Lake and the Shakers, and African separatist churches).

In Papua-New Guinea few adults are literate and fully trained for any sort of clerical employment. The majority have had at most a few years in a mission school under poorly educated teachers. This ignorance makes it impossible for the prominent men to understand the administration, economy, and technology in which they live or towards which they are moving. Yet some of them are remarkably adaptable and enthusiastic for economic and political development. One such man is Kondom, a Chimbu who was a boy when the first Australian patrol explored the New Guinea highlands in 1933. Without any formal schooling, he has during the past twenty years, with administrative support, been a *luluai*, member of the District Advisory Council, observer at the pre-1961 Legislative Council, observer at conferences of the South Pacific Commission, President of a Native Local Government Council, and elected member of the Legislative Council for the Highlands 1961-4 (Brown 1963). He failed to be elected to the House of Assembly in 1964, but is President of the newly-formed Co-operative Society in Chimbu. He led the local people in developing cash crops and growing coffee, and in 1954 built a large hall of woven bamboo with a thatched roof and instituted meetings to encourage reform and development. A sort of record was kept of points made in these meetings either by a native recorder or government officer attending. The introduction of cash crops and problems of processing coffee and marketing produce were the main matters for discussion. A set of rules was put forward:

> My name is *luluai* Kondom. The meeting is about the government laws. I want the natives to hold these laws. These are the rules:
> 1. Man must not kill other human beings.
> 2. Man must not commit adultery with young girls and old women.
> 3. Men must not burn the house.
> 4. Men must not steal someone's property.
> 5. Men must listen to their head man or *Luluai* or *Tultul*.
> 6. The women must not kill the young child that was born.
> 7. Man must not play with someone's wife.
> 8. The best and most important one is education.[2]

Meetings I attended in 1958 were of a similar character. An agenda in Pidgin-English was put on a blackboard, with items on cash crops, schools, taxes, prohibition of fighting, and the beginning of local government. On these occasions leading men spoke in favour of progress, and the audience cheered, expressing unanimous approval. In 1959 a Local Government Council was established in central Chimbu. The councillors elected were, in comparison with the previous appointed officials, young, progressive, and mostly fluent in Pidgin-English. The monthly meetings of the Council are held in a building of timber and corrugated iron; members sit on benches facing the President, who wields a gavel and proceeds formally through an agenda, with the help of the clerk and supervising officer. Members stand to address the chair, propose motions, vote, form committees, and so on; the ritual of procedure is more or less learned, but it has no meaning beyond being the white man's way of conducting Council meetings. The main Council business concerns the use of the few thousand pounds' tax: proposals for

[2] From a notebook given to me by Kondom, with spelling corrected, entry dated 19 July 1954.

expenditure on certain projects, estimates, and calculations are made by the supervising officer. Chimbu Council meetings are occasions for government officers to speak to Councillors and announce new developments. The Councillors raise questions of interest to them—such matters as payment for work on roads and the sale of coffee. The Council is more of a centre for complaint and information than an organ of government in the terms of the Ordinance.

The confusion of the people can perhaps be conveyed in a few examples. One Councillor bought a cow, and then at a Council meeting asked the government to provide a milking machine. In discussing the high price of locally raised chickens and the relatively low price of imported tinned chickens, Kondom remarked that the tinned ones are cheaper because they are made in a factory. Although the decline in world coffee prices was responsible for lower payments for coffee beans in Chimbu, this explanation was never accepted by the people; lower prices were responsible for much anti-European feeling.

Such an atmosphere of ignorance is a fertile field for the Melanesians' belief that the desired manufactured goods may be delivered to them by their ancestors. 'Cargo' beliefs and incipient cults are common in Melanesia; many of them fail to attract sufficient followers to become a cult, or are stopped by government officers, or die out before many communities are involved (Salisbury 1958; Read 1958; Berndt 1952-3; Burridge 1960, on Manam). Firth (1955:131) calls them 'prototype cargo-cult phenomena'. He says there can be a 'cargo'-cult type of behaviour, without its attaining the organized coherence of a movement or cult development.

CULTS

The desire for social and economic improvement may be expressed in social movements which include confused and mistaken beliefs about money and the manufacture of goods. A 'cargo' cult is one form of such a movement. A message is communicated in a dream or vision, the prophet foresees a millennium of prosperity and plenty, nearly always of European goods. To attain this the believers carry out rites, often destructive of traditional property; they may appear hysterical, entranced, etc. Other common beliefs are that the Europeans have the secret of obtaining wealth which had been withheld from the natives, and that the ancestors or spirits have now sent a ship or aeroplane loaded with cargo for the natives.

During the time the white man has been present in our land, so it was told, we have seen the many 'good things'—steel tomahawks, steel knives, laplap [cloth], saucepans, etc., and the good foods, which have all come to our country from outside . . . these good things have always been sent to us by our predeceased forefathers, but instead of finding their way direct to us, the white man knew how to intercept them and did so. Then instead of passing the goods on to us, they put them into trade stores, and we had to work very hard to get even a part of them. However, our predeceased forefathers have found out what has happened to all these goods and now they will be bringing them direct to us.[3]

A few studies have traced the origin and development of such movements. Lawrence examines traditional beliefs and the several stages of contact, including elements of Christian belief.[4] His study of Yali, a cult leader, first shows him being supported by the Administration in his efforts to raise the standard of living in his area of the Rai Coast, Madang District. At that time there was no cargo cult dogma involved, but later some members of the Letub cult group took charge of the movement and it became a cargo cult with Yali as its figurehead. Lawrence concludes, 'Although Yali was the accredited leader of the pagan Cargo Cult, I do not believe that he was its sole or true originator' (1955:12).

Yali seems to be a different sort of man from Mambu of Bogia, who had an entirely mystical programme in which the secret of the white men was revealed; Mambu performed miracles and produced money. However, in the stories of their followers, both Yali and Mambu were mythical figures, 'symbols which focus ideas in Cargo. . . . So far as they exercised political authority in accord with the myth-dream, they were as divine kings' (Burridge 1960:207).

Perhaps the fullest documentation to date on any movement in New Guinea is on the one led by a man named Paliau in the Admiralty Islands. Several phases were observed and reports and analyses were given by Mead (1956) and Schwartz (1962). The people of Manus were greatly affected by troops stationed there during World War II; American Negro soldiers especially impressed them. After the war their discontent with the old way of life was expressed both in social movements and in cult. In his monographs on the Paliau movement, Schwartz distinguishes various phases:

1. Local phase: secular and partial programmes of change were organized independently by leaders in their own villages to eliminate certain aspects of the old culture.

2. Initial movement: Paliau instituted a programme of social, economic, political, religious, and cultural transformation in a movement for all Manus. This rejected the old culture and drew on Christian belief for new goals.

3. First cult: during the events which are known as 'The Noise' people destroyed their property and had convulsive seizures. The cult spread rapidly and collapsed rapidly in many villages. The first cult maintained Paliau's original goals; Schwartz

[3] From Report: Lieut. R. J. Stevenson, P.O., Akuna Police Post, 28 October 1944 to D.O. Bena Area; Patrol Report, Bena No. 8 of 1944/5; Agarabe area, p. 12. Quoted in Berndt 1953:231.

[4] Lawrence's major study (1964) was published after this paper was written; these remarks are based upon his earlier work (1955).

characterizes the belief system as sparse, underdeveloped, unstandardized.

4. Organizational phase: the movement was in the forefront, and the development of a council, native courts, and co-operatives was anticipated by new forms of organization. New villages were built on the beaches, government recognition of new forms of organization was sought, and government schools were requested.

5. Plateau phase: a period of imposed waiting, drift, and decline in morale, and conservatism.

6. Second cult: the main emphasis was on ghosts and the reconstruction of cemeteries. This developed at a time when establishment of a council and of a co-operative were expected shortly. However, these were considered to require hard work. The cult was a short route to Paradise.

7. Officialization phase: the council was established, and a co-operative was to be instituted. This phase has not yet been reported upon by Schwartz or Mead.

The people of Manus wanted the sort of wealth they saw among the American troops. Several local leaders had small-scale programmes to achieve this. Then Paliau developed an inclusive programme. After this, cult and movement alternated: the movement demanded hard work for modest rewards; the cult promised easy success. It may be that the obviously slow progress of secular cultural transformation produced strains and impatience which inclined the people towards the immediate rewards promised by the cult. Collapse of the first cult was followed by a more practical programme, but morale declined with delays, and yet another cult spread through the area.

Schwartz's account is the fullest yet available, and we can only inquire whether this alternation of movement and cult is usual. Reports of cults in Biak (de Bruyn 1951), the Vailala River (Williams 1934), Tanna (Guiart 1952b), and Buka (Worsley 1957) show that cult beliefs often persist after the ritual stops and that the cult behaviour may recur. 'The persistence of these movements on Buka shows that mere failure of a prophecy is no assurance that a cult will lose its hold on the people' (Worsley 1957:122). Descriptions of Melanesian traditional religious cults with the aim of increased food, pigs, shells, etc. suggest that they have many characteristics in common with cargo cults (Williams 1930; Blood 1946; Ryan 1961).[5]

[5] The belief systems involved in New Guinea cults have been studied by only a few scholars; the accounts of Schwartz (1962) and Burridge (1960) should be compared with one another and with that of Lawrence (1964). Further examination of the similarities and differences between cults and social movements would be of interest; so would a study of those Melanesian communities which have neither. The influence of traditional beliefs and Christian teaching on modern beliefs also needs to be studied.

Attempts to understand and direct the course of social change in Papua-New Guinea have been bedevilled by the consideration of cargo cults as enigmatic phenomena and evidence of primitive gullibility, suggestibility, and credulity (Williams 1934). Officers and settlers are apprehensive of any suggestion of the presence of cargo beliefs and cults. But while only some of the movements have as their aim the ousting of the Administration, missionaries, or settlers, many Europeans assume that all the cults are anti-European. However, some movements, for example Marching Rule (Allan 1951), John Frum (Guiart 1952b), and the 'Johnson movement', merely want to replace the present administrators with other Europeans.

The destruction of property and neglect of subsistence, the refusal to pay tax, the mass hysterical demonstrations and false hopes are indeed serious matters for the Administrators who must restore order. Overt cult manifestations can be stopped by police action. However, cult belief pervades even where no ritual is observed. Cults thrive on ignorance and wishful thinking. Cults may alternate with secular movements or with a rather static and apathetic state. Movements which are practical both in their ends and in their means may incorporate the sort of false beliefs which are common in cults, for example members of his movement believed that 'Tommy Kabu was married to a daughter of the king of England and that they had two children' (Maher 1961:61).

OTHER FORMS OF POLITICAL AND ECONOMIC CHANGE

The movements which have been discussed are on a fairly large scale for New Guinea, bringing together several communities in a secular movement or a cargo cult. There have been many small-scale communal enterprises led by local men with a little education and entrepreneurial ability, such as Numbuk of Erap (Crocombe and Hogbin 1963), Gulu at Amele, and Simogun at Dagua (Anon. 1951). Other community projects have had no single leader but a small group of men have taken charge, as at Milne Bay (Belshaw 1955), or a group of villages have joined together, as at Sissano Lagoon. Such undramatic enterprises, with or without official support, are a common form of development in all colonial territories.

In Papua-New Guinea the government has sponsored Native Local Government Councils, rural progress societies, co-operative societies, agricultural extension projects, marketing projects, and other political and economic programmes. Most are still in their early stages, and without detailed studies it is difficult to assess them. The best known and apparently most successful of these has been the development of cocoa as a cash crop, combined with advances in education, health, and local government, among the Tolai of the Gazelle Peninsula, New Britain.

From time to time New Guineans demonstrate against govern-
ment-sponsored activities. They may refuse to support a project or
to pay a tax. These actions are sometimes attributed to cargo cult
beliefs, but they are nevertheless protests: they are organized
oppositions to the Administration. Our knowledge of their origin,
leadership, and organization is unfortunately slight. They seem to
be short lived and do not become social movements.

Papua-New Guinea has had few associations of employees or
trade unions. Several organized political and economic actions have
taken place or been led by police or military groups. Twice, Rabaul
has been the locale of a strike. In 1929 a one-day general strike was
organized by the police and extended to include other employees. It
was quickly suppressed. In June 1964 the native police in Rabaul
went on strike for some hours for better working conditions and
pay. The Pacific Islands Regiment has also demonstrated against
its rates of pay in recent years. The structure of these groups, the
skills and continuous service of their members give them the basis
for organized action which has not developed in labour lines on
plantations or among the employees of small private firms. When
such a group strikes, their action may be viewed as disloyalty rather
than as the expression of a labour grievance.

The labour movement in New Guinea has barely begun. When
the Public Service was reorganized in 1964 there was an immediate
reaction against discriminatory salary scales. But as work associations develop, employees must be expected to strike or protest to
demonstrate their views.

CULTS AND OTHER MOVEMENTS

In his discussion of the Mansren cult, de Bruyn (1951:3-5) makes
some significant general points about these movements. He says
the movement is

> a communal expression of the renunciation of the struggle for
> life. It symbolises the efforts of a people to re-order and re-
> organize its way of life as a result of changed conditions. . . .
> Such movements, although they sometimes show strongly re-
> ligious, syncretic features, are, I believe, merely psychological
> reactions to existing situations. They are the people's attempt to
> gain relief or release from their distress, through the intervention
> of supernatural powers in the efficacy of which they firmly
> believe, which powers either belong to the indigenous religion or
> are an element in an alien religion with which the people have
> become familiar. . . . There is no essential difference between
> these mystical and religious cults, and the aggressive movements
> whose political nature is becoming more and more prominent.
> From the psychological point of view both types of movement
> are the same.

Social movements are common in Papua-New Guinea; the Melanesian type of movement is most often directed towards obtaining an improved standard of living, including the accumulation of European goods in quantity, and often the obtaining of political power. It is a form of 'revitalization' movement: 'a deliberate, organized, conscious effort to construct a more satisfying culture' (Wallace 1956:265). It is not nativistic or revivalistic, but reformative and/or millenarian (Voget 1959).

Movement and cult have many common characteristics, but, as in any historical event, each phase of a movement or a cult is in some ways distinctive. The overthrow or departure of Europeans is not always part of the programme. Nor need it include destruction of property. In both the secular and cult movements the programme commonly includes a list of reforms—leaders urge the people to reject their old evil ways and become tidy, peaceable members of the new society. The rejection of the past is accompanied by a strong desire for a future in which the people have wealth and power. The preparation for the arrival of new property may include the re-siting of villages, new community plans, and new buildings. The new property may be expected to arrive as cargo gift from ancestors or as a result of community enterprise.

Various attempts have been made to pick out the defining features of cults. From Stanner's list we might select three: contact with the spirit world, prophecies, and hysterical mass demonstrations. But these characteristics are not limited to cults. Prayer is a common preliminary to political meetings in New Guinea; when a co-operative society was discussed in Chimbu, increased wealth was prophesied as the result; and Kondom's meetings were a mass (but not hysterical) demonstration of a desire to change.

Hogbin (1958:215) has advanced a somewhat different set of common characteristics of cults: the belief in the cargo, the ceremonies, the feasting, the constructional work, the emergence of leaders with their codes of correct behaviour. But while the belief that cargo is being sent is a defining feature of cargo cults, ceremonies and feasting can be part of any cult ritual; and leaders and codes of correct behaviour are as characteristic of social movements in general as they are of cults.

Margaret Mead distinguishes cult from movement while noting that they can occur in combination. She concludes that:

> The essential features of a cargo cult manifestation are these: An innovator, inspired by a supernatural revelation, announces . . . the arrival, by supernatural agency, of a cargo made up of a large assortment of objects emanating from the world of the European; at the same time, the invading whites will go away. . . . The inauguration of the new order may be accompanied by some natural hazard . . . those who will be its beneficiaries are urged to prepare themselves for the millennium by destroying their

property. . . . Acceptance of the prophecy usually is followed by a period of great excitement, often accompanied by convulsive seizures of a contagious nature (1964:194-5).

Movements . . . include programmes of directed change, modeled on Euro-American culture, that call for local autonomy, political identity and the adoption of real (not merely symbolic) aspects of modern culture (ibid.:196). Sometimes cargo cults and movements have occurred in association; at other times they have occurred separately. But they do have several features in common . . . both are future-orientated. . . . Leadership also is very important. . . . Whereas cargo cults had become endemic in the New Guinea area, political movements were epidemic in the immediate post-war atmosphere. Cargo cults depended on supernatural means of bringing about an immediate Utopia, and thrived on dreams, visions, and suggestibility. In contrast, movements depended on politico-economic means of realisation and thrived in the political atmosphere in which colonialism was being abandoned (ibid.:197-8).

Jarvie (1964:64-6) summarizes the distinctive features of cargo cults under eight points:

1. Cults are founded and led by a single prophet who receives the revelation and propagates it.

2. Prophets are hardly educated and are misinformed about the workings of society outside Melanesia.

3. Cults borrow European rituals, both secular and religious. They have a charter of systematic instruction.

4. New beliefs are grafted on to older local beliefs.

5. Cults predict the coming of a millennium in the very near future, and in material form: the cargo will be of non-traditional wealth.

6. There is organized activity of gardening and building, and various kinds of collective hysteria—visions, seizures, dancing, manias, etc.

7. The area is colonized but economically underdeveloped, isolated, politically acephalous and not given to violent resistance to white rule.

8. There have been attempts to Christianize the natives by missionaries.

This, too, is a mixed aggregation of criteria. The fourth, seventh, and eighth are true of nearly all rural communities in New Guinea; the second characterizes all members of the community, not merely prophets. The other characteristics are true as well of secular movements, when the non-magical, non-supernatural, and abnormal are removed. Thus movements have leaders with programmes, not revelations; movements use European rituals and make new rules of behaviour; movements state that the people will obtain non-traditional wealth; movements organize their adherents into working parties for construction and gardening. In fact these things—leadership, new procedures, expectation of material improvement, communal activity—are common to any ordinary development programme, but enthusiasm and conviction may be lacking.

The distinctive features of cargo cults are the dream or vision of the prophet, the belief in access to supernatural beings, miracles, the swoons, and seizures of individuals, and massed dancers, etc.—those elements of belief and behaviour which are magical, supernatural, and abnormal.[6]

CONCLUSION

The natives of Papua-New Guinea are going through a difficult transitional period. They have a strong wish for the power and wealth which they see held by the white man. Their own traditional beliefs, and some of the Christian influences which have reached them, sometimes make them expect wealth as a gift from gods or ancestors. Few natives have even now reached a standard of education to comprehend Western culture; beliefs in sorcery and other unscientific notions of causation are prevalent among schooled and unschooled. Dreams and visions told by prophets are readily accepted, especially when no alternative mode of attaining the unsatisfied desires has succeeded.

New Guineans lack both the general education to understand Western history and technology and also the training for skilled or professional work. They depend upon Europeans, mostly officers, but to some extent missionaries and settlers, for all of their information about the outside world. Only a limited number are now receiving the education which will give them this understanding and skill; the majority of today's youth will become illiterate subsistence farmers with very small cash incomes. Their longing for power and wealth it not likely to be satisfied by political means; their envy is likely to remain hopeless. In this situation they may find the rate of change unbearably slow. Their ignorance of technical processes, combined with their awareness of the inequalities of wealth and power between Europeans and themselves, produce movements aimed at social and economic improvement, millennial cults, and social protests. If these are to become increasingly realistic and progressive, it will be necessary to introduce a practical programme which will include fundamental education under enlightened leadership. One most important requirement of this programme is that its results be visible to those people of New Guinea who are supposed to benefit from it.

---

[6] Sinclair (1957:44) sees the cults as 'a false belief . . . a resulting dislocation of normal thinking and activity with its replacement by abnormal thinking and behaviour of an hysterical nature'.

9

Women in Transitional Society[1]

MARIE REAY

THE CUSTOMARY STATUS OF WOMEN[2]

PAPUA-NEW GUINEA, with all its linguistic and cultural diversity, was originally a man's world. Female members of the traditionally fragmented societies were kept busy with routine drudgery and had little place in public life. Some women of outstanding personality and strong character were able to influence events indirectly through their menfolk, but the scales were weighted against them so long as the important matters of life, including warfare and politics, were explicitly the concern of men. Woman was 'completely overshadowed by the male', as Williams (1930) put it, and in many regions she was ill-treated, though the cultures of the Territory differed greatly in what compensations, if any, they allowed women for the disadvantages.

Women have occupied an anomalous place in a set of social, economic, and ceremonial transactions carried out by men, namely the payments connected with marriage. In many regions women have been objects of exchange between groups of men, often with pigs and material valuables being exchanged too. The Orokaiva of the Northern District of Papua gave an initial payment (a-dorobu),

[1] The Department of Territories, Canberra, kindly allowed me to consult a useful report on the status of women and also supplied me with specific information when this was available. My particular thanks are due to Miss Patricia Rossell, Senior Welfare Officer (Female), Social Development Section, Department of District Administration, Territory of Papua and New Guinea, for giving me detailed information on women's clubs and discussing problems treated in this chapter; also to Lady Cleland, President of the Girl Guide Movement in Papua and New Guinea, for detailed information on the movement; and to Mr David Moriewitz, vacation scholar, Australian National University, for information on the Young Women's Christian Association.

[2] References to the Orokaiva are from F. E. Williams, *Orokaiva Society*, 1930, and those to the Minj people are based on my own fieldwork in 1953-5 (Reay 1959) and 1963-5. The position of women in matrilineal societies of the Territory does not seem to have differed from the situation in these patrilineal ones, except in detail, according to the literature.

which had to be reciprocated with a return payment (*bi-dorobu*). The Minj people of the Western Highlands District of New Guinea had to balance their primary payment (*amp kolma*) with 'adequate return'. The term for the Minj people's initial payment means literally 'a woman's *kolma*', but the word *kolma* occurs in no other context and cannot be directly translated into English. It was as much a 'repayment' as a primary payment: public recognition of a marriage was the occasion for its giving, but it was really a clan's method of rewarding or expressing material thanks to another for having borne and cared for a vehicle for its own continuance. The debt to the bride's clan was for bringing to maturity her capacity for child-bearing and making this available to the groom as a member of the clan providing the *kolma*.

'BRIDE-PRICE' AND CONFLICTING VALUES

A widespread misunderstanding of the obligations and sentiments involved in this transaction has altered radically the local people's own idea of marriage payment in recent years. The misunderstanding came about partly through resident Australians' tendency to view marriage as a bond between particular persons, rather than a transaction between groups, with a bride and a groom as principals rather than simply instruments in group relations. *Baiim meri* is the only concise Pidgin expression for the transaction, and the common use of this term in the Trust Territory has contributed to the misunderstanding through emphasizing a word which can express no subtler payment than purchase or bribery and gets readily translated into English as 'buy'. These days, many men do indeed 'buy' women, or at least seem to hope they are doing so, when they make their marriage payments. Government officers have often contributed to this change by making the transfer of the primary *a-dorobu* or *amp kolma* the critical criterion for the legality of marriage. They have insisted on the groom handing over his 'bride-price' at the time he receives the bride, though some New Guinea societies did not traditionally require any payments to be made until the marriage was well established as a social fact. They have neglected to sanction the *bi-dorobu* or 'equivalent return' in a parallel way, partly perhaps through unawareness of this reciprocal obligation and certainly sometimes because they have judged that the bride is 'worth' every penny of what the bridegroom has given for her and that he should not be encouraged to claim any of it back. Government officers have tried to peg the price of brides, and some have advised people that a physically unattractive girl should go for relatively little whereas a real peach (*gudpela meri tumas*) could be expected to bring an unusually high price. This idea is acceptable to men who view their own daughters and clan daughters as attractive and use it as a ground for wrangling with bridegrooms and their clansmen over how much money should change hands at the marriage of particular girls. The custom of men transferring to other men payments connected with marriage has spread widely and rapidly as pacification has enabled them to negotiate for brides from different cultural regions. Men who are seeking brides when marriage payments in their own region are grossly inflated can get them more cheaply from regions where such payments are novel and girls' male relatives are not aware of their cash value. The idea of a 'bride-price' as the valuation of a bride and her subsequent purchase is modern, not traditional, custom among people who used to barter bride for bride and pay not for a woman herself but for rights over her offspring. Being modern, however, makes it no less valid as custom when European acceptance has frozen it in this form.

The increasing substitution of money for traditional items in the transfer of bride-wealth has weakened the ceremonial aspect of marriage as well as strengthening its modern resemblance to a cash purchase. People whose experience of using money has been short and who still have very limited access to it need to have some on hand to contribute to marriage payments and to pay taxes. On the one hand, they have to participate to an unprecedented extent in a modified exchange system which deprives them of traditional return payments. On the other hand, they have to be in a position to withdraw annually from the funds circulating in intergroup exchange an amount of money sufficient to cover the taxes due from the members of the group. Often the two needs are conflicting, and in many areas the dilemma evokes response in cults with novel foci and in a social climate dominated by widely held, unstable fantasy structures (made up of rumour, folk legend, and local reinterpretations of religious and political evangelism). A balanced appraisal of scarce money as a reward for service and a means of achieving a satisfactory and enjoyable life is unlikely so long as men have to buy their way into marriage and pay in hard cash for the right to have children.

Some of the leaders in the Highlands recognize that the obsession with money for marriage payments is obstructing development and have voiced the private opinion that their people cannot benefit from their access to money without a total ban on its use in these transactions. Five councillors told me that they would suggest this course in formal meetings if they were not in danger of depriving themselves of payments due to them later or of being accused of trying to avoid their obligations to contribute. All are personally involved in the delayed exchange of money to such an extent that they cannot afford to take a public stand on the question, even when they recognize in private conversation the magnitude of the problem. For most, however, the total banning of 'bride-price' appears to be impossible as well as undesirable.

Attempts to peg the price of brides offer no complete answer to inflated marriage payments. It is hard to see how such attempts can be successful: so long as a man can expect to be sooner or later a direct or indirect recipient of a cash payment he will resist strongly (and, if need be, surreptitiously) any attempt to deprive him of the chance of getting the greatest amount he can prize from the donors. In areas where local government councils are required to prohibit cash payments over a certain amount, councillors can be tempted to act corruptly. I propose to cite three instances (from the Highlands) of such temptation.

A councillor who told me later that he had been on his way somewhere else heard the shouts of joy that greet the appearance of a marriage payment coming clearly from a site not far from the road in a certain clan's territory. He knew the families of the bride and groom and was aware that the ceremony of presentation was due to occur, for the question of this marriage had recently concerned the courts. It was well known that an Administration officer had sanctioned the marriage in the teeth of strong opposition from the bride's group, provided the bridegroom gave the bride's father exactly £40 on this particular day and received her in exchange the same day. The bridegroom's family accumulated hurriedly as much money as they could scrounge from relatives who had a traditional obligation to contribute and on the appointed day they gave the bride's group £75. The councillor had no traditional right to any part of the payment, but he stayed on for the distribution and accepted about £8 when it was offered to him. The bride, a girl of unsettled character at whose instigation the marriage had taken place, changed her mind several times and soon learned that she could earn more money for her brothers and her father by going home to them then agreeing to return to her husband as soon as he added a few more pounds to the already inflated payment. By the time she appeared to be settled finally with her husband, the amount he had given to her family was over £90 and at least one penniless close relative of the harassed bridegroom had committed a theft to make this possible. Having entered the transaction in a manner that was explicitly prohibited (giving a higher 'price' than the one specified by the court), all were anxious to prevent the question of this marriage from reaching the courts again—with the possible exception of the bride, who threatened on one occasion to run away to a certain other man if her monetary demands were not met. The councillor who had witnessed the original presentation of the payment followed all the subsequent events with interest but evidently felt no obligation to report either the events themselves or the original flouting of the prohibition.

I have described this case in some detail because of its relevance to some of the other problems mentioned in this chapter. Another illustration is the presentation, a few days after an official had pegged the price of brides at no more than £50, of a marriage payment in which the dominant item was £169 10s. in cash. This presentation was organized by a man whom the president of the council had charged with the duty of seeing that his people knew about and respected the ban on large payments. Yet another example is the payment by a councillor of a much larger amount than this for an extra wife at a time when he was well aware of the prohibition and indeed had based his own court judgment of another man's marriage on the assumption that the pegging of 'bride-price' was law.

A Highlands councillor named £1,000 as the payment he wanted for his daughter. He knew that no local man could raise this amount but hoped that her good looks and education (Primary-T standard) would induce a white man to pay it. He saw a white son-in-law as a means of access to unlimited wealth, but had not found one at the time of writing. Hoping for one presupposed that a white man would be willing to pay a 'bride-price' proportionate to his apparent wealth, and that a white man, like a local man, would be proud to be known to have given a large marriage payment. Much of the 'anti-European feeling' observers have noted in centres where sophisticated local men are concentrated is directly due to their resentment at white men evading the obligation to pay 'bride-price' when they enter extended associations with native women. This resentment is understandable when the modern custom of 'bride-price' (as distinct from the traditional custom of payments connected with marriage) is one of the few native institutions that have been respected and preserved in Papua-New Guinea.

Even in more backward areas, the traditional exchange of women between groups is tending to become an exchange of money involving at each step the purchase of a young girl for cash. A girl may suffer a personal indignity by having a price put upon her eligibility for matrimony when her bridegroom's group or a councillors' court decides that she is not worth the price her clansmen are asking. In areas where the traditional pattern of behaviour was for her to protest vehemently against being treated as a chattel in exchange, humane officials have encouraged her rebellion against the authority of the men and have insisted on her being allowed untrammelled freedom of marriage choice, in the belief that this is a necessary step in raising the low status of women. A rule known by the Pidgin term *laik bilong meri* ('what a woman wants') prevails in formal and informal courts dealing with marriage and divorce. This rule has so dominated litigation in these matters that equality in marriage choice can only be achieved if a counter-principle is introduced to consider also *laik bilong man* ('what a man wants'). Insistence on the rights of women has led ironically to a neglect of the rights of men, and youths who want to delay settling down until they have received further education or seen more of the world are often coerced into uncongenial marriages through a coalescence of interests between heavy fathers and would-be brides.

Ironically, too, it has led to group relations, which are still crucial in every sphere of Highlands life, being determined by the whims of the least responsible members of society: teenage girls who are no less a beat generation because they strum tradestore jews' harps instead of more sophisticated instruments, and who prolong the patterns of adolescence beyond marriage because the maturer people now lack real sanctions to ensure that change of residence brings about a rapid transition to adulthood. Without raising in any way the position of the women who do the work their sex is heir to, girls are able to flaunt traditional marriage prohibitions when they are too immature to realize that these expressed a society's standards of decency and decorum and when they have not learned any other settled *mores*. In fact the older women's burden is heavier than ever, since a young man's family and clanspeople are no longer able to discipline his bride and ensure that she does her share of work.

Men in Papua-New Guinea take for granted the inferior status of women, though women themselves are no longer accepting every aspect of this inferior status without question. This has occurred also in some parts of Africa (Baker and Bird 1959:120-1). Opportunities to get 'cheaper' brides from areas where 'bride-price' has not long been established have hastened the spread of the custom to such areas. Educated men giving their opinions on 'bride-price' discuss women as bought and paid-for possessions of their husbands; one even defined a wife as 'a piece of furniture that does the housework' and justified 'bride-price' by saying that a man had no means of preventing others from removing household goods he had not paid for. It is extremely unlikely that the men of Papua-New Guinea will appreciate their women as human beings so long as the cash purchase of brides is not only permitted but sanctioned as 'native custom'. An outright ban on 'bride-price' would be unpopular with those men who have already bought their wives; but is the only way women in the Territory would be able to achieve any firm status as persons.

STATUS-RAISING AND WELFARE POLICIES

The official attitude towards native women seems to have been advancing quickly beyond the policy of deliberate (and abortive) status-raising towards an appreciation of women as ordinary citizens, as an earlier emphasis on 'the education and advancement of women' gives way to broader approaches to community development. The status-raising approach fitted well with the concept of 'welfare' that had been central to native policies in Australian territories during the last few decades. The conception of native peoples as 'under-privileged', like the poor of earlier times, was essentially patronizing. Women's clubs were established with a tendency to emphasize the teaching of elementary hygiene and something called 'social advancement'. This was vaguely defined but generally involved persuading people to turn their backs on their own methods of organizing social life to adopt new ways somehow judged to be better for them. The clubs developed in a governmental climate dominated by the official idea of female indigenes as a stodgy pudding that could not be ignored so had to be stirred for its own good. One suspects that a good deal of the emphasis on 'welfare' has been window-dressing. Unsuitable females have been pushed embarrassingly into public office, and yet the administrative centre of the Territory (Konedobu) still has at least one lavatory with labels directing 'Women' to use one section and 'Hahine' (Papuan women) to use another.

One may deplore a particular policy and yet admit that the achievements of this policy have been remarkable, probably on account of the abilities and interests of the persons charged with putting it into effect.

Positive achievements. Women are being trained as schoolteachers, welfare officers, and nurses. Because they are women, they tend to give up using their training professionally quite soon after they have qualified, even when they have managed to complete their training before marriage. I know of only two exceptions to this, a confirmed spinster and one who is still young by Australian standards but who is getting too old to expect a native of her own country to seek her as a wife. There may be others I do not know about, but the proportion of trained women who give up work in order to become fulltime wives and mothers is undeniably high. Certainly we can expect them to influence the narrower circle of their own families, and perhaps they may be more confident and vocal in the affairs of their village than they would have been without vocational training. Nevertheless, practical difficulties in the way of enabling more than a thin trickle of girls to undertake vocational training at anything approximating to Australian standards make it impossible to contemplate an occupational structure of Australian type as a feasible development in the foreseeable future.

One of the traditional careers for women in Australia, general nursing, became available to girls in Papua-New Guinea only in 1958 when a training based on Australian standards as to length of course and the subjects studied began. Up to this time the local equivalent of a nursing service had been the corps of native medical assistants, who still serve in hospitals and aid posts throughout the Territory. These were men, and it was natural that the establishment of a training course in general nursing should attract men also. In contrast to Australia, where male nurses are still a minority, only

A young woman in traditional dress, Nondugl

A women's clubhouse, Oki Yufa village

Social mixing on the sports field

46 of the 102 persons who had graduated in nursing by mid-1963 were women.

It is hard to secure the exact rates of failure in various training courses and of leaving the service soon after training is completed, but everyone directly concerned with training whom I have consulted is unanimous in the judgment that the number of trained women who continue to practise their skills professionally is discouragingly small. In view of this loss to the professions, it may be wiser to encourage the continuation of general nursing services as a predominantly male concern and encourage girls who are interested in this kind of career to consider some of the alternatives available to them. By mid-1963, 496 young women had successfully completed their training as infant and maternal welfare nurses, 141 holding both certificates. These figures are impressive, even when compared with the total number of nearly 900,000 females of all ages in the Territory. This particular occupation is evidently one which girls find congenial, and it is the one most relevant to most of their lives when they decide to cease professional practice. At 30 June 1962, 13,048 girls were enrolled at Administration schools, and although female pupils in some areas seem reluctant to outshine and shame their brothers, it is reasonable to suppose that in a few years a number of girls from these schools and also from some schools of equal standard conducted by missions will be prepared to seek higher education, vocational training, or employment that requires a measure of literacy. One may hope that when these girls drop out through marriage they will do so in circumstances which allow them to use their education and training to advantage in supporting the aspirations and social adjustment of equally educated husbands; but comparability in educational background often appears to be irrelevant to marriage choice. The unique experience of one such woman in the Highlands is lost to her people through the inability of her husband, who has had no formal education or special training himself, to appreciate and understand it; similarly, many men who become prominent in modern political affairs keep their unsophisticated wives away from the public eye to avoid embarrassment. A study of marriage choices among the younger sophisticates, however, may reveal that the children of educated Papuans tend to marry each other, irrespective of where they come from; if so, they may form a core of educated families whose common culture consists of what they have learned at school.

Women's clubs. In June 1964, 513 women's clubs had been set up by the Social Development section of the Department of District Administration. During the two preceding years the number of these had increased by 100 per annum, despite an evident shortage of trained welfare officers. These clubs are more developed in Papua, where the movement began and where 317 such clubs now operate together with some 250 village women's committees in the Milne Bay District. In the most populous part of the Territory, 30 women's clubs are operating in the Eastern Highlands and 7 in the Western Highlands. These are all very recent and it is early to judge their success, but from the sketchy information available they seem to be popular and effective means of diffusing an unusual range of skills (from baseball to needlework) previously unknown to women in these regions. In areas where women's clubs are still contemplated but not yet started, local women find it hard to grasp the idea of a 'club' that is not specifically a place for men to meet and drink liquor. The success of some of the women's clubs in the Highlands seems to be due largely to enthusiastic campaigning by influential men, and this suggests that it may be advisable to integrate women's clubs with other community ventures through a committee with people of both sexes serving on it. Indeed this is already being tried, though only in exceptional circumstances.

EDUCATION AND URBANIZATION

There is a growing recognition in the Social Development section of the Department of District Administration that 'female indigenes' are not an undifferentiated lump of common problems but an analytically separable segment of a population which embraces communities in a variety of social contexts. In many areas people usually described as 'station women' and 'local women' (native women living off the government station) are recognized to be facing very different problems of social adjustment, and women in the greater urban centres such as Port Moresby, Lae, Rabaul, and Madang are differently situated from those living on the largest stations. I have met various women in Goroka, Mount Hagen, Port Moresby, and other places, but know well only five 'station women' in the Highlands—two at Minj (the Papuan wife of a station employee, and a 'local' girl married to a Papuan) and three Minj girls living at Goroka, Kundiawa, and Mount Hagen. I know well many more of the 'local women' of the Minj area.

There is no common meeting ground and mingling between the 'local women' and the 'station women', with the exception that 'station women' who are 'local' girls by birth maintain strong ties with their relatives and age-mates in the bush, even when they are able to hold their own with the more sophisticated Papuan and coastal women in the town. These latter have sometimes had experience of women's clubs in the phase when these stressed elementary hygiene and social advancement. They tend to disdain the 'dirty bush kanakas' as people who have no sense of hygiene, not understanding that 'kanakas' have a different idea of hygiene which places less importance on personal cleanliness but often includes some realistic measures to protect public health. An English-speaking Papuan woman once told me that it was impossible for her to associate with the 'local' women. 'They can't help it,' she said condescendingly. 'They're primitive, like our ancestors.' The gulf between 'station' and 'bush' is greater for the women than for men who can come together on a football field or at the bar of their club. It is less likely to be bridged by periodic interaction, and indeed such bridging may have a disorganizing effect. 'Station' women have fewer domestic chores and much greater leisure than 'local' women, who have to devote their time to growing vegetables, caring for pigs, and picking home-planted coffee; and mothers with young children in both town and bush are limited in the amount of travel they can comfortably undertake.

It is consistent with the change in emphasis of government policy from uniform development to the encouragement of *élites* to concentrate on educating the women of the great urban centres and the townships. Although the majority of women's clubs are ostensibly for 'village' women, the 'villages' affected are all too often those in the immediate vicinity of the station, with mainly 'station' women as office-bearers. While welfare programmes divert the leisure interests of an under-employed class on the government station from quarrelling and gambling to games and useful crafts, the 'local' women emerge from their remote homesteads or villages only to dispose of vegetables they have grown for sale or to attend a court case or visit a relative who is in hospital. Meeting and growing to know women of both classes makes one regret that recruitment to female *élites* takes place only on the basis of degrees of or access to urbanization. It would be a pity if leadership in women's organizations and prominence in public life depended simply on an ability to be in the forefront of a group of women united only by a knowledge of the lingua franca, an interest in gambling, and an absence (imposed by residence among people from different cultures) of other aspects of a shared way of life. In some areas, however, a particular village or local group has been selected as the spearhead of women's organization in the district and the women of this village become prophetesses or forerunners of a different kind of life, more akin to that of European women and 'station' women, with access to sewing machines (and hence to clothes that fit properly), participation in sports, and the chance to meet women from other places without being snubbed. Women of widely varying abilities and ranges of informal influence, including the village shrew, the eccentric intellectual, the public-spirited rebel or conformist, and so on, are neglected in both cases unless they live close to the station or in the particular village selected. It would seem opportune, therefore, to consider whether opportunities granted to a random *élite* could be extended to all women through links which would require as little organization as possible.

A danger in such a procedure is that it could easily stimulate quite embarrassingly a demand for women's clubs and similar institutions for community development far exceeding the capacities of persons available to guide them. Such institutions cannot, of course, develop without external stimulation of some kind, but the idea of starting them is readily acceptable to women both on out-stations and in the bush and is often met with great waves of spontaneous enthusiasm. This enthusiasm is not always enduring. Indeed, complaint is sometimes made that clubs decline and even wither as soon as a European officer ceases to visit them. I would endorse the judgment of Patricia Rossell that 'enthusiasm should be geared towards particular projects which will not be of too long a duration'. A related difficulty is that 'local' women are slow to realize that these clubs are appropriate vehicles for the expression of personal initiative and the development of leadership, so they tend to wait for a European officer to come and tell them what to do or at least make concrete suggestions they can follow. Perhaps this difficulty may be overcome in clubs being freshly formed by the officer initiating a project which logically requires further steps which the club women themselves are likely to suggest without prompting.

Social welfare work. The danger of engendering enthusiasm which may be wasted because there are not enough officers to guide it is a real one. There was only one welfare officer in the Highlands (stationed at Goroka) until a second one was able to go to Kundiawa in July 1964. One trained social worker for every 200,000 head of population (the proportion employed in 1965) seems pathetically meagre, and much of the burden of welfare work among women has had to be borne by experienced immigrant and expatriate women, mostly trained nurses who have lived in the Territory for some years. These include Miss Fairhall of the London Missionary Society and eight wives of present or former Administration officers. The participation of these women of varied experience in a government welfare programme has inevitably given a special character to the service itself and particularly to the training of local girls to help in this field. The present training of local social welfare assistants entails twelve months' apprenticeship (preferably in their own districts), then nine months at the Ahioma Training Centre, and finally three months' more intimate work with individuals and families in urban areas. The course has been shortened by one-third with the reorganization of the public service, and the number of girls in training has been increasing swiftly in 1964-5 from twenty-three to thirty or so. Two of the present local women working as social welfare assistants were originally teachers who transferred to do this work. The demands of a woman's domestic roles intervene in this modern career as in others and it is not expected that many will complete their training. As with certain kinds of nursing, however, the skills acquired up to any stage of training are likely to be a help to a woman engaged fulltime as a family member. A special homecraft officer runs courses to disseminate these skills.

Welfare officers are stationed in at least ten of the administrative districts of the Territory, and the diversity of their background and experience suggests that it would be misleading to generalize too broadly about the effects welfare programmes have been producing on the women of the Territory. When more detailed information is available, we may find diverse patterns emerging in different regions in respect of such questions as the emphasis of welfare programmes on homecraft and family life or the participation of women in public affairs. How enduring these special influences may be can only be tested in areas such as Hanuabada in the vicinity of Port Moresby, where the valuable work of Miss Fairhall and similar outstanding persons engaged elsewhere in the Territory has been continuous over many years. I do not know enough of the special history of welfare work in particular regions to form an opinion on whether the missionary zeal of some secular welfare workers, who tried with different degrees of success to organize local women in urban areas to protest against liquor reform, has managed to develop a formidable female sector of public opinion in those regions, nor even whether these 'organizing angels' (as another research worker in New Guinea has dubbed them) are common in the service: certainly the actions of two such welfare workers were out of harmony with the officially held aim of the Social Development section to stimulate local people to express their own opinions and form their own decisions. The point I wish to make here, however, is that welfare work seems to have followed such diverse courses in different regions that certain generalizations one would like to be able to make about women in the Territory are impossible. This situation has stemmed directly from the shortage of trained staff of particular kinds and the consequent necessity for administrations to choose whether to use the severely limited staff with the appropriate training for the benefit of a select few or to disperse the energies of those persons who, while lacking professional training in the appropriate field, have had considerable experience of the problems in the local situation and often have some skills which are somehow relevant.

Education for what? The danger of engendering enthusiasm which may be wasted because there are not enough officers to guide it (mentioned in respect of women's clubs, above) points to a grave weakness in any kind of training schemes in New Guinea, particularly but not only for women. The staff resources for educating people whose need for education grows increasingly urgent are so far from adequate that the trend is to teach few people besides those who will themselves be teaching. This has the effect of keeping standards low by beginning teacher training (and the training of trainers) at a low academic level and shortening the training itself. Thus two girls sat for the Intermediate Certificate only after beginning their training as social welfare assistants, and the educational standards of other trainees are evidently variable. The work allotted to them at the end of their training seems equivalent in duty and responsibility to that of a junior almoner or some other kind of social worker with a brand-new diploma.

A serious effect of the shortage of staff in all fields of training is that few, if any, local people in the Territory receive an education adequate to allow them a genuine choice of occupation. The only female university student from the Territory has done two years of social work training at the University of Queensland. Her course has recently been suspended while she has a baby, and it seems unlikely that she will continue. If she should do so, her Administration scholarship does not formally require her to return to her country when she has finished her studies; but her legal rights might be unclear if she wanted to stay in Australia permanently, and in any case she would be under considerable pressure to return to work for the Administration. Some of her energies will inevitably be diverted and much of her privacy is bound to be lost as she satisfies predictable demands to contribute to public relations— conversing with visiting United Nations officials; being interviewed by press, radio, and television; representing Papua-New Guinea in overseas conferences—as a mainland aboriginal girl has already interrupted her studies to represent Australia; above all, being a living demonstration of what Papua-New Guinea can achieve against formidable odds.

The old idea of an *élite* was of 'the privileged few', and there have been phases in the history of democracy when it has been hard to justify the encouragement of such a class. In Australian territories, however, the continuing pattern of 'welfare' and 'social development' has brought about a sharp division between an *élite* whose superior access to information and to official aspirations has obliged them to bear the heaviest burdens and the masses who are still able to enjoy some of the leisure and privacy that were originally among the diacritical privileges of *élites*.[3]

The *élite* is expanding. But it is losing its *élite* character. The handful of students in Australian universities will be returning to the Territory, it is hoped, as graduates of equal standing with Australians who have graduated with them. They will be outnumbered by local people who have never left the Territory but who have pursued the essentially makeshift courses available to them there. It is important that those who stay in their own country to acquire the training offered there, which is almost invariably adapted to the special conditions of the Territory, be acquainted with its makeshift character from the start. Any uneasiness in race relations can find quick expression in allegations of equivalences that do not exist,

[3] Cf. Weber's idea (1947:352) of a 'ritually trained' class and honoratioren; also Mannheim's ideas of *élites* as 'classes which create and assimilate culture' (Mannheim 1946:84) and as specially privileged classes (ibid.:92).

such as the wild assertion a man trained as 'Assistant Medical Officer' once made that he would be taking over the post of the Regional Medical Officer (who was much better qualified) as soon as the white people left. I am certain that this man saw the training he had received as equivalent to that of the European medical officer. If Papua-New Guinea is pushed too speedily towards independence, his allegation may turn out to be true and the health and hospitalization of the people of a vast region may become the responsibility of a man whom no junior interne in an Australian hospital could accept as a professional colleague.

FUTURE PROSPECTS

The training and general education of women cannot be considered out of the context of the education of people in general in Papua-New Guinea, nor apart from the probable structure of the society that will use their training and benefit from their education. Any estimate of likely trends over the next decade must be conditional on highly unstable circumstances remaining constant or changing in specified ways. Some predictions can be made if we assume (1) that the Territory is pushed into independent nationhood within ten years; (2) that recent evidence of official thinking in terms of a black New Guinea, pruned of expatriates, continues to be borne out; and (3) that 'bride-price' continues to be regarded as inviolable native custom.

The first prediction that can confidently be made is that the handful of students at present doing courses in Australia will swiftly accede to positions of unusual seniority for persons of their particular training and experience, compared with the posts available to Australians who graduate with them. A girl with a diploma in social work is likely to go to the top quickly in the Social Development section if she stays with the Administration and does not resign for domestic reasons. Primary degrees in law, agriculture, and economics are likely to lead other students (all males) to top postings for which Australians have had to spend decades waiting for the appropriate grades of seniority and the right opportunities.

By 1974 we can expect the nursing service and hospital administration in the Territory to allow for the unusually high proportion of males undertaking and completing training and the still higher proportion of males, compared with females, remaining in the service. Within the context of both local and Australian attitudes towards women in employment, it would be unrealistic to envisage a local matron of a general hospital with predominantly male nurses on her staff. Probably the only top posts open to women would be those as matrons of specialized obstetric and children's hospitals and also in infant welfare services; any girl who seeks a nursing career in the general hospitals would be able to aspire no further than being an officer in charge of a specialized section (for example, female wards) requiring only female nurses. Similarly, women schoolteachers are only likely to become prominent educationists so long as they contain their ambitions within the context of special girls' schools and do not hope for advancement in competition with male teachers.

There will be a comparatively low percentage of girl university students in the Territory. Given the continuation of local attitudes, those girls who do become undergraduates are unlikely to find themselves interacting with male students on conditions of intellectual equality. We can expect females among the earliest graduates to be unusually subdued in their expressions of opinion and timid in making independent decisions, a tendency already observable in female teacher trainees and social welfare trainees in the Territory.

No women seem likely to become national leaders within ten years. In a few regions where they may be able to influence public opinion they are likely to do so indirectly if at all. Public opinion in 1974 may be sharply divided into two sectors. Vocal public opinion is likely to express the dissatisfactions shared by a substantially literate *élite*, consisting largely of public servants either with no direct involvement in national politics or with experience of political defeat. There is likely to be, in addition, a substratum of public opinion with no effective organs of expression apart from direct acts of displeasure which need not stop short of rebellion. Resentments already expressed in populous, underdeveloped areas against certain aspects of selective development could easily crystallize in unwillingness to recognize the legitimacy of an indigenous public service recruited from more favoured areas. Trouble over women and 'bride-price' is not likely to be resolved without violence, and lawlessness among men would lead almost inevitably to violence against and reactionary suppression of women. There would seem to be no means available to avert such a situation, provided the three conditions outlined above continue. In case such a pessimistic view of the future should be borne out by events, it is relevant to inquire how the women of the Territory are being prepared to live in a changing, difficult, and perhaps even chaotic world.

VOLUNTARY WORK

The Girl Guide Movement. Even more striking than the achievements of governmental agencies have been the efforts of individual white women to prevent the local girls from lagging too far behind the men in learning to live in a new kind of society. As early as the 1870s, women missionaries and wives of missionaries were trying to teach native women practical items of home care and handicrafts. In 1928 Mrs Chatterton, of the London Missionary Society, formed a Girl Guide company in Hanuabada, Port Moresby. By the beginning of World War II the movement was well established in Port

Moresby and Rabaul and Mrs Ure, also of the London Missionary Society, had been conducting a company of Rangers at Hanuabada since 1934. While the Administration was still primarily concerned with pacifying the increasing number of native communities being contacted by white people, these women concentrated on bringing to native women in long-pacified areas some character-training and practical skills which they assumed quite rightly would be needed in the years to come. The Girl Guide Movement, though interrupted by the war, has nevertheless grown to include 154 Guide companies and Brownie packs with at least 3,240 local girls being trained in company with Australians and Chinese in places as widely scattered as Daru in the south-west of the Papuan Gulf and Kavieng in New Ireland, as far apart as Wewak on the north coast of the Trust Territory and Bwagaoia in the islands off the south-eastern tip of the Papuan mainland. Residential training centres have been established in Port Moresby and Rabaul, and at least 180 of the 230 Guiders are local women. Many more have been trained but have been lost, as in other fields of training, to the necessity to devote themselves to domestic tasks. The loss is not, however, so permanent as it seems to be in fields where women have to be employed full-time if at all, and they tend to resume Guiding activities when their children have grown old enough to be independent of close maternal care. The training does not differ materially in content from that given to Guiders in Australia, though it is given in a simplified form. Two of the twenty-eight trained Commissioners and eight of the ten salaried Guide Trainers are local women. Seventeen of the sixty-six members of the Girl Guides' Territory Council and three of the twelve elected members of the Executive are local women.

The remarkable success of the Guide movement in Papua-New Guinea seems to rest on three factors that have been missing from bureaucratically processed programmes of development: the simple determination of a few women to carry out clear and realizable goals; the assumption, which seems to have been acted on early, that companies and packs should welcome members of all races; and that consistent character-building offers a way of preparing people for life in a changed society, where they will have to work out valid values. The Guide Law, here as in other countries, stresses honour, loyalty, service, amity, courtesy, kindness to animals, obedience, cheerfulness, and thrift. It may be a rare girl who manages to develop this full constellation of virtues, but at least everyone who enters the movement becomes aware of this set of values, and there is a good chance that women who have been Guides will try to instil them into their children. An explicit aim of the movement in the Territory is to ensure that an *élite* of educated local leaders will be able to find wives who can live in equality with them. There is no guarantee, of course, that character-training of the kind the movement offers will increase the attractions or availability of a particular girl for an educated local leader who is looking for a wife. Such evidence as we have suggests that local leaders may admit the general desirability of education and domestic virtues for women and yet choose their own marriage partners on the basis of totally different considerations.

This situation contrasts strangely with that in some African and Asian countries which have gained independence in recent years, where education is an asset to a girl in the marriage market and legend has it that even a girl who is a failed B.A. has a better chance of making a good match than one who has not completed secondary schooling. There is no doubt that schoolchildren of both sexes benefit greatly when the parent they are closely associated with in their developing years is well educated, and this parent in Papua-New Guinea will be the mother. It may be significant that although educated men of the first generation in Papua-New Guinea do not tend tb choose educated wives, their sons seem to do so.

The Young Women's Christian Association. The aims of this association in Papua-New Guinea are to 'encourage amongst women and girls the development of balanced personality and self-government through a programme of recreation, study and service on the basis of Christian principles' and to 'strengthen Christian character by training of body, mind and spirit'. The activities of the Y.W.C.A. in Port Moresby have included various training courses embracing training in 'good housekeeping', cooking demonstrations, and a leadership training club. A teenage club has met once weekly, and an evening coffee club enables members to discuss 'interesting features of life in the Territory'. The association aims to develop in young women a sense of social responsibility and 'a right public conscience with regard to civic, national and international affairs'. It emphasizes the participation of native women, and although the constitution stresses 'bringing together women and girls of all classes, creeds, nationalities and races' the absence of Australian and Chinese girls from ordinary membership gives it an appearance of do-goodery which the organizers may not have intended. The absence of Australian girls from the teenage club and the house-keeping classes is commonly attributed to this section of the population being at school or at work in Australia; but young Australians are numerous enough in all urban centres to organize dances and other forms of recreation among themselves, so clearly this is not the entire explanation. Australian girls in the Territory are not likely to be interested in receiving training in domestic skills and social graces in company with and on a level with native women, and they are unlikely to see the work of the Y.W.C.A., here as elsewhere, of 'integrating members into their social environment', as relevant to themselves (Fiawood 1959:95).

The Y.W.C.A. is building, with the help of the Administration, a hostel for girls in Port Moresby. This is not explicitly planned as a segregated hostel, but it is plain from the proposed design and from the expressed hopes concerning the problems it may help to solve that it will serve largely as a residential centre for native girls undergoing various kinds of training in Port Moresby. The proportion of unmarried girls whose training is interrupted by pregnancy appears to be high, though it is hard to obtain precise figures, and some responsible persons see stricter supervision of residential arrangements as a possible control.

WOMEN AS CULTURE CARRIERS

Far from transforming the oppressed creatures of traditional Papua-New Guinea into latter-day feminists, aggressive towards their menfolk, the government's programmes of social development and the voluntary work concerned with character-development and moral stability in changing times have both proceeded on the assumption that a woman's most important role will be as fulltime family member during the period when her children will depend on her personal care. Where these influences have affected local women, there has been a considerable increase in the self-sufficiency of the individual family unit. Where these influences have been absent, change has proceeded in a less directed way and has resulted in disorganization of old ways without any stable forms of some new kind replacing them. I mentioned earlier the tendency for teenage girls in a part of the Highlands to use a kind of surreptitious feminism to demonstrate their recently acquired power over men and free themselves from the burdens of undergoing traditional character development and accession to social maturity. The programmes of governmental and voluntary agencies are geared for continuing expansion, and it is reasonable to expect eventually a Territory-wide increase in the self-sufficiency of the individual family unit which will make the typical family of Papua-New Guinea resemble the Australian family more closely than any of the local traditional forms of domestic organization.

Along with this tendency we must expect trends in change which will reduce the cultural diversity of the country to strands of uniformity which will have in common with each other close resemblances to the Australian system. The special adaptations of this system to Territory conditions will not be enough to fill the cultural vacuum created by the removal of diacritical aspects of traditional culture. This situation, in which cultural and spiritual impoverishment seems to be the fate of the majority of the Territory's inhabitants, calls for a special kind of applied anthropology: one which can suggest how to introduce compensation for cultural losses. One suggestion can be made immediately, in which local women would have an important part to play. Every people has its past, and every literate people has some kind of written history. When the people of Papua-New Guinea are substantially literate, it is important for their history to recount more about their past than the discovery and development of 'primitive stone-age savages'. Many traditions, which are fast disappearing not only from communal life but also from 'memory culture' (the remembrances of the past), should be recorded as a matter of urgency before it is too late. Insights from archaeological and other research can be used for interpreting mythological accounts of the past prior to European contacts.

Much of Papua-New Guinea's cultural traditions will remain the specialized province of anthropologists and ethno-historians, but much can also be preserved in the family circle. As this becomes an individual family of the Australian type, women will be taking over from the men the chief role in transmitting awareness of the past. This can easily be misinterpreted as women learning by rote exotic little legends to tell their children as bedtime stories; but what I really have in mind is women, as carriers of culture, learning to appreciate that an essential part of their heritage is belonging to a lively people who worked out for themselves certain modes of adjustment that were different from the modern modes. With this as background, a child need not grow up ashamed of a black skin that prevents him from being more than an imitation white; instead, it can be a symbol of his distinctive identity and history. There should be no need for him later to rely on the biased accounts of people who see unadulterated evil in pre-Christian, pre-pacified life, nor to choose between discrediting the past and developing a nostalgia for it. The people of the Territory are under considerable pressures to accept all we have to offer them, and the pressures are so strong that there is little alternative besides total acceptance and total rejection. As we prepare them for fuller participation in the modern world we offer them the skeletal framework of our own social forms and political institutions. We (and they too) must see that the skeleton is clad healthily in the flesh and blood of personal and cultural identity.

IV

Political Problems

10

The Growth of Territory Administration

R. S. PARKER

BACKGROUND

ADMINISTRATION is important for the success of any kind of government. In a colonial territory like New Guinea the Administration
(capitalized to denote the whole Territorial apparatus of public
officialdom) is synonymous with the government, though subject to
control from Canberra and to some influence by the House of
Assembly on the law it administers (see Chapter 12). Moreover, the
Administration there helps to shape the whole community's affairs
to a degree unparalleled in those developed societies which are not
totalitarian. There are some obvious quantitative measures of this.
Expatriate members of the Territorial public service form well over
half of the non-indigenous breadwinners in the Territory. In the year
ended June 1963 the Administration was responsible for about £10
million in capital investment in the Territory, compared with £6
million by private enterprise—the government share being spent
mainly on public works to provide the basis for a modern economy.
Qualitatively, the influence of public servants is more dominant still
—through their work in promoting education, social services,
economic development, industrial and employee organization, and
extending the rule of law and order which is also a basic prerequisite
to the building of a unified modern nation. Hence the staffing,
education, organization, co-ordination, and morale of the Administration can make or mar the whole process of growth and change
to which New Guinea is committed.

Perhaps this was why the first Minister for Territories, Mr Paul
Hasluck, counted administrative reform high among the memorials
of his régime. Looking back in 1958 'with something of personal
pride', he claimed 'with complete confidence that one of the substantial and lasting achievements has been the building of sounder
foundations for a better public service' (Wilkes 1958:114). Among
these foundations he listed the reorganization of the Territorial
departments, raising the levels and rates of recruitment, improved

187

training and education, the systematic classification of officers, the introduction of 'Organization and Methods' techniques, the establishment of the Auxiliary Division to admit and train indigenous people, and the strengthening of the Department of Territories in Canberra. This chapter describes and appraises such administrative changes since 1945 and estimates the significance for future development of some trends and problems not mentioned in Mr Hasluck's 1958 review.

The environment of administration. There is always a clash between the addiction to uniform structures and practices among sophisticated architects of administration and the need to adapt every administrative system to its particular natural and human environment. An acute form of this clash occurs in colonial situations, where the administering power is tempted as a matter of course to transplant its own institutions to the dependent territory. Mr Hasluck's list of reforms, and the manner in which they were applied, clearly reveal this tendency, and any appreciation of them must begin with a reminder of the special problems the New Guinea environment sets for a European-style bureaucracy.

The difficulties of communication across mountains, valleys, swamps, and straits have a number of administrative implications. They break the country into distinct districts, regions, and island groups, each of which needs to be relatively self-sufficient in some basic services. They increase administrative costs through unusual dependence on the radio and aeroplane, expensive methods of communication whose rapid expansion has possibly discouraged to some extent the growth of other forms, especially roads. They subject many officers to working and living in sustained isolation from their fellows, calling for special care in recruitment and training. They demand unusual delegation of discretion to field staff if local decisions are not to be intolerably delayed. At the same time they hinder the flow of information from the centre to the field and back and hence the adaptation of policy to local needs and of local action to changing policy.

The regional diversity of the country, combined with its transitional social and economic condition, calls for a highly decentralized system of administration by districts, but with strong integration of effort at the district level. There is diversity not only in the value and kind of economic resources and potential in different districts, but also in the stages of development they have reached and the relative rates of change that are possible. It is diversity that requires considerable local autonomy in the application of policy in a district. It is the need for co-ordinated growth along all fronts together that requires a firm integration of administrative effort within each district.

The poverty and primitiveness, by Western standards, of the New Guinea economy narrowly limit the sources and amount of local

An Assistant District Officer supervising villagers at work, Eastern Highlands, 1957

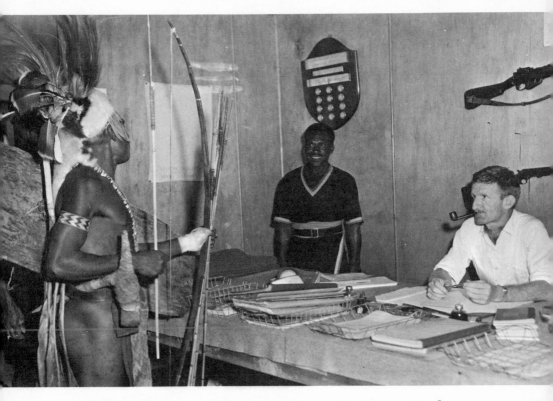

A luluai discusses a gardening programme at Lufa, near Goroka

A meeting of the Kui Native Local Government Council, Mount Hagen

A meeting during the 1964 elections for the House of Assembly

public revenue, though demanding substantial public investment and public services of all kinds in order to combat them. The expense of rapidly expanding administration since 1950 has had to be borne in increasing proportion by Australia, which now supplies about two-thirds of it. But the total government expenditure is still at an extremely low level, serving a population of over two millions with a budget about the same size as that of a middle-sized state business enterprise in Australia. Thus, although the public service is so important among Territory institutions, in numbers and outlay it is tiny compared with the public bureaucracy of a modern state with a similar population.[1] Tropical and otherwise exotic conditions of service require special forms of compensation for expatriate staff, and together with political uncertainty cause exceptional staff turnover and recruitment problems. 'Localization' (replacement of expatriate by indigenous staff) is a corollary of the advance to self-government, and presents its own challenges. It seems inherent in the situation that the tasks to be faced will long be in inverse ratio to the administrative resources available.

There are other challenges which, like these, are common to colonial administrations elsewhere, though perhaps more acute in New Guinea. The language barrier, a largely illiterate population, racial tensions, are some of them. Indeed, although the Australian government dislikes the term 'colony' being applied to New Guinea, and insists on the Territory's uniqueness, very little of the basic context of politics and administration is peculiar to it, though that little is quite important. It consists chiefly in the very limited extent of alien economic exploitation, which is related to the long-standing policy of protection of native interests, most significantly reflected in the fact that over 97 per cent of the country's land still belongs to the indigenous people (though the alienated land includes some of the best and most accessible). This has both positive and negative implications for administration. Most importantly, it has minimized overt conflicts of interest between the minority and majority races, and so has created on the whole a receptive or at least acquiescent attitude towards the Administration's policies and programmes. It has thus simplified the problem of planning for the peaceful and evolutionary development of a substantially indigenous-owned economy. On the other hand the long decades of inaction before 1940 and relative inattention to economic development up to 1960 have left a great leeway to be caught up under insistent pressures of time and external change. And popular acceptance and acquiescence also mean dependency and economic conservatism, where

[1] The total of employees of the Administration in June 1964 was 26,891, including Administration servants, warders and police, and unskilled labourers, and excluding local government employees (see Appendix). The population was estimated at 2·2 millions. At the same date central government employment in New Zealand, with a population of about 2·6 millions, totalled at least 126,000.

they do not conceal that frustrated sense of inequality and inequity which finds disguised expression in cargo cults. It is this subtle blend of economic and psychological factors, of compliance and tension, that comprises whatever is unique in the New Guinea context of administration.

Impact of the Japanese war. The present Administration is in membership and structure largely a post-war creation, but it inherited important legacies from the past. Outstanding among these were the system of district administration and a core of experienced officers who had helped to operate it in the two pre-war decades. The decentralized system of divisions under Resident Magistrates, following British colonial practice, had been introduced by Dr (later Sir) William MacGregor as soon as he became the first Administrator of British New Guinea (later Papua) in 1888.

> The Resident Magistrate system formed the backbone of the whole administration, for on these men devolved the task of applying in detail, in the areas under their control, the policy formulated at the centre. Almost nothing was beyond their competence. Theirs was the responsibility of maintaining order and settling disputes; of arresting offenders and trying them; of opening up the country and establishing relations between government and native village; of supervising the smooth functioning of labour ordinances; and, in general, of directing all functions of government in their respective divisions (Legge 1956: 62).

The conditions calling for this type of administration still exist in large and populous areas of the Territory, some of which have been 'opened up' as recently as coastal Papua had been when Mac-Gregor took charge. He, too, founded the native constabulary and the system of village constables to represent governmental authority at the grass roots.

A system of essentially similar constituents had been inherited by the Territory of New Guinea, seized from Germany in 1914 and placed under League of Nations Mandate to Australia in 1919; the administrative divisions were there called 'districts' and the local native headmen, appointed in the villages by the Administration, were called *luluais* and *tultuls*, as they had been by the Germans.

Following the Japanese attacks on Rabaul and Port Moresby in January and February 1942, civil administration was suspended in both Territories, and by the end of March the Army had appointed most of the officers of the two civil services, and many other men experienced in the territories, to the Australian New Guinea Administrative Unit (ANGAU), which administered the areas under Australian and Allied control for the rest of the war.

The régime of ANGAU had permanent effects on the shape of New Guinea administration. It paved the way for the administrative union of the two territories of Papua and New Guinea, having itself been formed by merging, after only a few weeks, the two separate units at first set up in March 1942 to establish military administrations. It also confirmed, on a uniform pattern for the whole country, the system of integrated administration within relatively autonomous districts. The former New Guinea terms 'District' and 'Sub-District' became universal, replacing the corresponding terms 'Division' and 'District' in Papua. The general administrative officials in charge in these respective areas became the District Officer and the Assistant District Officer, superseding the Resident Magistrate and Assistant Resident Magistrate. Their responsibilities during the war became even more extensive. In addition to maintaining patrols, law, order and police, and seeing to the feeding, clothing, health, and welfare of the people, they had to provide and control native labour for the war effort, prevent fifth column activities, operate radio stations, provide guards for vital routes and installations, and generally keep close liaison between the fighting troops and the supporting activities of the local communities. The range and exercise of their functions were supervised by the District Services Branch of ANGAU. The rehabilitation and management of food, rubber and copra plantations and the provision of civilian transport were controlled by the Production Services Branch, whose functions were transferred to a Production Control Board in 1943. The post-war trend to separation of specialized functions from district services was foreshadowed by the successive establishment within ANGAU of a Native Labour Service, a Medical Service, and a Legal Service. The war period saw an unprecedented expansion of medical services for the people and the beginnings of governmental educational and agricultural services. All of these activities, uninhibited by the pre-war doctrine of financial self-sufficiency for the Territories, resulted in a greatly expanded Territorial service, including field staff, by the end of the war. And in February 1944 the G.O.C. ANGAU summoned the first general conference of headquarters and district staff ever to be held in either Territory, when discussion ranged over native administration, medical and dental services, native welfare, education, labour and land policy, and native agriculture.

Return to civil control: the Provisional Administration. At about the same time the preparation for the post-war administration began. A standing sub-committee of the Australian Cabinet on Territories was formed, with a small Department of External Territories (which had been separated from the Prime Minister's Department in 1941) acting as its secretariat. Simultaneously a small 'Army Research Section', which had established itself in Melbourne under the Adjutant-General, was re-named the Army Directorate of Research, attached directly to the Commander-in-Chief, and charged with advising him on the exercise of his powers in respect of the administration of Papua and New Guinea, maintaining liaison between the Army and the Department of External Territories, and undertaking research on Army administration and on matters of post-war policy in the Territories referred to it by the Cabinet sub-committee. This eccentric military formation was a way of legitimizing one of the enterprises of the redoubtable Mr Alfred Conlon, who had gained the ear and the confidence of the Prime Minister and General Blamey and gathered round him a group of like-minded enthusiasts, mainly academics and lawyers, in the hope of injecting some constructive thought into the rehabilitation of New Guinea.

The group was re-formed by Cabinet in March 1945 as the 'Pacific Territories Research Council', with the Commonwealth Director of Education as formal Chairman and with the addition of officers from the Territories administration. The most constructive achievement of this group was the planning of a School of Civil Affairs to train patrol officers for ANGAU and become a permanent research and training institution. First established in Canberra in February 1945 under the Directorate's control, a year later it was transferred to the Department of External Territories and moved to Sydney, and in May 1947 given a continuing role as the Australian School of Pacific Administration with its own semi-autonomous Council (swallowing, incidentally, its own parent, the Pacific Territories Research Council). Imaginatively conceived and ably headed and staffed, this School laid firm foundations for administrative training and education in the Territory, under the uneasily watchful eye of a Minister and Department always sceptical about the value of free discussion for this purpose.

Meanwhile civil administration of the Territories, on a unified basis as under ANGAU, had been restored. In July 1945 the Papua-New Guinea Provisional Administration Act was passed to provide tentative arrangements for civilian control until the fate of the Mandated Territory should be decided. By the end of October a single Provisional Administration Public Service had been inaugurated and taken over from ANGAU all of the Territories south of the Markham River. In June of the following year the Provisional Administration assumed full control of both Territories under a single Administrator, Colonel J. K. Murray, a former Professor of Agriculture at the University of Queensland who was then Chief Instructor at the School of Civil Affairs. In December 1946 the United Nations General Assembly approved a Trusteeship Agreement for New Guinea which permitted it to be brought into 'a customs, fiscal or administrative union' with other Australian territories. In November 1947 the government announced its intention to form a permanent administrative union with a single administrative head, a single legislative body, and a common public service. These aims were effected by the Papua and New Guinea Act, 1949, which retained the single Supreme Court already established, ratified the Trusteeship Agreement for New Guinea, and established a new Legislative Council for the combined Territories without altering their separate identity and status. This Act also replaced the pre-war Executive Council by an 'Administrator's Council', intended 'to advise the Administrator' but, unlike the Executive Council, including the Administrator himself, together with three official members of the Legislative Council and three non-official members of whom two must be elected members.

Post-war policies and administrative patterns. The general pattern of post-war administration was set by Mr E. J. Ward, Minister for External Territories, when introducing the Provisional Administration Bill in 1945. First he rejected the pre-war principle that the Australian official effort should be limited to what the Territories themselves could finance:

> This Government [he said] is not satisfied that sufficient interest had been taken in the Territories prior to the Japanese invasion or that adequate funds had been provided for their development and the advancement of the native inhabitants. Apart from the debt of gratitude that the people of Australia owe to the natives of the Territory, the Government regards it as its bounden duty to further to the utmost the advancement of the natives and considers that can be achieved only by providing facilities for better health, better education and for a greater participation by the natives in the wealth of their country and eventually in its government (*C.P.D.* 1945 Vol. 183:4052).

Next he proposed to abolish the indenture system of securing native labour for European enterprises and to establish a separate Native Labour Department to improve and supervise working conditions and pay for natives. Third he promised 'a vigorous programme of education in its broadest sense controlled and directed by the Administration' (which had left education almost entirely to the missions before the war). Fourthly he announced that in future the basis of the economy of the Territory would be native and European industry, 'with the limit of non-native expansion determined by the welfare of the natives generally', rather than, as before the war, 'by the markets available and the supply of native labour that could be obtained'. With the exception of the last point, these policies of the post-war Labor government were accepted by the Liberal government which succeeded it at the end of 1949. An unprecedented expansion of Administration expenditure, staff, and activity followed, especially under Mr Hasluck, who held the Territories portfolio from 1951 till the end of 1963.

In June 1946 when the Provisional Administration was fully established the public service consisted of 643 Australians and some thousands of native people known as Administration Servants and engaged in minor skilled and unskilled labour. They were organized in eleven departments: the Government Secretary's (then including the Registrar-General's Branch, Crown Law Office, and Police Force); the Treasury (including the Government Printing Office, Government Stores, and Post and Telegraph branches); District Services and Native Affairs; Native Labour; Education; Public Health; Agriculture, Stock and Fisheries; Trade and Customs (renamed Customs and Marine in 1948); Forests; Lands, Surveys and Mines; and Public Works (which operated under the authority of the Commonwealth Department of Works and Housing). By the time of the passing of the Papua and New Guinea Act, followed by the change of Australian government in 1949, there were about 1,200 expatriate officers and about 8,500 Administration Servants, while the Government Secretary's Office had absorbed the Department of Native Labour.

By a Territory Ordinance of 1949 this public service was placed in the care of a Public Service Commissioner, whose duties were to effect economies, promote efficiency, and check and supervise the activities and methods of each department. The Commissioner and his staff were located in the Department of the Government Secretary. Though given a separate department in 1954 the Commissioner has never had the quasi-judicial independence of Public Service Boards in Australia. He holds office at the pleasure of the Governor-General and reports to the Minister for Territories. And his jurisdiction does not extend to those Commonwealth agencies outside the Territorial public service, such as the Departments of Works and Civil Aviation and the Australian Broadcasting Commission, which operate extensively in the Territory.

The tasks of this administration were unusual not only by reason of their special environment but also because of the constant change in that environment produced largely by its own activities, and the different stages and rates of change existing simultaneously in different parts of the Territory. The pattern of change is not uniform, but the first stage in each area is 'to make contact with the people of the country, stop fighting among those who have been traditional enemies, and establish law and order'. Then follow (as the Native Affairs Department has described them) the tasks of improving village sanitation and hygiene, developing inter-village roads and tracks, applying the laws of the Territory as required, introducing improved food crops and methods of cultivation, encouraging reforestation, supervising recruitment and employment of labour and through various field surveys, compiling data on which to base future work. The next stage is to apply and develop the special techniques of local government and co-operation. This requires more detailed supervision and instruction by the field staff. Next, when a group of peoples has been in contact with European ways for some time (and the time varies greatly), new economic activities may begin, often meeting problems of land usage and tenure, capital investment, resettlement, and labour relations. This stage may call for more differentiated and specialized public services, and as the spread of communications makes the more recently opened areas safer and more accessible, experts from various functional departments can establish more formal provisions for agricultural, experimental, and extension work, for the protection of public health, for education, public works, afforestation, and the administration of lands and justice.

To increase the scale, the level of technical competence and the concentration of effort in these functional departments was one of the chief administrative concerns of Mr Hasluck from 1951, when he became the first Minister for Territories and the first Minister who had ever been given the Territories as his sole responsibility (they included the Northern Territory and a number of other Australian dependencies). He later said of this time:

> Quite frankly, . . . I was appalled at the state of the Territory Public Service, . . . dismayed at the delays and the ineptitude and indeed the lack of the basic craftsmanship of the service (Wilkes 1958:115).

And so, 'as one who had had some experience on the public service side of handling public business' (he was an officer of the External Affairs Department during and after the war), he set out from the beginning to impose his own pattern upon the administration—a pattern of specialization and centralization as he foreshadowed in his first year of office:

> For some years to come, it is inevitable that Papua and New Guinea will be administered as a territory and that the administration will become increasingly centralized in Australia. This is due to the fact of the constitutional superiority of the Commonwealth Parliament, the fact that the expenditure in the Territory will be financed by the Commonwealth, to the fact that the Commonwealth Government alone holds the responsibility before the world and (in the case of New Guinea) to the United Nations for administering the territory according to certain standards and cannot delegate that responsibility to anyone else, and to the fact that the Commonwealth Government must of necessity maintain the security of the Territory and the observance in the Territory of the fundamental principles of national policy. This centralization of administration will also be promoted and facilitated by the improvement of communications and by the growing specialization of all human activities (Hasluck 1952:227-8).

THE ADMINISTRATIVE STRUCTURE

'Centralization and specialization'. With Mr Hasluck's appointment to the new portfolio of Territories in 1951 the former department of External Territories and the Northern Territory section of the Commonwealth Department of the Interior were amalgamated into a single Department of Territories in Canberra, with a total

staff (including the Northern Territory administration) of 623. Within a year the division of the Department into sections dealing with each territory as a whole had been superseded by a 'functional' organization so that 'problems of a like nature in all Territories', as the Public Service Board said, 'will now be handled by a common staff'. The main Divisions dealt with General Administration, Welfare and General Services, Industries and Commerce, and International Relations. Despite some internal reorganization and changes of Division titles, this structure has remained essentially the same, but in the thirteen years to mid-1964 the size of the Canberra staff rose to 1,771—an increase of 184 per cent. (In the same period the Papua and New Guinea Territorial Public Service was increased from 1,174 officers and employees, all expatriate, to 6,473, of whom 1,384 were indigenous people—a total increase of 451 per cent, most of it in the territorial headquarters at Port Moresby.)

Within the first year of his administration Mr Hasluck terminated the appointment as Administrator of Colonel J. K. Murray, known for his firm views on native policy, and replaced him with Mr (now Sir) Donald M. Cleland, former Chief of Staff to the Military Administration and wartime chairman of the Production Control Board, and later W.A. Vice-President and then Federal Director of the Liberal Party in Australia. The Administrator has 'the duty of administering the Government of the Territory on behalf of the Commonwealth', but geographical proximity to Australia and modern communications have enabled his role (like those of his counterparts in other Australian territories) to be confined within much narrower limits than that of a Governor in a traditional British colony. Though he has the right of direct access to the Minister, his more important decisions are normally subject to Canberra approval of recommendations submitted through the officers of the Department of Territories. In some matters involving the functions, organization, and staffing of the public service his recommendations must be countersigned by the Public Service Commissioner; in purely public service matters the Commissioner alone makes recommendations. Though his Administration is responsible in New Guinea for nearly the whole of the functions which are carried out in Australia by state and federal governments together, his administrative discretion and authority are in practice scarcely equivalent to those of a single departmental permanent head in Canberra.

So much for 'centralization'. The growth of 'specialization' was encouraged by the development of a departmentalized Territorial Service on the model of the Australian public services. In particular, specialized functional departments were multiplied and expanded both numerically and geographically. Former sections of existing departments which were made independent included the Crown Law Office (1950), the Departments of Posts and Telegraphs and Public Works (1955), and of Labour and Police (1961). In 1961, also, a new Department of Trade and Industry was created, absorbing the functions and staff of the former Department of Customs and Marine. In the following year the Division of Extension Services in the Administrator's Department was given full status as the Department of Information and Extension Services, its function being to promote understanding among the local people of the policies and measures of the Administration. At the same time high priority was given to the growth of previously established specialist departments such as Agriculture, Education, and Public Health.[2] In addition, most of these departments were steadily developing their own field organizations, at District and Sub-District levels, while some of them introduced a new 'Regional' level of organization of their own, intermediate between the District and headquarters.

The policies of 'centralization', in the form of a large and powerful bureaucracy in Canberra, and 'specialization', in the form of multiplied functional departments with their own local hierarchies in the Territory, were complementary to each other. The strengthened lines of command, from every specialist officer in the field through his own departmental headquarters in Port Moresby to the Department of Territories and Minister, were calculated to concentrate decision-making in the hands of the Minister and his immediate advisers. To be fully consistent, such a system could scarcely tolerate other points of strong co-ordination and authority (even though delegated), the obvious candidates for which were Port Moresby and the Districts. It is not surprising, therefore, to note a distinct Ministerial resistance to fully co-ordinated administration at these levels.

Co-ordination at Port Moresby. The relatively limited autonomy

[2] A rough indication is given by the following comparison between public service increases in two broad groups of departments and in the Department of Native Affairs (District Administration), in two successive periods. The first group 'Law, order and basic services', includes the departments of the Administrator, Civil Affairs, Customs, Lands, Law, Police, Posts and Telegraphs, the Public Service Commissioner, Public Works, and Treasury. The second group, 'Specialist services', includes Agriculture, Education, Forests and Public Health, all in existence in 1957, and Trade and Industry, Labour, and Information and Extension Services, all created since 1960. (The movement of some staff from the Department of the Administrator and the Customs Department into Group 2 departments after 1960 makes little difference to the basic comparison. If Public Works and Posts and Telegraphs had been included in the second group the contrast in rates of growth would have been more striking, as these departments also grew rapidly.)

Increase in Public Service Staff

Departmental groups	1957-60	1960-4
	%	%
Law, order and basic services	45	16
Specialist services	60	123
Native Affairs Department	29	21

of the Administrator has already been noted. Other potentialities of
concerted decision-making at Port Moresby were avoided with
equal care. In the immediate post-war structure, for example, there
was an appearance of traditional colonial practice in the survival of
a Government Secretary's Department, which had had a certain
primacy over other Territory departments as the right hand of the
Administrator. Even then, however, this department was not the
co-ordinator of district administration. As an experienced critic
observed in 1951:

> At the centre, the dualism of the Government Secretary's office
> and the Department of District Services comes straight from the
> primitive colonial past. It is a reflexion of the view that the
> control of 'native people' is some kind of esoteric art divorced
> from the ordinary matters of government. . . It makes a properly
> co-ordinated policy impossible. For this reason, the former 'native
> affairs departments' . . . in territories under the United Kingdom
> have in every case been abolished, and their duties have been
> transferred to a central Secretariat (Davidson 1951:6).

In New Guinea, by contrast, the Department of District Services
and Native Affairs was perpetuated and in 1955, as if to emphasize
the limited, functional conception of its role, was renamed simply
'Native Affairs'; while in the same year the Government Secretary's
Department was abolished and its staff transferred to a Department
of the Administrator which had been created in 1952.

The history of the last-named department is instructive. Despite
its title, it never has been directly headed by the Administrator. At
its foundation a new post of Assistant Administrator was created to
provide it with a separate departmental head. After an important
general administrative reorganization in 1955 the official description
of its functions made it look like the true heir of the Government
Secretary's Department. They were to include responsibility for:

> The smooth working and efficient functioning of all the Depart-
> ments of the Administration; organisation of research for and
> planning and promotion of developmental policies; investigation
> and co-ordination of the plans and programmes . . . prepared by
> Departments and the determination of final programmes in re-
> lation to available resources; co-ordination of Administration
> activities with those of Commonwealth Departments and Instru-
> mentalities operating in the Territory; channels of communication
> with the Department of Territories; and so on.[3]

But it is doubtful whether the Administrator's Department ever
played such a role, since six years later the Minister was impatiently
telling his advisers that there was still a marked tendency to over-
elaborate the structure of the Department of the Administrator. He
directed that it was to be mainly a secretariat in the narrow meaning
of that term and was not to be a clearing-house, brains trust, or a

[3] Circular Memorandum H.H. 180, issued by the Administrator on 15 June
1955.

planning authority for the whole Administration. Instead, he approved (in 1961) the appointment of a second Assistant Administrator; the separation of both these offices from the headship of any individual department; and the creation of a Central Policy and Planning Committee at Port Moresby, consisting of the Administrator, the two Assistant Administrators, and the Territory's Treasurer. (The Director of Native Affairs was added in 1964.) The Department of the Administrator was to be headed by a Secretary, but it was explicitly stipulated that he should be in the 'second grade of Departmental Heads', with a lower salary than his predecessor, and was *not* to be a member of the Policy and Planning Committee.

Reminiscent of the 1955 announcement of the functions of the Department of the Administrator was the 1961 public description of those of the Central Policy and Planning Committee:

i. To ensure consistency in the overall application of policy in all departments of the Administration;
ii. To bring under notice all phases of the administrative effort and of the situation in the Territory before recommendations on policy are made to the Minister; and
iii. To ensure that forward planning is realistic and comprehensive (T.P.N.G. 1963b:3).

More indicative, as before, of the real state of affairs was the Minister's instruction to his own officers that the Policy and Planning Committee should not bring any change to the processes of planning or making policy. All the planning, all the prompting of policy and all the detailed investigation were to come upwards out of the functional departments and not out of the Department of the Administrator. This showed pretty clearly where the Policy and Planning Committee stood, and this is pretty much where it has remained—as an occasional sifter of departmental propositions. Probably at least as effective, as a gesture towards co-ordination at Port Moresby, was the 'assignment' under the 1961 arrangements of the general oversight of three groups of departments respectively to the Administrator and the two Assistant Administrators.[4]

[4] The 'Assignments' were authorized by the Administrative Arrangements Ordinance, 1961. The grouping arranged at that time was:

Administrator	Assistant Administrator (Services)	Assistant Administrator (Economic Affairs)
Department of the Administrator	Education	Agriculture, Stock and Fisheries
Treasury	Public Health	Forests
Law	Native Affairs	Lands, Surveys & Mines
Police	Labour	Trade and Industry
Information & Extension Services	Public Works	Posts and Telegraphs

Since the replacement of the Department of Native Affairs by that of District Administration, the latter has been 'assigned' to the Administrator and the Department of Information and Extension Services has been transferred to the Assistant Administrator (Services).

Alongside the Policy and Planning Committee as potential planning and co-ordinating bodies at the Territory level are the Land
Development Board, consisting of the Assistant Administrator
(Economic Affairs) as Chairman, with the Directors of Agriculture,
Lands, Forests and Public Works; and the Administrator's Council
(see Chapter 12). Between the three of them as they actually
function it seems safe to assume that Port Moresby cannot, as a
co-ordinating or planning centre, seriously purport to challenge the
more closely knit Department of Territories.

The problem of district administration. It has already been
suggested that the New Guinea environment makes the role of that
Territory department which has variously been called 'District
Services', 'Native Affairs', and 'District Administration' unique
among its fellows, both in principle and practice. And yet, partly
for this very reason, partly as a by-product of the policy of 'centralization and specialization', and perhaps partly from accidents of
personality, its organizational status has always been equivocal.
Among landmarks in its chequered post-war history were, first, the
creation outside this Department of the new office of District Commissioner (see below); next, the reorganization of 1955 which erased
'District Services' from its title, transferred some of its more routine
functions to a new Department of Civil Affairs, and nominally
shifted the Government Secretary's co-ordinating responsibilities to
the Department of the Administrator; next, a connected series of
official investigations, reports and recommendations in 1959-61
which only resulted in removing further functions from Native
Affairs; half-despairing suggestions at various stages for dismember-
ing what remained of the Department and ending its identity; in
1963 another official investigation and report; and finally, in 1964,
another change of title to Department of District Administration
and one more definition of its 'role . . . in Territory administration'.
And throughout this period until the 1964 reorganization, no statement of the Department's functions (though many were tendered)
was ever formally approved by the Minister. Instead, it suffered
steady attrition by *ad hoc* transfers of activities to the specialist
departments—its Labour Branch to the Department of Labour, the
Co-operative Section to the Department of Trade and Industry, its
Publications, Radio, and Films services to the Information and
Extension Department, and so on. Threats of further surgery were
endemic: a new department of Local Government and Community
Development should take over these functions; field officers should
shed their police powers and authority in land matters; and so it
went on.

Behind this vacillation lay sharply conflicting views of the Department's proper status. Territory officials—and sometimes also
those in Canberra—who examined the problem posed the issues
very clearly. The 1959 committee of review was sure that the line

of command was confused by the implication in the 1955 reorganization that the Department was *unus inter pares*, that it was another technical department with technical functions 'to take care of the Natives' as though this was something quite distinct from the responsibilities of other Departments. It was asserted that the 1955 reorganization failed to make clear that the responsibilities of the Department of Native Affairs were essentially of a general administrative nature involving the integration and co-ordination of the work of other Departments.

In 1960, nearly ten years after Professor Davidson had made a similar observation, the 'overwhelming view' of local officials, as one of them put it, was that 'the present status of the Department of Native Affairs as an organisation distinct from the Department of the Administrator, and in the field, as concerning staff, distinct from the District Commissioner, was a source of confusion and frustration'. They accordingly advocated 'the removal of the separateness' between these departments. Their conception was that 'the primary role of the present Native Affairs organisation is to serve as the instrument of central administration at lower levels', especially in 'the co-ordination of planning at the district level'. But the authoritative view, as published by the Administrator himself in 1958, was quite different. He said it was the Department of the Administrator which was, 'in broad terms, responsible for the general co-ordination of the work of other Departments', while

> The Department of Native Affairs is primarily concerned with the detailed aspects of native administration in the field. . . . Its activities include—to mention but a few—establishment of patrol posts, patrolling, administration of law and order, Courts of Native Affairs, native land matters, and the control and protection of those indigenes who enter the field of employment (Wilkes 1958:xiv).

As a matter of history, the deep ambivalence of administrative practice lent some plausibility to each of these views simultaneously. Because of its title, and because in more recently-opened areas it acted as agent for all other departments, the Department of Native Affairs had indeed been tempted to 'regard itself as the whole Administration in so far as natives are concerned'. Truly, 'native administration' could involve every activity and therefore every department of government. But the whittling away of its own functions, as well as the transfer of its agency functions to 'technical departments' in more settled areas, seemed to imply in the long run a limited, 'functional' role for Native Affairs. This did not mean that 'native' concerns as a whole could be segregated from other policies and programmes of the government, but that this Department might be confined to certain aspects of 'native' administration: exploration and pacification of new areas, establishing and maintaining patrol stations, acting as a primary point of contact with

native communities, and advising other departments on the application of their specialist techniques at the 'grass roots'. This was the
concept distinguished in one report as 'bringing the natives to some
stage of development after which the technical Departments will
take over'. It was given some countenance by Ministerial directions
about the investigations of 1959-62. They were to explore the
Department's handing over of magisterial and police powers in
certain areas, its liaison in the field with other departments, the
relief of Native Affairs officers from the performance of agency
functions. The Minister was unconvinced by arguments in favour
of placing 'direct administration, exploration and agency functions'
(he was referring to Native Affairs) within the Department of the
Administrator, presumably because he saw these as specialized,
technical functions in which that 'secretariat' should not become
involved. On the other hand, the Department of Native Affairs was
entrusted with the initiation, development, and continuing supervision of the native Local Government Councils, which were seen
as the means of introducing the people to organized political life
and as an important medium of general economic and social development. Surely this was a 'generalist' responsibility which might
be thought to involve the Department in the co-ordination of many
other departments' efforts in the field? These ambiguities were
puzzling enough. But the strangest anomalies of all were generated
by the system of District Commissioners.

Before 1951 the District Officer, belonging to the Department of
District Services and Native Affairs, had been the nearest approach
to a co-ordinating authority in the field—if only because the field
organization and activities of other departments were still relatively
rudimentary. In that year a new office of District Commissioner
was established, outside the Department of District Services, and
with 'a dual administrative role':

> Firstly—As senior executive officer he is responsible to the Govern-
> ment Secretary for the co-ordination of all the activities of the
> Administration within the District in respect of matters other than
> those concerning native administration.
> Secondly—In relation to all matters concerning native admini-
> stration he is responsible to the Director of District Services and
> Native Affairs.[5]

On the face of it, this arrangement was consistent with the notion
that District Services was a purely technical department, and that
an independent authority was required to co-ordinate its district
offices with those of other departments in the field. However,
authority (as distinct from 'responsibility') was precisely what the
District Commissioner was not given. He also had no staff of his

[5] Circular Instruction G.H. 548 issued by the Territory Administration on
13 January 1951, para 7.

own, and was required to divide his administrative allegiance between two masters. Naturally enough, it was soon being said that 'the position of District Commissioner is far less attractive than that of pre-war District Officer',[6] and a state of uncertainty and periodic exasperation set in among field officers, calling forth successive 'clarifications' which remained obstinately beside the point, and if anything rendered confusion worse confounded.

Following the 1955 reorganization, a new Memorandum announced that the District Commissioner was the representative of the Administrator within a District and was now on the staff of the Department of the Administrator.

> District Commissioners will be responsible within a District for the observance by all Departments of the Administrator's directions on policy and for the achievement of the objectives of policy. Additionally, they will ensure smooth working and co-operation between Departments working in the District.

This time the withholding of the authority necessary to achieve these results was made explicit:

> The direction of the policy of a Department may not be restricted by a District Commissioner in any way, but should a District Commissioner consider that some feature of the policy of a Department is not in the best interests of a District, he is to communicate his views to the Departmental Head or the Assistant Administrator as the case may require.[7]

It was also provided that District Commissioners should be kept acquainted with policy changes and departmental actions, that they could call conferences of departmental representatives to secure co-operation in the District, and that they should continue to preside over Town and District Advisory Councils (see Chapter 12) and transmit their advice when necessary to the Administrator.

Two years later, at a District Commissioners' Conference, it was still 'apparent that some uncertainty exists as to exactly what his position is, particularly in relation to Departmental and Technical Officers and to the general co-ordination and direction of administration in his District'. Yet another Memorandum was issued, talking of 'the need for the closest co-operation between Departments and District Commissioners', 'mutual consultation', 'the District team', 'the general supervision of the District Commissioner',

---

[6] Remarks of a senior District Services officer in 1953, listing some anomalies that would arise 'while this Instruction remains in force'. Incidentally, one of the reasons advanced for the establishment of District Commissionerships was that existing District Officers were men of 'insufficient education' for the post-war tasks of district co-ordination and leadership; however, up to 1962 at least, every post of District Commissioner was filled by a former District Officer.

[7] Both extracts are from Circular Memorandum H.H. 180, issued by the Administrator on 15 June 1955.

'common objectives', 'endeavouring to secure agreement on measures' at the monthly meetings of district departmental representatives; reiterating that the D.C. was 'personally and directly responsible to the Administrator for the peace and good order of his District and for the . . . observance by all Departments of directions on policy'; and yet reaffirming that:

> The District Commissioner will not normally intervene in Departmental matters, but *in matters of detail and routine* any *reasonable* request addressed by him to local Departmental Officers should, as a matter of course, be honoured.[8]

His only power to issue orders on his own responsibility was 'in cases of emergency'. Unsupported by membership of any departmental hierarchy in the District, without command of any executive apparatus of his own, and facing specialist officers whose allegiance, interests, and primary duty of obedience lay firmly with their own departmental headquarters in Port Moresby, the D.C. was in reality no more than a liaison officer, dependent on persuasion and personality for whatever influence he could wield.

The difficulties of this system were repeated at the Sub-District level, where Assistant District Officers, responsible in matters concerning their own Department of Native Affairs to the District Officer, and also for agency functions on behalf of other departments, were 'to be regarded . . . as the agent of and responsible to the District Commissioner' for the purpose of inter-departmental co-ordination and co-operation at Sub-District level. Relations with other departmental representatives in the Sub-District were prescribed in the same hopeful terms as for the District Commissioner, and the rest was left to the 'good sense of Officers and their common devotion to the interests of the public and of the Service'.[9]

The 1964 reorganization. It took thirteen years of protest from within the service and a change of Minister to amend the more obvious defects of this system of district administration. The consensus of those who had to work it was remarkable, as expressed in reports of District Officers' and District Commissioners' Conferences, Senior Officers' Courses at A.S.O.P.A., interdepartmental 'Policy Workshops' (conferences of senior officers), and the 1959 and 1963 Committees of Review. As crystallized in the last-mentioned report, the consensus ran as follows.

The very creation of the office of District Commissioner recognized the need for integrated execution of policy by all departments in the field. Unified planning and budgeting on a District basis were also necessary. But all of these, to be effective, required a

[8] Circular Memorandum H.H. 1/57, issued by the Administrator on 16 May 1957. My italics.

[9] Circular Memorandum H.H. 2/57 (undated).

unified executive authority and administrative apparatus in the District which the D.C. lacked. Moreover, he needed the support of an effective policy-framing and executive co-ordinating machine at the Territorial headquarters. In fact he was attached to the Department of the Administrator which had been denied both policy-making and executive functions and had no organization of its own in the field. There he was required to rely on the help of the A.D.Os., thus straining their obligations to their own Department, but he was denied that of the most experienced potential adviser, the District Officer, who as a result was kept less informed about overall district administration than his own A.D.Os., yet was expected to deputize for the D.C. when the latter was absent or on leave! The A.D.Os. in their turn had to spend more time on agency and general administrative work than on native advancement problems, which tended to be left to very junior officers. In the absence of authoritative co-ordination at the District level and a unified chain of command from the centre, the advantages of decentralization were lost and integrated decision-making had to be concentrated in Port Moresby or Canberra. We have already seen that this was precisely what the Minister wanted in 1952, but the conclusion drawn from the 1963 investigation was that the organizational separation of District Commissioners from field officers of the Department of Native Affairs had proved inadvisable. The present system was formally unworkable, had resulted in considerable confusion in most districts, and worked satisfactorily in others only through the good sense of the officers concerned. There should be a reversion to the single chain of command which existed prior to the 1955 reorganization.

The reorganization of 1964 accepted most of the recommendations which followed from this analysis. The Department of Native Affairs was renamed 'Department of District Administration', whose functions as announced by the Administrator 'include a clearcut co-ordinating role within administration districts and responsibility for promoting political awareness at all levels'.

> The Director of District Administration is directly responsible to me and is a member of the Central Policy and Planning Committee. . . The strengthening of the generalist administrative organization, both at the central level and within administrative areas, and the establishment of a unified chain of command from the Administrator to the effective contact level, will be achieved through the transfer of District Commissioners from the Department of the Administrator to the Department of District Administration.
>
> District Commissioners remain my personal representatives. . . They are responsible to the Director of District Administration for the administration of their respective Districts. . . .[10]

[10] Circular Memorandum A.D. 128, issued by the Department of the Administrator on 18 November 1964.

District Officers are renamed Deputy District Commissioners, become in practice 'the District Commissioner's Executive Officers',
and are directly responsible to him. Officers in charge of Sub-
Districts are now called Assistant District Commissioners and are
responsible directly to the District Commissioner for administration
and the co-ordination of all departments operating therein.

The problem of interdepartmental relations in the District is not
definitively resolved, as District Commissioners are still given no
authority over officers of other departments except 'in times of
emergency'. Each departmental head remains responsible for implementing approved programmes for his Department throughout
the Territory. However, a system of District Development Committees, comprising senior officers of major departments in each
District, under the Chairmanship of the D.C., has been established.
'The District Commissioner in this role must clearly be recognised
by the Departmental representatives as the chief executive and
co-ordinator in his District.' But conflict between departmental
plans and programmes in a District cannot be resolved by him. If
agreement cannot be reached on the District Development Committee, he must simply refer the matter to the Director of District
Administration, 'who will take necessary action to have the problem
determined at the appropriate level'. Thus no real decentralization
of decision-making has yet been achieved. At least the Director is
now on the Policy and Planning Committee, and the D.C. is
backed by his authority and the resources of the traditional
'generalist' Department in the field. And something, in turn, has
been done to restore the prestige and authority of that Department.
But it is still not the department *of* the Administrator, and it remains
to be seen whether its new Planning and Advisory Division at headquarters will develop as an aid to the Policy and Planning Committee in considering the problems of the Territory as a whole.

THE PUBLIC SERVICE

In 1964 the Territorial Public Service was organized in fifteen
functional departments, together with the Department of the Public
Service Commissioner. At 31 August the staff employed in these
departments numbered 6,535 under the Public Service Ordinance
of the Territory and 9,703 under the Administration Servants
Ordinance. In addition there were a separate Police Commission and
an Electricity Commission. Police and warders numbered about
3,400; over 6,500 indigenous people were employed under the
Native Labour Ordinance (mostly as unskilled labourers), and there
were about 800 students, apprentices, and other small groups in
Territory employment. The Public Service Commissioner's duties
included the promotion of efficiency, co-ordination of the work of
departments, recruitment and staff training, promotion of staff, and
supervision to ensure economy in the use of staff and other re-

sources. The Minister retained power in many matters, including creation and abolition of departments, the functions of departments, the classification of offices in the public service, qualifications for appointment or promotion, appointments of permanent heads and overseas officers (expatriates), rates of salary, and the making of Regulations under the Ordinance.

Until 1958 the public service proper was staffed exclusively by non-indigenous people, almost entirely Australians. Inducements to serve in the Territory included post-war improvements in salaries, special 'expatriate allowances' and generous leave conditions, and for some the interest and challenge of the job and prospects of rapid promotion. Nevertheless the post-war efforts to increase the public service rapidly for its new tasks of development were chronically hampered by scarcity of staff. Although the size of the service was doubled in the five years to 1958, the numbers on strength always fell a long way below approved establishments, and high rates of staff turnover set constant limits to efficiency. In this context and in that of political development an obvious need was to provide for a rapid transition from an expatriate to a largely indigenous public service. This step was inevitably delayed by the tremendous lag in native education. Intensive measures were necessary to qualify and train local people for clerical, professional, and administrative work. By the time these began to bear fruit, the prospects of increasingly rapid political change reinforced a growing sense of insecurity among expatriate staff, and it seemed likely that the wastage rate would exceed the rate of recruitment and training of qualified indigenous staff to replace them. Most problems of the public service are related to this basic situation.

Localization. The post-war public service was divided into three Divisions. The First Division consisted essentially of departmental heads. The Second Division contained most of the administrative, professional, and clerical staff, and required the Australian Leaving Certificate or Senior Examinations as a qualification for entry. The Third Division contained technical and routine clerical staff, and the entry qualification was the Australian Intermediate Certificate or Junior Examination or evidence of a trained technical skill.

Planning began in 1953-4 for the creation of a new Auxiliary Division, to enable increased participation of indigenous people in partly skilled, technical and clerical work in the Administration, to provide in-service training to standards qualifying for entry to the established Divisions, and ultimately to give them scope for higher advancement in those Divisions. In 1955 the Public Service Ordinance was amended to establish the new Division, to open the service to competitive entry by indigenous people, and to grant them salary, status, and conditions equal to comparable expatriate officers (except for the Territorial allowance and expatriate leave conditions).

At this time only three indigenous persons were known to be qualified to enter the Third Division of the public service, and it was necessary to set lower standards for entry to the Auxiliary Division. Between 1955 and the end of 1957, 360 positions were established in the Division, and divided for entry purposes into three categories. For the 'clerical and professional' category (Clerical Assistants, Teacher Assistants, and Health Assistants) two years of post-primary education were required; for the 'higher technical' category (Technical Assistants and Field Assistants), a completed primary schooling; and for the 'lower technical' category (semi-skilled), three years of primary school. In 1958 the first appointments were made to the Division—188 were admitted. In the following year a single public examination was substituted for the initial three standards, with an internal examination barrier before advancement beyond £509 (later raised to £530). By August 1964 there were 1,197 Auxiliary Division officers, almost all of them former Administration Servants.

A further amendment to the Public Service Ordinance in 1959 made the first provision for appointing indigenes to permanent positions in the regular Second and Third Divisions—to the latter either directly or by promotion from the Auxiliary Division. Positions were classified in three categories similar to those adopted for the Auxiliary Division, and for entry to both Divisions there was a reversion to differential entry qualifications for these categories, ranging from Junior Certificate down to Standard 4. The Junior Certificate was required for certain 'In-Training' positions, leading after successful completion of formal training courses, of from two to five years, to such positions as Assistant Patrol Officer, Assistant Welfare Officer, and Assistant Surveyor. A new Retirement Benefit Ordinance in 1960 provided a form of superannuation for permanent public servants born in the Territory. In June 1961 the first group of permanent indigenous appointments was made—26 to the Third Division and 2 to the Second Division. By August 1964 there were 19 permanent and temporary indigenous members of the Second Division, and 168 in the Third Division. These all received the same salaries as expatriate officers in corresponding positions (but not, of course, expatriate allowances and leave conditions).

The combined result of these measures was that by the end of 1964 about 21 per cent of Territory public servants were indigenous officers, very few of whom had had time to advance beyond the lowest ranks of their respective occupational groups. Localization was keeping pace with the five-year development programme announced by the Minister for Territories in October 1961, which provided for additional recruitment of 2,000 expatriate officers and not less than 2,500 indigenous public servants by 1967, giving the service in that year a total strength of 10,000, of whom one-third would be indigenous. But this was not at all pleasing to the United Nations Visiting Mission of 1962.

> To aim at permanently increasing the Australian staff of the Government Service to about 6,000—this increase to be progressively undertaken over five years—seems to the Mission to be a policy which would be open to grave doubt, if the expatriate recruitment were all undertaken on a permanent basis.

The Mission felt that the public service was to some extent over-centralized and over-complicated, and feared that the government was creating a bureaucratic superstructure too cumbersome for the country to afford. They also considered that the target of one-third indigenous officers by 1967 would 'fall far short of a reasonable objective' (U.N. Trusteeship Council 1962:para. 227). It would have been helpful if the Mission had indicated how a higher indigenous proportion might be attained, other than by allowing the expatriate service to wither. Indeed, its warning about permanent expatriate recruitment seemed to encourage government moves in that direction. Speaking to the Annual Congress of the Territory Public Service Association in September 1962, the Minister for Territories announced a change in recruitment policy:

> For some time past the policy has been not to appoint an expatriate officer to any permanent position for which indigenous candidates will shortly be available. Our judgment is that in a great number of positions expatriate officers will be required for many years to come. For such positions permanent appointments will continue to be made. For other positions we will give only temporary, exempt or contract appointments to expatriates . . . (Hasluck 1962a).

It was perhaps not so much this frank and specific statement, as the general assumptions behind it, and the beginning of short-term appointments in practice, which increased the sense of insecurity among expatriate officers. The change seemed likely also to increase the difficulty of recruiting needed Australians for the service and to complicate the problem of training new entrants.

Training and education. Both the Papuan or New Guinean and the European, when engaged for any but the most menial work in the Territory public service, are plunged forthwith into an alien culture—the one into the Western world of organized authority, written communication, and advanced technology, the other into the semi-savage environment of Melanesia, with the primary task of helping to transform it. Add this to the urgency of all that the public service must do, and it becomes obvious that experience 'on the job' must be supplemented by intensive formal training if waste of time, errors, and disillusion are to be avoided. This was obvious to the creators of the Australian School of Pacific Administration (ASOPA) back in 1944, but the School's role never developed as they envisaged, and the growth of formal training provisions within the Territory, though recently accelerated, was extraordinarily tardy at first. The reasons for this are too complex to examine here, but the facts may be noted.

In 1947 when ASOPA began to operate in Sydney, staff training in the Territory was reported by the Public Service Commissioner to be 'virtually non-existent'. ASOPA's first (and always major) contribution was the training of Australians as Patrol Officers for field service in the Department of Native Affairs. From 1947 the Cadet Patrol Officers, who were required to have the Leaving Certificate or its equivalent, took a three months' Orientation Course at ASOPA, served for two terms (21 months) in the field in the Territory, and then returned to Sydney for a full-time two-year course of a standard which earned credits towards a degree of the University of Queensland. After finishing this course an officer could complete a university degree or diploma by correspondence from the field, or submit a thesis for a Diploma of ASOPA, or both. In 1954 the need to increase staff in the field and counter wastage was accepted as a reason for cutting the Orientation Course to three weeks, supplemented by a three weeks' induction course in the Territory, setting correspondence assignments to be completed during field service, and reducing the subsequent 'long course' to one year, entailing compression of the teaching to the point where university credits were no longer granted. This short-sighted policy was soon regretted in the Territory, leading to repeated recommendations for restoration of the two-year course, endorsed in 1963 by the committee of review on the Department of Native Affairs, and in 1964 by the Currie Commission on Higher Education and the Interim Council of the Administrative College (see below). Meanwhile, since 1963, expatriate Cadet Patrol Officers have been recruited on a six-year contract basis which precludes any thorough formal training. Since 1962 indigenous Assistant Patrol Officers-in-Training have been recruited in the Territory and given a one-year combined practical and rudimentary clerical course at Finschhafen. Proposals for an integrated training and education for District Administration field officers, including a two-year diploma course at the Administrative College, were adopted in 1965.

Quasi-professional training for the public service received sustained attention from the middle 1950s. From 1955, Cadet Education Officers recruited in Australia received a two-year training course at ASOPA with the help, in part, of lecturers seconded from Balmain Teachers' College, Sydney. Training colleges for indigenous teachers have been established in the Territory. A crash programme for increasing the supply of European primary school teachers was conducted at a special teachers' college at Malaguna, Rabaul, from 1960. The same period has seen the establishment of agricultural colleges, of a forestry school at Bulolo and of the Papuan

Medical College at Port Moresby for the training of indigenous staff to sub-professional levels. Other departments such as Posts and Telegraphs have training schools for technical officers. In most of these institutions part of the effort has to be devoted to raising the general educational level of the students before they can proceed to more specialized training. The Education Department also runs courses for this purpose.

Formal training conferences for middle-grade and senior public servants have also been a development of the past ten years. The first Study Group for Senior Officers from different Territory departments was held at ASOPA in 1956, and these have continued annually, producing reports which are valuable source material for the study of Territory administration and its problems. In 1961 a series of 'Policy Workshops' was inaugurated. These are conferences of two to three weeks in different Territory centres designed to enable officers to discuss policy issues and administrative problems of their districts with officers from other parts of the Territory Service and from the Department of Territories.

The conduct of central training courses in office methods of all kinds, and the encouragement of officers to undertake further education on their own account, have been functions of the Public Service Commissioner's Department since it was established in 1954. It has helped to administer the schemes in operation since 1956 for selected officers to attend courses conducted by the Australian Administrative Staff College, the Commonwealth Public Service Board, and Commonwealth specialist departments, and also the Territory scheme of Free Places for full-time or external university studies which was begun in 1958. In 1962 it awarded the first Public Service Secondary Education Scholarships for full-time secondary studies to enable indigenous officers in the Auxiliary Division to qualify for entry to the Third Division.

A good deal of this work was managed by the Public Service Institute, a branch of the Public Service Commissioner's Department established in 1954, initially to help develop training programmes for the new Auxiliary Division. In the following year it began to widen its scope, and by 1963 its activities included tutorial assistance to public servants engaged in part-time university studies, orientation and induction courses, typing, stenographic, and basic clerical training, courses in supervision and management, and refresher courses for specific occupational groups in the clerical-administrative ranks of the service.

In 1961 an interdepartmental committee in Canberra had prepared for the Minister the first comprehensive report on development of higher education in the Territory, including a recommendation for establishment of an Administrative College which was immediately adopted. In November 1963 this College was formally inaugurated at Port Moresby, absorbing the Public Service Institute and commencing a new training scheme for indigenous court officials. The College is intended to give special emphasis to the development of higher management and administrative education for the public service, and has embarked on the first stage of a scheme of combined formal education and planned experience intended to qualify a number of indigenous officers for senior executive posts within a period of ten years. Work has commenced on permanent buildings for the Administrative College, which will provide full residential, classroom, library, and recreational facilities for 300 students and the teaching staff. The Commission on Higher Education has recommended that any university established in the Territory should consider the future incorporation of the higher management and administrative education activities of the College in the University as an Institute of Administration.

'Reconstruction', 1961-4. In May 1961 the Minister initiated planning to change the structure of the public service 'to provide for the present and prospective increases in the number of indigenous public servants and for the day when the service will be predominantly an indigenous one'. The most important problems this raised were those of standards of entry, rates of pay and allowances, and terms of appointment, and of these rates of pay was to prove the most crucial issue. It was posed by the Minister—and his answer given, in his address to the Public Service Association in September 1962:

> The question to be faced . . . is whether an indigenous public service can be maintained at the Australian rate of salary and whether its members should receive the expatriate allowances and conditions given to the Australians. This is not a question of equal pay for equal work but a question of the capacity of the country to pay and a question, too, of social equality in the indigenous community. It will be bad for government and bad for the community if the self-governing country makes the bureaucrat a more highly privileged person than any other citizen. . . . In the territorial service [the Public Service Commissioner] will fix a lowest rate and a highest rate based on a broad judgment of the long-term capacity of the Territory economy, and within that range he will classify positions according to work value and qualifications required (Hasluck 1962a:9, 11).

The Minister went on to specify alternative ways of reconstructing the service to this end: first (which he preferred), an integrated service in which 'the indigenous and expatriate officers would be fellow members of the same service, the expatriate receiving his additional emoluments mainly in the form of expatriate allowances'; and second, 'a main service organised for local conditions and local rates of pay and . . . an auxiliary division which would be staffed wholly by expatriate officers'. He had been told by the Association

Executive that after discussion of these schemes with their indigenous and expatriate members, they preferred the second, and the government would adopt it. 'At an appropriate stage in the course of the work consultation will be arranged.' And the government would ponder the idea that the new expatriate service, and the payment of its emoluments, might be provided for under Commonwealth Acts rather than a Territory Ordinance, though he did not accept the Association's view that this was a necessary safeguard.

There appeared to be mutual agreement on these principles, but their subsequent history was a chapter of confusions and conflicts. When the Bill for a new Public Service Ordinance was introduced into the Legislative Council in September 1963, the Association Executive had seen it only briefly in final draft and under seal of confidence so that there could be no consultation with the rank and file. Indeed, it was not even discussed with Territory department heads until after its First Reading in Council. The Bill embodied the principle of separate Territorial and Expatriate Divisions, each to have its own salary scale, with a cumbersome system for reclassifying a position into one Division or the other according to whether a qualified indigene was held to be available for it.

The Public Service Association now declared itself opposed to a dual service. The separate Expatriate Division seemed to threaten an early Australian withdrawal (the very objection to this scheme raised by the Minister a year before), and its establishment under Territory legislation, and not a Commonwealth Act, would make the expatriates' position precarious when a native majority dominated a Territory House of Assembly. The Association also complained about the clumsy provisions for reclassifying offices between the two services; about the lack of a preference clause in favour of local officers; and above all about the failure to incorporate in this Bill, as a *quid pro quo* for the increased insecurity of expatriate jobs, a plan of compensation for premature loss of career through localization.

The government was prepared to revert to the principle of a unified service with its main corollaries, but refused to delay the Public Service Bill until a compensation scheme could be worked out. (Indeed, its anxiety to pass the Bill in the last hours of the old Legislative Council drew accusations that it was unwilling to run the gauntlet of the proposed new House of Assembly.) Relations between the Association and the Minister broke down; the Association had most of its proposed amendments introduced by private members of the Council; and when the Second Reading of the Bill was taken in November the government accepted without demur those calling for a single service. As passed, the Ordinance (No. 20 of 1964) retained the First, Second, and Third Divisions of the Service, omitted the Auxiliary Division, paved the way for officers of that Division and for Administration Servants to be transferred

to the Second and Third Divisions, and authorized different salaries
for offices in any of the three Divisions according to whether they
were occupied by local or 'overseas' (i.e. expatriate) officers. Provision was also made for preference to local people in appointments,
promotions, or transfers to prescribed positions or classes of position.
In effect this removed the right of expatriate officers to appeal
against promotions of local officers to positions so gazetted. Apart
from the Association objections to the postponement of a compensation scheme, there was general assent to the Ordinance both
inside and outside the Legislative Council.

It took a further year to work out the regulations and actual
salary determinations necessary to bring the Ordinance into effect.
Once again strict secrecy was preserved until the completed scheme
was announced on 9 September 1964. It immediately drew down a
chorus of criticism and protest from inside and outside the public
service, including both indigenous and expatriate elected members
of the House of Assembly. Native teacher trainees and medical
students staged marches on Administration Headquarters; leaders of
employee associations and other groups issued public denunciations;
public meetings passed resolutions of censure; the Public Service
Commissioner was besieged by deputations; and newspapers in the
Territory and Australia expressed measured disapproval. When the
House of Assembly met in February 1965 the elected majority
unanimously passed, over official opposition, an Ordinance introduced by an Australian elected member, to share control of the
Territory service between the Minister for Territories and the
Administrator's Council and a local public service board. This provoked a rift in the anti-Administration ranks: the President of the
Public Service Association said that overseas officers wanted to
remain under Australian control and feared a measure which could
subject the service to manipulation by Territory politicians. The
amending Ordinance was in due course vetoed by the withholding
of Vice-Regal assent. The Minister appointed a committee of
three elected M.H.As. and two government officers to report on what
changes should be made in control of the public service and how
localization could be accelerated. The question of local salary rates
was submitted by the Association to the Public Service Arbitrator.

Since there is nothing in the decisions announced in September
1964 which is inconsistent with the principles accepted by all
parties a year earlier, it is necessary to ask why they aroused such
resistance. The main reasons would seem to be as follows:

(a) Foremost and fundamental was the cold shock of the actual
salary differentials, unheralded by any prior consultation with the
interested parties—a case of tactical ineptitude. The rates for local
officers average about 40 per cent of those for overseas officers for
the same jobs at all levels—before the latter's territorial allowances
and leave conditions are taken into account.

(b) The change meant an actual reduction in the nominal salaries of indigenous officers already in the Second and Third Divisions on equal pay. Of course, it had always been quite clear that this would happen and that, on 'the principle of no reduction', they would receive allowances to make up the difference from their former salary until, by promotion, their new nominal salaries reached the former level. But somehow the announcement of the new rates brought home to them the indignity of future inequality—an inequality which, ironically, would only become apparent in their wage-packet as increased qualifications and meritorious service brought them formal promotion. Mr Lloyd Hurrell, an elected member of Legislative Council, had prophesied their dismay a year earlier when debating the Ordinance:

> The Administration committed an almost irreparable blunder when it placed several local employees in the Second Division, with salaries based on the Australian rate. This was done despite the fact that in September, 1958, provision was made in this Council for separate salary scales to be established. . . . These promotions have prejudiced any real hope of salaries being placed on a local economic basis without local employees being badly upset (T.P.N.G. 1963f).

(c) Some people felt that the uniform ratio of local to overseas salaries at all levels was particularly crude. They argued that, even though the principle of lower local rates overall were accepted, the margins might have been varied according to the responsibility of the job and the qualifications required and possessed by the incumbent. The margin might be relatively small in highly skilled and exacting jobs when the local officer had the advanced qualifications that would have been expected of an expatriate; margins might then be graded to a maximum where no skill or training was present.

(d) Another related argument was that local officers in clerical-administrative positions had become accustomed to European styles of living which they and their like would no longer be able to afford. Was it wrong for those who had acquired European skills and habits of work to aspire to something like European living conditions and so set an example of ambition to their fellow-citizens?

(e) Such critics were not necessarily questioning the need for some differential, but they joined with those who asked how so severe a differential was actually chosen. Administration spokesmen had talked of 'what the Territory will be able to pay when the people determine their own political future', and said the new local rates 'even at the levels proposed are in excess of what the Territory could afford without the direct financial assistance being given by the Australian Government' (T.P.N.G. 1964a). But none of them had offered a single argument or figure to support the alleged calculation that the new rates represented 'what the local economy could

afford'. The calculation was, in fact, based on the prevailing minimum urban cash wage in the three main centres, but, apparently for
tactical reasons, the explanation was withheld until the arbitration
hearing had begun!

(f) In any case, these references to the Australian financial sub-
vention were disturbing in themselves. Seeming to rely on a hint
that Australian assistance could be curtailed or withdrawn at any
time, they conflicted with other government assurances to the contrary. They provoked, moreover, the thought that if Australia did
decide to economize on New Guinea after independence, some
other countries would be only too willing to step into the breach.
In the meantime, such a severe curtailment of indigenous salaries,
announced just before the largely elected House of Assembly
rose, really looked more like Australian financial prudence than
tenderness for the future solvency or social equality of Papua and
New Guinea. It might have been left to their own independent
legislature to decide whether 'it would be bad for the government
and the community if public servants were to become more highly
privileged persons than other citizens'.

(g) Another government argument was that as the Administration
was the largest single employer of the Territory work force, regard
should be had to the influence its local salary levels must have on
'commerce and industry employment'. The critics were soon able to
point out that the levels actually fixed were below those of much
private white-collar indigenous employment: except for the banks,
the large private employers publicly declined the Administration's
request to bring their rates into conformity with its own. As for
the lower wage-rates for manual employment in private industry, it
was argued that a substantial rise in their levels could take place
with little other effect than to enforce much-needed improvements
in managerial and technical efficiency.

Most of these reactions and criticisms are of course debatable,
and many of them do not nullify the basic argument for some salary
differential in the public service. There were others suggesting that
the form of the differentiation could have been more tactfully
designed without altering the substance, but few Papuans and New
Guineans would have been deceived by this. It is true, again, that
many of the objections were made belatedly and not argued very
cogently. But the manner of bringing in the change had smothered
adequate prior discussion, giving a spurious impression of acquiescence, and it was the substance of the change, when finally unveiled,
that crystallized the latent, ill-formulated, and sometimes unreasoning opposition. Unreasoning or no, it is a warning that in this kind
of nation-building, economic prudence is not necessarily synonymous with political wisdom—and in the long run may be less
important.

CONCLUSION

This chapter has attempted to convey some idea of the development and shaping of Territorial administration since 1945, to give examples of some of its more important problems of organization and staffing, and to appraise in a preliminary way some of the methods adopted to meet them. Such an approach cannot by itself assess the substantive achievements of the Australian Administration in that time. It is probably still too early for this; in any case the range and magnitude of the achievement have been described at great length in a large number of readily accessible Ministerial statements, official reports on the Territory to Parliament and the Trusteeship Council, and publications of the Department of Territories. The yearly reports of the U.N. Visiting Missions on New Guinea contain many judgments on Australia's record—on some matters favourable, on others critical, but all somewhat cursory.

The chapter, also, has not addressed itself to the quality of the administrative effort: the ability and dedication of many Territorial officers, their patience in trying to understand the people's points of view and to ease, while accelerating, the transition to a new form of society; and the occasional obtuseness, prejudice, or lack of interest of a misfit minority. In terms of money, equipment, numbers and qualifications of staff, and formal organization, the administration has been greatly strengthened since the war and has been invested with a sense of urgency previously unknown. These changes have been due largely to dynamic and imaginative leadership at the Ministerial level—and one Minister held the portfolio for twelve of the most crucial years. Analysis of some of the strains of this régime cannot detract from its achievement. It can, or should, contribute to a more sophisticated facing of the future.

Some of the strains selected for analysis here were associated with deliberate political decisions on public service salaries and classifications. Others resulted, it seemed, from a declared Ministerial approach to administration—the approach of 'specialization and centralization'. Of these two elements, specialization is not wrong in itself, but only when pursued at the expense of co-ordinated planning and execution. In the Territory, it has possibly been reflected in a prematurely segmented organization—too many separate departments for a comparatively small total structure. This is a defect in so far as it is one of the many factors pushing the need for co-ordination to higher levels in the hierarchy where control of detailed administration is never easy. In terms of organization, therefore, specialization has been one aspect of the more general policy of centralization—and centralization is always administratively suspect.

The Territory experience confirms such suspicions. Concerted planning and co-ordinated action are inadequately provided for at the level of the District and of Territory headquarters. This must result—and, it seems, intentionally so—in concentrating planning and co-ordination (in short all important decisions) in Canberra. But what does this mean in practice? An excessive quantity of memoranda and recommendations moves between the Territory and Canberra. Only in this way—at second or third hand—can the decision-makers be informed on matters which could often be better decided nearer to the point of action. This process can mean that submissions from senior Territory officers are reviewed, and final recommendations made thereon, by people in Canberra who may be junior in status or experience and have never seen at first hand the places or problems they pronounce upon. (Exchange or secondment of officers between the Territory and Canberra is virtually non-existent.) This is, certainly, only one case of the universal tension between central and field staffs, but here it occurs at one further remove, and there are correspondingly more serious bottlenecks and delays in getting decisions—with no general presumption that they will be that much wiser.

Of course the Minister remains generally responsible to Parliament for Territories policy and administration, and he needs a secretariat in Canberra, for liaison with other Commonwealth departments, co-ordination of policy for different Territories, research, budgeting, and clerical services. But with New Guinea so accessible and modern communications so easy, it would seem possible, as well as desirable, to operate with a minimal interposition of policy-advising and executive officers between the Minister and his staff in the field. It is within the Territory that delegations of authority and subordinate decision-making centres, at district and Port Moresby levels, need to be strengthened. Apart from its direct administrative advantages, this could bring incalculable gains in restoring morale and self-respect, and eliciting initiative and enthusiasm in the Territorial Administration. Political insecurity and uncertainty about careers are not responsible for all of the 'wastage' of senior and experienced officers in recent years.

This analysis, incidentally, may be compared with the comments on administration by the World Bank Mission which recently reported on economic development in the Territory. For example:

> Administration is excessively centralized . . . Communications are frequently poor. The staff in several districts are quite isolated. These factors, coupled with the concentration of decision making in the headquarters staff at Port Moresby, frequently hamper effective administration in the districts. It is important that district staff be given authority to make decisions and implement programs and projects which have the general approval of the Administration. . . The staff in the district offices, as well as the staff in the departments in Port Moresby, should be made a part of the planning process. To date there has been a tendency to minimize the contribution district officials can make to planning. This is a mistake (I.B.R.D. 1965:46, 410).

To anyone moving in the field, these summary abstractions are brought alive by the obvious and widespread feeling among district officials that people at Port Moresby and Canberra hardly think it worth while to keep them carefully informed on current and future policy, still less to heed or even acknowledge their own views, even when painstakingly formulated in the reports of Senior Officers' Courses and Policy Workshops. Again, on Port Moresby's own role, the World Bank report deplored the lack of an economic development planning staff to give continuity and substance to the work of the Policy and Planning Committee, and criticized the restricted membership of the Committee and its failure to invite other heads of departments for direct discussions on matters affecting their departments. It suggested that the Committee 'be expanded to include the heads of the major departments primarily concerned with action programmes', and that these programmes should include 'plans for the districts' prepared by the District Commissioners (I.B.R.D. 1965:408-11).

The positive alternatives to centralization are reorganization and delegation of authority based on a different psychological approach. This would recognize the need for division of labour between broad policy-making and detailed administration. It would understand that the only workable relationship between the two is to invest confidence and trust in the loyalty and good sense of those to whom most of the work must, in the nature of things, be delegated, and to safeguard this investment first, by selection of staff for their independence and initiative, and second, by imparting the broad aims of policy wherever possible through face-to-face discussion and explanation. Constant tapping of field experience and opinion should go without saying.

A few years ago Sir Ivor Jennings (1956:125-6) wrote:

The notion that a country is governed by politicians is fallacious. The task of the politician is not to govern but to supervise government, to take decisions on questions of principle which are submitted to him, and to maintain a close relation between public opinion and the process of administration. The actual business of government is the function of professional administrators and technical experts. . . . The Minister is concerned with policy. He is responsible for the efficiency of his Ministry, but he does not administer.

To overlook this conventional maxim of modern parliamentary government would be a natural temptation for a Minister who valued his own 'experience on the public service side of handling public business'. Yet if this maxim is applicable to the Ministerial direction of a single department, how much more so to the control of all functions of government in at least two huge Territories. When the Minister tried to administer the whole machine in detail, as well as making policy and maintaining public relations, the result was inevitable. He would engage in approving appointments of expatriate typists, awards of secondary school scholarships, and nominations of individual officers to attend training courses, while allowing the key department of his administration to remain disorganized and discouraged for a decade. He would meticulously check the details of an organization chart but fail to see the need for a more rational thinking and planning machine at Territory headquarters. He would create an elective House of Assembly and legislate for the appointment of some 'Under-Secretaries', but leave no sign of any coherent preparation whatever for the orderly evolution of a responsible indigenous Executive (see Lynch 1964). All this being said, however, a substantial administrative apparatus has been created; it has considerable momentum and potential; it has been given resources which by now are probably as great as it can effectively manage and as the Territory can absorb at its present stage of development. These are firm foundations.

APPENDIX

Government Employment in Papua and New Guinea at 30 June 1965

Public Service of the Territory—

Expatriate	5,290	
Indigenous	4,046	
		9,336
Administration Servants		5,596
(Indigenous routine, technical, and semi-skilled workers)		
Students and apprentices		1,362
Other employees (incl. police and warders)		13,059
Total, Territorial Administration		29,353
Commonwealth Departments and Instrumentalities—		
Department of Civil Aviation	342	
Department of Works	817	
Other agencies	150	
		1,309
Approximate Total, Government Employment		30,662

Note: Comparison of this table with the 1964 figures in the text shows that large-scale transfers of former Administration Servants to the public service under relaxed entrance conditions have radically altered the percentages criticized by the Foot Mission without altering anything else of substance.

11

The Expatriate Community

D. G. BETTISON

APART from the effects of any serious worsening of Indonesian-Australian relations, the future of the expatriate community in Papua-New Guinea over the next ten years rests to an important extent on its handling of relations with native people. The emphasis of this chapter is on the expatriate community in terms of the situation it is contending with inside Papua-New Guinea. It examines the nature of expatriate organization with particular reference to the position adopted by large-scale private enterprise. The chapter concludes with an examination of the conditions needed for the continued prosperity of expatriate interests in Papua-New Guinea.

The term expatriate denotes those residents of the Territory who feel an allegiance not only to the country itself but to Australia or some other overseas country as well. It includes the overwhelming majority of the 11,685 male and 8,277 female Europeans enumerated in the 1961 census. A small number of these say they are quite happy to spend the rest of their lives in Papua-New Guinea, and some even argue that, whatever conditions emerge, it will remain their home. The expatriate community includes some of the 2,319 full-blood Chinese and some of the 375 people from other Pacific islands as well as some of the 2,717 mixed-race people recorded in the 1961 census, though what proportion of these ethnic groups could rightly be so considered is unknown; certainly some Chinese deliberately attempt to adopt Australian status symbols such as sending their children for education to Australian Church schools. Similarly, some mixed-race persons have sought press publicity in their attempts to gain Australian citizenship.

The term 'expatriate' is less easily defined than 'non-indigenous', which has long been favoured by census officials and statisticians as a classificatory convenience to distinguish indigenous from non-indigenous people. At 30 June 1961 the non-indigenous people numbered 25,330 (Australia 1962:T.4). By 31 March 1964 the

number had risen to almost 28,000, about 1·4 per cent of the estimated total population of Papua-New Guinea. At a guess, the
expatriate part of the non-indigenous population might have been
24,000 in 1964.

The European came to Papua-New Guinea in the early years in
search of treasure or adventure, or with a sense of mission, or
perhaps even with a lust for power. Many Chinese were originally
introduced by the Germans in New Guinea as a source of labour.
The imperial powers' acceptance of political responsibility for
Papua and New Guinea introduced the expatriate civil servant and
simultaneously determined the distribution of status both within
the expatriate community and between it and native people. Up to
1964 the senior government officer remained the principal dignitary
in any locality where the expatriate community was found. During
the early decades of settlement the readily observable differences in
dress, language, technical skill, and customs between the expatriate
and native people were sufficient to keep the communities distinct.
Over the past fifteen years, however, the rapid development of
education, governmental institutions, co-operatives, etc., has removed many of these clear-cut differences and blurred the distinction between individuals. There is a small but growing number of
natives with qualifications better than or at least as good as those
of many expatriates. The grounds of distinction are decreasing,
particularly in towns.

Despite this, one recent American observer used the word
'caste' in describing the social distance between the expatriate and
native people (Watson 1964). For various reasons most expatriates
tend to hold themselves aloof from all but the most advanced
natives. This fact, however, should not necessarily be seen to mean
that they are unpopular or unwanted in the country, although
certain political implications may follow from its persistence. It
would be assuming a good deal to think that the expatriate's future
in the country is doomed on the basis of this alone.

Native people sense the separation but are concerned about it in
differing degrees. The country fellow, whose interest and aspirations are contained largely within his traditional culture, recognizes
a difference between himself and the expatriates he meets, but it is
of little concern to him. It is the younger, up-and-coming, more
educated person with aspirations towards expatriate positions,
income, and status who feels the difference most. Mr Lawrence
Waide, a medical student at the Papua Medical College and
recently returned from a conference in Perth, is reported as saying
that 'for the first time he had been able to see Australians as they
really were. The Australian community in Papua-New Guinea was
so close knit that it was possible for Papuans to live among them
and not really get to know them' (A.B.C. 1964).

In Papua-New Guinea the individual expatriate is conscious that

at least his way of living (and for most people the work they do
and the very purpose of their endeavours) is different from what it
would be in a society such as Australia's. Though some expatriates
are concerned only with what they can get from the country and
its people, almost all are aware of an element of personal
responsibility towards fellow expatriates *vis-à-vis* indigenous people.
Speaking of Australians collectively, the Prime Minister remarked:

> We regard ourselves as trustees for Papua-New Guinea. . . . We
> are not oppressors. On the contrary, our dominant aim is to raise
> the material, intellectual, social and political standards and self-
> reliance of the indigenous peoples, to a point at which they may
> freely and competently choose their own future (A.B.C. 1963).

Government policy over the past five years at least has been aimed
at removing any formal discrimination between the racial groups.
The enacting of the Discriminatory Practices Ordinance, 1963, the
opening of public bars to all races, and proposals to minimize
differences in school curricula for expatriate and local children are
examples of this trend.

But the legal suppression of discriminatory practices does not
necessarily encourage expatriates to mix with indigenous people. It
does little towards removing from the mind of expatriates the notion
that group loyalties demand they defend another expatriate's wrong-
doing against outsiders. Though this may be a general feature of
the relations of one closed society to another, it does little to further
the development of Australian ideals of equality both before the
law and in the application of principle to human behaviour
irrespective of race or creed. This is one aspect of the expatriate's
dilemma.

Subtle means of discrimination in public facilities have been
attempted since the passing of the 1963 Act. They have not always
gone unchallenged. The challenge has come both from native and
expatriate sources. Some expatriates are deeply and personally concerned over discriminatory acts. Such people are found mostly in
the educational services of the country, both inside and outside the
civil service. Their concern is motivated largely by personal
conviction and a belief that greater mixing is necessary to loosen
the close-knit bonds of the expatriate community. Their attitude is
that the future of expatriates generally is dependent upon the
creation of friendships across colour differences as much as upon
the opening of opportunities for advancement to native people.

It is important to distinguish increased mixing and expanded
opportunities for native people from reduction in the political and
administrative authority of expatriates, and the expatriates' superior
economic status and standards of living. An interconnection among
them is admitted, but expatriates show much confusion of thought
over the connection and its relative importance in determining the
future.

This distinction has more than academic significance. Papuans and New Guineans show little inclination to enhance the sense of cultural and political difference by suggesting, for example, that Australians 'go home', or indicating in any specific way that they are unwelcome in the country. This does not mean that such remarks have never been passed. They have been, but by individuals, and the same remark has been made of Sepiks by Tolais and reinforced by practical demonstrations on more than one occasion. The application of the attitude to expatriates is possibly outweighed by the number of genuine expressions of goodwill in public and private. This is certainly connected with the clearly expressed intention of Australia to grant political independence when indigenous leaders feel they can stand on their own feet. But the matter goes further. It reflects, at least at the present time, a suspicion on the part of the native people that the differences among themselves are as great as those between themselves and expatriates. It also reflects a hard-headed recognition by indigenous leaders of economic dependence and the advantages of defence relations with Australia.

The native's attitude to the expatriate reflects to some extent at least the nature of relations he had with other native groups—and still has today in many areas of the country. The small scale and closed nature of traditional societies, language differences, and the absence of superior political authority made for difficulty, uncertainty, and a lack of institutional persistence in inter-group relations. These were personal and individual. Papuan and New Guinean societies showed an ability to deal with each other without any pronounced assimilation of one group by another. The expatriate's enforcement of peace, his provision of expanded opportunities, and the introduction of new tools and techniques have gone some way in providing recognizable benefits, but he remains a member of a distinct and separate group. The handsome annual grant from the Commonwealth of Australia, though almost half of it goes into expatriate salaries, assists in providing proof that the expatriates' presence is beneficial. The speed of development is becoming demonstrable as ever-greater quantities of expatriate effort and money are devoted to extension and development work. If the speeches of indigenous members during the first meeting of the House of Assembly, when their requests for roads, hospitals, and schools poured out *ad nauseam*, are anything to go by, they lack nothing in awareness of what benefits might yet accrue! These speeches also reflected the shortfall between present efforts at development and the felt needs and aspirations of the people.

Though I know of no study on the point, I suspect that the indigenous Papua-New Guinea person tends more than most people to judge a man in terms of what he can do and what can be done through him. His judgment in the past was made largely within the confines of his own limited group. Modern influences are extending

his opportunities, and his basic approach to man is extended
accordingly. Though pronounced stereotypes and suspicions about
other tribal groups remain, the indigene's basic attitude towards
mankind persists. Preconceived notions about other individuals, in
terms of what they belong to or who their ancestors were, give
way quickly to an overriding estimate of others in terms of their
practical bearing on current human relations. In short the indigenes
are pragmatists; and this attitude is applied to the expatriate just as
to others. They are not unlike Australians in this.

At the practical level, the freedom of association with strangers
provided by Western forms of organization, such as shareholding
co-operatives, private companies, church membership, and sports
clubs, offers excellent opportunities for the practising of this basic
pragmatism. Not only by enlarging the scale upon which activity
can be carried out, but also as a means of making effective their
view of others and of mankind in general, the Western form of
association is likely to prove a powerful instrument. The committee,
as a technique of decision-making and of reconciling different
points of view, is likely to prove important as soon as the advantages of co-ordination are perceived.

The expatriates do not attempt to justify their superior status by
asserting a mystical prowess or claiming supernatural qualities
possessed by them alone. In this respect they differ markedly from
the Europeans of South Africa. The Australian artisan or clerk will
complain about natives working under him—and often in not the
most savoury of language—and may occasionally say 'it will be
years before they do a job properly'; but there is little evidence of
any fallacious theorizing over the innate qualities, or lack of them,
of local people. Differences of performance are acknowledged to
exist, but the answer to the problems to which they give rise is
seen to be in more and better training and education. The individual
expatriate has an easy and fairly adjustable approach to race
relations, and the almost complete lack of expatriate organizations
clustering around particular points of view on 'the native question'
or the place of the expatriate in the country's future emphasizes the
personal nature of decisions on race relations. Such a situation
certainly gives the government a much freer hand to advance its
egalitarian policies. As will be seen later in this chapter, it is certain
kinds of large-scale expatriate associations that most clearly require
to modify their terms for the participation of indigenous people.

The individual expatriate has placidly accepted the government's
intention to remove discrimination by legal means. He is aware that
political independence is coming shortly. No expatriate organizations have been formed deliberately to oppose these policies.
Reassured by his belief that he could leave if conditions became too
unpleasant, the expatriate is assessing the situation largely in
individual terms. His interpretation is influenced by the ease with

employers remarked that over 50 per cent do not renew their contracts. The secretary of Burns Philp (New Guinea) Ltd said it was his experience that if a man returned for a second contract he was likely to stay indefinitely. An important reason for the non-renewal of contracts is said to be isolation and dissatisfaction with the lack of public amenities and entertainment.

The short-term resident, new to the country, probably arrives with an open but receptive mind regarding the type of relation he will establish with indigenous people. He quickly learns that the ways of life and standards of the expatriate and most of the indigenous communities are widely different. His accommodation is likely to be in an expatriate residential area. It is convenient and not very expensive to employ an indigenous servant. Piece by piece his behaviour comes to conform to expatriate standards. His increasing involvement with expatriates encourages his acceptance of their reasons for their behaviour and standards *vis-à-vis* others. Though his personal attitude to indigenous people may remain very friendly, congenial, and even egalitarian in principle, the day-to-day behaviour he adopts marks him off as an expatriate in the eyes both of his fellows and of the indigenous people. On occasion, however, some short-term residents (who are usually single) may associate with indigenous women in conventional and illicit relationships—a factor often leading to inter-racial difficulties.

Considered as a discrete group, the expatriate community believes in its own superiority over all other groups. The dominant position of its members in all major institutions of Papua-New Guinea society, its higher income and privileges, and the educational and technical superiority of its members confirm this belief. Yet the belief gives rise to twinges of conscience. Aspects of religious teaching, values generated by other sources of knowledge, the Australian notion of egalitarianism, and the particular role of the expatriate in Papua-New Guinea impinge on the conscience of many expatriates. Yet the pricks of conscience need to be repressed in the face of day-to-day relations with expatriate friends. The personal cost of resisting the accepted patterns of behaviour needs to be weighed. Support for those encouraging change is not always readily forthcoming, whether the direction of suggested change is towards or away from closer relations with native people. Inter-racial behaviour is constantly in the forefront of expatriate thought.

Inter-racial social mixing takes place in Papua-New Guinea under something of a strain. It is easiest and most natural when members of both racial groups acknowledge the importance of an egalitarian philosophy in its own right. They gain confidence from the fact that non-discrimination is government policy and that they are bringing into being the state of affairs that ideally should follow from such a policy. There is, too, the feeling on both sides that at a mixed gathering some insight into the workings of the other's mind may be obtained. Something may be learned; some clearer understanding of the other's motives and attitudes may be achieved. Yet inter-racial mixing is hardly spontaneous, if only because the differences in living standards, the different network of friendships, and the varying degrees of personal involvement in public problems and national ideals inhibit a free, emotional expression of unity and common purpose.

The topics of conversation at racially mixed gatherings are themselves illuminating. They are most frequently on serious issues. There is little chit-chat about trivial matters. The people most often discussed are not friends held in common but rather people holding important offices or participating in important events. This is explicable in terms of the things the parties have in common. Their daily round of living in separate communities limits the range of mutual contacts. Yet this limitation emphasizes the importance of even the most trivial form of contact and communication. Inform-ation obtained and the opinions of native leaders expressed at racially mixed social gatherings, large and small, can markedly influence the decisions taken by expatriates in the formal meetings of established institutions.

EXPATRIATE ORGANIZATION

In New Guinea the indigenous culture's organizational techniques did not include that form of long-term, specifically purposeful association typified by the Western company or voluntary welfare association. The co-operation of members, themselves voluntarily participating through formally agreed upon articles of association; the election of office-bearers by vote; the recognition of legal personality and liability of members, these are among the features of Western organization that offer advantages for modern develop-ment over the organizational forms of indigenous societies. Such associations can be highly influential in the process of social change.

The government recognized their importance as instruments of capital accumulation and public control when it fostered Native Local Government Councils, Native Co-operative Societies, the Tolai Cocoa Project, and similar associations for indigenous people. Largely by a policy of non-interference, the government did not discourage the growth of companies among expatriates. Its most serious attempt at interfering in expatriate associations was the introduction of income tax—a matter immediately challenged in the courts. In prescribing racially mixed Town and District Advisory Councils and most recently by facilitating the indigenous majority in the House of Assembly the government introduced the principle of extending racially mixed associations. It has amended its former policy of exclusively native local government councils and co-operatives by opening membership to expatriates also.

Most sporting clubs spontaneously open membership to all races.

Social and recreational clubs are more restrictive—thereby embarrassing ex-servicemen's clubs at least—and tend to use the right of exclusion on grounds of race, culture, and class. With some exceptions the small-scale, non-power-oriented club or association does not have formal provisions to obstruct multi-racial membership. Cost of membership and lack of interest are cogent reasons for membership to be confined to a single race.

It is as employees that most expatriates are linked to large-scale organizations. Whether as an officer in the Administration, an employee of one or other of the large trading or plantation companies, or a missionary occupying the managerial position in church affairs, expatriates are part of organizations very much larger than any so far attempted, perhaps even contemplated, by local people. With the exception of the individual settler, the European or Chinese small retail store-owner, builder, or business-owner, the expatriate serves the interest of well organized commerce, plantations, airlines, religious missions, or government. Many of the smaller organizations openly admit their dependence, in one way or another, on large-scale private enterprise, and all except the missions acknowledge their basic dependence on government and its policies.

Official statistics give little indication of the distribution of the expatriate community among government, private enterprise, and missionary organizations. An examination of relevant reports suggests that the Territory Administration in 1965 employed about 5,300 expatriates. Expatriates in Commonwealth departments and instrumentalities in the Territory numbered in round figures 1,250. Thus the government generally has approximately 6,550 expatriates in its employ.

Non-indigenous persons engaged in mission activities at 30 June 1963 numbered 2,556, of whom 1,365 were men and 1,200 women (*N.G.A.R.* No. 76 (1964):App. xxv, p. 300, and *P.A.R.* No. 77 (1964): App. xxv, p. 263). It is difficult to estimate the number of expatriates engaged in private enterprises; but if by 1964 the number of non-indigenous persons outside the work force numbered 12,000[1] and the total non-indigenous population in June 1964 was 28,000, then some 6,500 or 42 per cent of the work force was engaged in private economic enterprise of some sort.

Private enterprise takes many forms, from individual landholders on properties of a few acres to large-scale companies operating very mixed businesses including plantations, shipping, merchandising, garages, hotels, as well as wholesale distributing. The three largest distributive companies are Burns Philp (New Guinea) Ltd, W. R.

[1] This figure assumes that the proportion of persons outside the work force enumerated in the 1961 census could be applied to the 1964 estimate of the non-indigenous population. The figure probably slightly overstates the number outside the work force in 1964.

Carpenter Ltd, and Steamships Trading Co. Ltd. All have sub-
sidiaries. Steamships Trading Co. is registered and managed entirely
in the Territory, though it is heavily dependent on capital from
overseas. Its management is entirely European.

The Territory Administration has adopted a policy of increasing
indigenous participation in the civil service and has provided
varied educational and technical services to raise indigenous standards and abilities. Its long-term aim is the granting of political self-
determination. Similarly, a number of missions in Papua-New
Guinea have handed over senior positions to indigenous people, and
in the case of the former London Missionary Society, a transfer to
indigenous control and the formation of the Papua Ekalesia Church
has been accomplished. Many other missions are increasing their
training facilities for indigenous people.

It is in private economic enterprise that expatriates practise exclusion of indigenous people most strictly and widely. The need to
make a profit is undoubtedly a serious factor in their thinking about
increasing indigenous participation. Directors of large businesses
claim their profits are not excessive by Australian standards. They
fear that any reduction in efficiency through employing indigenous
people at supposedly uneconomic rates of pay, or investment of
capital in questionable indigenous enterprises, could speedily place
them in difficulties. In a letter explaining his company's policy
regarding staff, the managing director of Burns Philp (New Guinea)
Ltd said,

> Our executives in Papua-New Guinea are in precisely the same
> position i.e. they are employees who have climbed within the
> structure, and this process is open to any local inhabitant with
> the necessary education, experience and ability behind him. We
> will even train any prospect for these positions, provided we see
> a chance of the prospect being able to advance.

A similar view is expressed by the management of other large
companies. However, its implementation is a difficult matter.

Some of the practical considerations that influence the low status
of natives in private companies are the difficulties of promotion,
due to the native people's status in the community at large and the
senior positions held by expatriates in the firm; the conduct and
behaviour of the native people themselves; the paucity of in-service
training facilities and the absence of governmental incentives to
encourage private enterprise to train and educate; the wide range
of skills required by large-scale expatriate enterprise as it is presently
organized.

The highest wage paid to a native in one large Port Moresby
company in 1964, a man with very long service, was approximately
£800 per annum. The presence of expatriate employees, themselves
with long service, makes difficult the promoting of non-expatriates

to positions equal to or better than expatriates', unless particularly good grounds are evident to all. Private companies are very conscious of their dependence on expatriates in sub-managerial capacities. Despite the cost of their salaries, services, and recruitment, management prefers them to indigenous employees; any move likely to cause resentment among expatriates is avoided.

The manager of the Port Moresby Freezing Co. expressed the view that the native people expect to become managers before they have learnt the lower levels of work. He said that they have not yet learnt to work hard, and that the paternalistic approach of government to indigenous people has contributed to this. As an example, he quoted the decision of the Administration to label the heads of small co-operative societies 'directors', their clerk 'secretary' or 'manager', etc., which had given a false impression, he argued, of their abilities and powers. In his view, such a situation gives the native people false hopes and misguided aspirations.

Attempts have been made to place native people in more responsible positions than they held four years ago. Steamships Trading Co. and Burns Philp (New Guinea) Ltd are considering offering long-service indigenous employees the right to join superannuation schemes. The difficulties lie not so much in company policy as in the absence of life tables on which to assess insurance risks. The British New Guinea Development Co. has attempted to use Papuans in responsible positions on its rubber estates. As explained by Mr B. Fairfax-Ross, C.B.E., indigenous employees have difficulty in exerting authority over their own people at the level of organization demanded in large-scale enterprise. On small coastal vessels or small estates employing perhaps up to ten labourers, indigenous supervision is effective. When in port, small, locally-crewed ships come under expatriate inspection and control. In large-scale enterprises, authority can be wielded by a local foreman if an expatriate is in the vicinity, but it breaks down quickly in his absence. Local people educated enough to keep the required statistics are, it is thought by management, too young to be respected. Younger men appear to be particularly frightened of controlling 'bush' or primitive people in the labour line, while expatriates tend to prefer them. The present use of the Highland Labour Scheme to obtain labour from the more backward areas of the country probably encourages the continued use of expatriates. Indigenous supervisors are also said to care little for the health and conditions of the men they control and in general to show irresponsibility. The managing director of Burns Philp (New Guinea) Ltd remarked that it was not the wages paid to indigenous drivers that counted but the cost of the damage done to the company vehicles they drove. Businessmen argued that the natives' lack of diligence and apparent confusion between the demands of regular attendance at work and those of the traditional society's obligations to relatives make them generally poor employees. These circumstances pointedly raise the question of their economic value under the present system of large-scale organization.

The attempts of management, limited as they have been, to provide in-service training have been unsuccessful. The larger companies have tried courses for particular non-expatriate employees, but they were poorly attended. Apparently no inquiry was made into the reasons and few active steps at training are presently being taken. Yet this is clearly what must be done both to improve skills and to increase native participation in private companies. The high cost of expatriate labour should, one would think, encourage management to be active in this regard. The managing directors of large Port Moresby companies were unanimous in their view that it was the duty of government to train and educate. Private enterprise could not afford to carry overheads of this nature, particularly following the introduction of income tax. In the interviews held with managers, there was apparent an almost bitter feeling towards the government's ability to hold the native trainees it produces from its own courses. Managers complained that few natives were willing to work for private enterprise and that promising students from high schools were earmarked for definite postings with the Administration. Higher wages and career opportunities in private enterprise were not seen by the managers to be a reasonable way of competing for scarce resources.

A further difficulty for private enterprise is said to be the variety of skills for which training would be required. The range of interests of companies like Burns Philp (New Guinea) Ltd and Steamships Trading Co. is very wide. It includes plantations, garages, hotels, shipping, wholesaling, retailing of most everyday commodities, timber, sheet metal working, etc. The training for skills in this variety of interests is viewed by management as an overwhelming task. Apparently no study has yet been made of which skills are most readily acquired by native people or where their advancement would be resented least by expatriate employees.

The present inertia in training and promotion of native people is a serious matter. The country's development needs private enterprise. It would be detrimental to all concerned if native people came to resent expatriate activity for private profit. The limited possibilities offered native people for promotion in the larger companies and the natives' unwillingness or inability to participate through shareholding are likely to encourage any tendency on the natives' part to view the expatriates as alien and exploitive. As the government has seen fit to limit the free entry to the country of expatriates on political grounds, it might serve a purpose also to limit entry to certain grades of skill. Tax rebates for the cost of training indigenous staff in the grades of skill to be restricted would help to offset the additional cost to the company concerned. Government action of this nature might well give business managers the opportunity to implement their professed policy without being themselves the subject of resentment from expatriate staff.

Promotion inside the firm is only one way of increasing the participation of natives in this form of expatriate organization. It is also possible to provide opportunities to indigenous entrepreneurs by extending credit to them and offering advice on the management of their young businesses. Such a move would mean a change in the role of the large companies. It would involve limiting the range of their present interests and emphasizing the wholesaling, manufacturing, and similar activities where their greater organizing skill and capital would be an advantage. When asked about this possibility one manager replied, 'We will not put money into a project we cannot control; that is company policy.' Examples were quoted where small entrepreneurs had failed and money had been lost. If the only function of private enterprise is to make money, this policy is justified; but under the conditions evolving in Papua-New Guinea it is shortsighted. The role of expatriate private enterprise in Papua-New Guinea is clearly more than this.

The management of private enterprise feels personally proud of its contribution to the development of the Territory. Directors of two companies mentioned that in the case of one, in the eighteen months to December 1963, no less than £853,000, and in the case of the other, in the two years to mid-1964, £670,000, had been invested in the Territory from profits or as new money. This, they felt, compared favourably with the smaller investments of recent new enterprises that had been given considerable publicity. They emphasized, too, the long-term interest their companies had had in the Territory, and expressed the hope that their contribution would continue.

In addition to evolving practical means of increasing native participation and interest in private enterprise as a method of organizing, large private companies need in the future to evolve new relations with the government. The era of mutual disregard of each other's activities will increasingly give way to a time when mutual co-operation and understanding are important. The increasing part played by Papuans and New Guineans in all aspects of government will make it increasingly necessary for expatriate private enterprise to heed indigenous points of view, use indigenous potential at all levels, understand indigenous fears and aspirations, and incorporate indigenous people into its organization. One managing director, when asked why his company had not found it expedient to appoint one or two native leaders to its board of directors, replied, 'It would be merely a political act and hypocrisy to do so.' Yet political leaders need practical experience of the problems, and also to see for themselves the advantages to the country, of expatriate private enterprise. Development, as well as profit, is everywhere dependent on the privileges and laws of the country at any given time.

Many indigenous members of the House of Assembly are intensely interested in the workings of big business as well as in its contribution to development. Their interest stems as much from the emphasis their own culture places on the acquisition of wealth as from suspicion of 'unfair' means expatriate enterprise may adopt to acquire it. The more sophisticated members are now more concerned over the latter, but the interest is widespread.

Managers feel strongly that changes introduced by the government in the past five years have been too radical and hasty. In particular the urban wage agreement and the encouragement of workers' associations were, it is argued, quite uncalled for: the people had neither asked for them nor wanted them. Managers favoured a recommendation of the Report of the Tripartite Mission on Labour Matters, 1960. (The Mission consisted of representatives of government, employers, and unions.) This brief report recommended, *inter alia*:

> In short, just as we think it desirable that there should be no legislation about industrial organisations as such at this stage, so we think no legislative provision should be made at this stage determining the form of industrial relations machinery.

The Mission recommended the matter be re-examined in about two years' time by another, similar, tripartite mission. Instead the government went ahead with industrial legislation. Since 1961 the urban cash wage has been established by negotiation and has been extended to five towns. Eight workers' associations have been set up in the Territory with a membership approximating 10,000. Though it may be true that indigenous people did not press for these changes in 1960, it appears that they have made some use of them since.

Indigenous people are slowly coming to understand that a powerful means of improving their conditions is organization. The government has seen fit to provide through legislation machinery likely to direct labour disputes into reconciliatory processes comparable with those in Australia. These processes, if seen to be effective by native people, might come to be viewed as alternatives to more drastic means of ensuring their participation in economic enterprises. The extreme forms of expropriation of foreign assets that can be quoted from Burma, Indonesia, and Africa are constantly in the minds of expatriate managers. One director said he considered ultimate expropriation was inevitable. While it is likely, in the years ahead, that the conflict between management and worker will remain largely between expatriate and native, the absence of a rabid nationalist movement in Papua-New Guinea may affect the expatriate's position. If managements could genuinely demonstrate that their decisions were not taken on racial grounds, the chances of avoiding expropriation after political independence would be greatly enhanced. The successful examples of readjustment made by large-scale private enterprise, such as the United Africa Group in West Africa, should be studied in good time (United Africa Company 1963).

Most sections of urban expatriates are critical of the big companies. All manner of innuendo, gibe, and semi-humorous comment passes in everyday chatter. Expatriate employees feel hardest the prices they have to pay for imported goods. They resent paying 10s. for a cabbage they feel could be grown for less locally. Imported oranges, at 1s. each for large ones, seem exorbitantly priced when they will grow in Papua-New Guinea. On the other hand, the management of big retail firms argue that their prices are competitive and fair. Small independent businessmen quote examples of the effects of their dependence on established shipping lines which are in turn coupled to retailing and wholesaling concerns. Freight charges appear to be exorbitant. Small concerns get little in the way of commercial franchise and view themselves as unable to compete fairly in any significant line of trade with the large organizations with interests in almost everything.

These are the complaints one hears spoken of: they are what people are thinking. Whether or not they are valid would require a major examination. But expatriate managers ardently seek to avoid publicity. The public press rarely mentions their affairs and is uncritical of them. Managers are concerned more about defending private enterprise as a principle and mentioning in platitudinous terms the significance of its contribution to the country than about quoting facts and examples to prove their efforts. Chambers of Commerce rather than individual firms are thought to be the better instrument for defending their activities. But it is a defence, rather than a promotion of their position and potential.

At the present time, both the promotion of private enterprise as a method of organizing and the integration of native with expatriate efforts are most evident in small-scale, rural enterprises. Though it is not everywhere the case, there are examples of very close and intimate relations between expatriate and native landholders; the managers of some plantations, country stores and other small enterprises are similarly placed. Advice, the lending of equipment, common processing and marketing facilities, common membership of farmers' associations, etc. are examples of a recent growth in partnership among people with common interests. The co-operation is often face to face and concerned with everyday problems. It often rests upon individual regard and affection. Neither natives nor landholding expatriates show any inclination to frown on private profit honestly and efficiently obtained. There exist no powerful political parties or philosophical schools demanding the sociali-

zation of the economy on principle. The embryo trade union movement has not yet considered the matter.

During the past ten years, government has implemented a policy
aimed at the settlement of both natives and expatriates on small
farms. In many cases the farms of expatriates have common boundaries with those of natives. Many farmers of both racial groups
come from distant parts and conditions appear good for the sharing
of advice and facilities and for mutual co-operation. But expatriates
received considerably larger areas of land, and the racial differentiation in the size of loans in favour of expatriates amounts to as
much as 33:1—a maximum loan to expatriates of £25,000 as
compared with £750 to natives. The differential might temporarily
have passed notice had government policy in general moved in the
direction of encouraging social and political differentiation in the
status of the races. Government policy's actual trend towards
equality of the races has highlighted the differences in the scale of
its assistance. Discontent among some native farmers is already
evident. It is made worse by the failure of some expatriates to
develop the land allotted them while some natives are seeking more
land to develop. Despite these difficulties there are signs that
farmers are working out a common approach to their mutual
problems.

The possibilities of inter-racial co-operation among these farmers
contrast with the rather sharp division of interest found in other
areas between native villagers and the large company-owned
plantations in their midst. These plantations commonly have exclusive marketing channels and sources of supply. Their capitalization, order, and efficiency contrast with native subsistence agriculture and limited attempts at cash cropping near their boundaries.
The contact of native neighbours with these plantations is often
confined to envious eyes looking over land that once was theirs, to
the possibility of employment at rates of pay they often scorn, and
possibly to purchases from trade stores at prices they suspect.
Though it is not everywhere the case, plantation management often
feels it can disregard the local pressures its presence and self-
contained organization give rise to. It feels it need pay little
attention to local native aspirations or the mutual resolution of
common agricultural problems.

Despite these difficulties, throughout Papua-New Guinea in
general there is emerging in both racial groups an increasing awareness of common interests. In both town and country, people of all
races are experiencing common problems and difficulties. There is
a common aspiration—to develop the country and its people. Native
people in all but the remotest areas see something worth having in
expatriate material wealth, standard of living and, in some areas,
methods of organization. Their wish is to participate in what the
expatriate has and what he is doing. Active membership by both

races of the smaller organizations appears to be increasing, though measurement of it is difficult. Recently some small business companies with extensive native shareholdings have been registered. Leadership in small organizations generally is still largely expatriate, but native participation in all forms is often encouraged. On the other side of the coin, when membership of exclusively native co-operative societies is opened to expatriates, and when they come to play a significant part in Local Government Councils, the area of mutual co-operation will be substantially widened.

Recently natives have come to carry increasing responsibilities in government. The expatriate has yielded many points of power he formerly controlled. Full control of their country's affairs by the native people is the aim of the Australian government. The problem of the next ten years is to bring about much more extensive participation by native people in large organizations presently dominated unyieldingly by expatriates. The size of these organizations involves them in problems of communication and co-ordination of staff and activity. Their staff must be responsible; otherwise, large sections of their organizations, and hence the whole, are threatened with collapse through inefficiency. The running of the country's services depends very much on them. There are thus good reasons, other than threats to profit margins, why increasing native participation is resisted. Yet the increasing involvement of natives in power positions of government will pose a threat to the independent attitude of expatriates in their large organizations. The immediate task is to remove the conditions likely to encourage the growth of an attitude among native political leaders which rejects as unacceptable large expatriate organization because it persists in maintaining an exclusiveness and independence in activities critically important to the running of the country as a whole. Exclusion and independence were acceptable in the tribal era. They are no longer.

Expatriates feel strongly the presence of large numbers of local people around them. Differences in language, dress, and custom exaggerate their fears. They sense the potential for ill will their privileges, standards, and independence might generate. There is good reason for them to understand the world around them in racial terms. The uniqueness of their expatriate position further encourages processes of thought which lie along racial rather than functional lines. They tend to group people in racial, tribal, or cultural contexts rather than functional and associational ones. Race, expatriateness, and sexual fears are dominant overtones in their thought processes about the native people. Yet despite these overtones, most expatriates are disposed to accept native people for what they are, or offer them equality and a fair go. There are few fallacious rationalizations about the nature of man. They admit their authoritarian position is temporary. This is the nature of the ambivalence, the expression of paradox, in the Papuan-New Guinean situation, that in turn provides its opportunities.

Government policy has recently been aimed deliberately at removing the grounds of racial discrimination. It has taken a timely lead in this regard. Though removing many forms of discrimination it has not removed expatriate privileges. These tend to emphasize the specialness of the expatriate's position and cause jealousy. The civil servant's overseas service is a ground for a special allowance; his leaving the service on grounds of redundancy is considered to warrant a special pension or grant; his training involves special courses on government policy and the handling of native people. Local private investors—most frequently the small man rather than the foreign-based company—make pleas for special assurance to cover political risks on new investment, and abnormally high profits are justified on the grounds of excessive risks. The missionary's special task is bringing to local people the Christian faith and its particular denominational attributes. It is a task pursued by altruistic men in the service of God.

In expatriate terms there are justifications for all these positions, but they are exclusive to the expatriate and mark him off from indigenous people.

The expatriate community over the next ten years is faced by the need further to remodel its relations with native people. Some sections, most notably large-scale business, will need to make drastic changes in their approach, attitude, and method of organizing their affairs. The decision to mix and co-operate with native people can be made only in the minds of individual expatriates. It is a personal decision and a personal challenge. It has been encouraged by the lead of government. In many spheres of thought and activity an acute sense of fair play and a willingness to ensure a fair go for all are shared by natives and expatriates alike. Although there is not always agreement on what is 'fair', there appears to be no substantial reason why co-operation cannot be extensive, or unity achieved, and successful means of developing the country worked out through mutual give and take. But time is running out on the expatriate community both in local and international terms. The opportunities are still there, the necessary conditions appear to be present; the question is whether the expatriate, individually and through his organizations, can continue to adjust his ways to take advantage of them.

12

The Advance to Responsible Government

R. S. PARKER

POLITICAL ADVANCEMENT: THE NEW GUINEA CONTEXT

AUSTRALIA's legal and moral responsibility in New Guinea is for a country comparable in size and population to the Dominion of New Zealand. In practice this responsibility is shouldered on Australia's behalf by a single Commonwealth Minister and Department (who also manage the Northern Territory and some others) working through a very small Territorial public service (see Chapter 10) and by a few hundred Australians and other expatriates in missions and similar avenues of private service.

The problems of political development in New Guinea are urgent and challenging—largely because they were never squarely faced by Australian governments until after World War II, and now have to be faced in a context of impatient international pressures and accelerating economic and social change, among local communities which in many areas are rather nearer to the stone age than to the nuclear age. The majority of the people still live by subsistence agriculture in small hamlets, with comparatively recent conscious-ness of a wider world beyond their immediate contacts through warfare or trade.[1] They are separated, as well, by language barriers; few adults know English, and the rest can communicate, if at all, only through the limited media of Melanesian Pidgin (mainly in the Trust Territory but steadily spreading), Police Motu (in Papua), or one of the 'mission vernaculars'. Within each social group the idea of a stable, impersonal political authority is traditionally unknown. As they are what the anthropologists call 'segmented societies', co-ordinated Territory-wide political activity faces tremendous obstacles. Indigenous political institutions are inadequate both in

[1] For example, an elected member from the Highlands, in his first speech in the House of Assembly, said: 'I never knew before that Port Moresby was on the mainland of New Guinea, and I thought that Port Moresby was beyond on another island' (H.A. Deb. I, i, 35).

243

scale and function as a basis for a modern polity. The number of
people who have received any systematic Western technical or
agricultural education is extremely small. There are few indigenes
with any executive or administrative experience beyond the exercise
of minor police functions at the village level.

These facts pose formidable dilemmas for the policy-makers of
Australia as the trustee power administering the Trust Territory of
New Guinea and the colonial power 'owning' Papua. They might
not want to impose a single 'foreign' system of government upon
New Guinea as a whole. But the alternative might be to leave this
great region fragmented and rudderless. And since by universal
consent it is headed for self-government in some form, and has no
suitable political institutions of its own, what more natural than to
offer it the only form of government that Australians know well?
The policy-makers might not want to insist that New Guineans be
imbued with the same ideals, values, and conceptions as Australians.
But could Australia afford to leave her island neighbours to embrace
potentially hostile conceptions—either of their own accord or at the
behest of some other external power? The Australian Administration
might want to encourage spontaneous political aspirations and
organization among the New Guinea people. But it is hard to induce
spontaneous receptivity to an introduced plant; and it is equally
hard though of course desirable to create sufficiently sensitive communications with the local people to notice and exploit the natural
growing points in their own barely nascent political consciousness.

Whether or not there is any theoretical solution to these dilemmas,
in practice Australian policy since the last war has assumed that
Eastern New Guinea must move, or be moved, towards some form
of self-determination, through increasing degrees of representative
government at the local and national levels, culminating in a responsible Cabinet facing an elected Assembly. In this context the
more 'advanced' of the New Guinea people, appearing (at least) to
be grateful for the personal security and social improvements that
accompany Australian rule, and anxious to please in return, do
their best in a bewildered way to play some part in the exotic
institutions proffered by the Australians. At the same time, but
beneath the surface appearances, and so far much more slowly,
they are beginning to develop a distinct political life, consciousness,
and organization of their own. The remainder of this chapter seeks
to analyse New Guinea political advancement under these two
broad headings of Australian measures and autonomous New
Guinea responses.

Australian measures for political advancement

A rounded policy of political advancement comprises many elements,
of which the provision of formal government institutions is only
one. Those which are relevant in New Guinea include: general

education in the European culture; the conduct of new institutions in the society as examples for the people; providing local leaders with opportunities for observing 'model' institutions abroad; creating new institutions in which the people can be represented and practise responsibility for themselves; formal instruction for their leaders in the new political and administrative processes; providing the people with informal channels for consultation, advice, and complaint; and, finally, facilitating any efforts the people may make to develop forms of political activity of their own.

General education. In the nineteenth century it was assumed that a literate public was a necessary condition for responsible democracy. This would have been an impossible condition to set as a prerequisite for the self-government which has been claimed so imperiously for so many illiterate people in the present century. The inevitability of self-government preceding 'capacity' for it, in this as in other respects, has been accepted in the case of New Guinea, where universal suffrage and a representative legislature have been granted long before universal education is in sight.

The main reason why education is lagging so far behind political advancement is that until after World War II the Australian Administrations had done very little directly or indirectly about native schooling. At the beginning of the 1950s there were about 100,000 indigenous children receiving primary education, and these almost entirely in mission schools and attaining a rudimentary level of bare literacy; there was not one indigene receiving secondary or tertiary education of any kind.

The policy developed by post-war governments has been, in the first place (to quote Mr Paul Hasluck when Minister for Territories),

> to establish a broad primary school base so that the development of the country rests upon a wide distribution of education. This will permit a broad stream to enter secondary and tertiary education thus obviating the creation of a narrow educated elite.

The expansion of Administration schools has been accompanied by efforts to raise the standards of mission schools to levels recommended and recognized by Department of Education inspectors. Figures given in Chapter 6 show that between one-quarter and one-third of the native children of primary school age 'attend' schools of recognized standard.

The beginnings of native secondary education came in the mid-1950s. In 1954 the Administration began awarding up to twenty scholarships a year to enable promising native students to attend secondary schools in Australia (Chapter 6 outlines the development of post-primary schooling in the Territory). The progress of secondary education has been hindered, however, less by inadequacy of provision for it than by the return of many primary pupils to their villages before completing their schooling, and by the attraction of many others from secondary school prematurely into employment— including until recently employment by the Administration itself. The progress of all schooling has also been limited by one severely restricting bottleneck: the difficulty of recruiting and training teachers.

As for tertiary education, a number of young native people have been trained, some at Suva and some in the Territory, as assistant medical practitioners and medical assistants, and a number of others in a few agricultural and technical vocations. No indigene had entered a university before 1960; by the end of 1964 there were about a dozen native undergraduates, all at Australian universities, where the first New Guinean graduated in 1964 and one other completed his course at the end of 1965. In April 1962 the Minister announced plans for setting up a university college in the Territory 'not later than 1966'. Statistical forecasts suggested that in that year there might be about 100 students from secondary schools eligible to matriculate—and perhaps 200 in 1968. In 1965 the government took steps to establish an independent university at Port Moresby, on lines recommended in the report of the Commission on Higher Education in New Guinea which was submitted to the Minister in March 1964.

The ministerial announcement in 1962 coincided with the report of the Fifth United Nations Visiting Mission to the Trust Territory, under Sir Hugh Foot's chairmanship, which criticized what it called the imbalance in the education system and the diversion of young people from school into more or less menial employment.

> The main reason why the present education programme is inadequate [said the report] is that it pays little or no attention to the need for higher education . . . [The Minister] noted that in five years it is estimated that the enrolment in post-primary and secondary schools will rise to 10,000. But there is no indication at all of how many students will be completing their secondary education, let alone how many will be taking and completing university courses (U.N. Trusteeship Council 1962: para. 198).

It added that if such a state of affairs continued, it would be impossible to develop the standards of professional, administrative, and political leadership which are vital to any territory preparing for self-government.

If Australia's belated start with an educational programme of any kind is, as suggested earlier, the main reason for the present shortfall, there are also critics, including previous U.N. visitors, who agree with the Foot Mission's view that the lag in higher education could have been less if the programme *since* 1950 had not concentrated so long on the 'broad primary base' but had diverted resources earlier to the development of secondary and tertiary institutions.

The former Minister (Mr Hasluck) made two replies to this which are not entirely consistent. The first has already been quoted: it seems to imply that he has deliberately held back higher education to enable all groups to start on an equal footing with primary education—this to prevent the creation of a narrow *élite*. There could indeed be seeds of serious future conflict in such an uneven rate of advancement of different regional and tribal groups as would enable some of them to secure an early monopoly of positions of power and influence. There is a good deal of regional chauvinism in New Guinea, and an overriding sense of nationhood has scarcely begun to rival this. However, these are forces which are hardly likely to be influenced by a schooling programme. Even now, 'uniform educational development' would be a misnomer for a school system which is inevitably denser and more advanced in the longer controlled parts of the country. Moreover, it is questionable whether primary schooling, as distinct from, say, agricultural extension work embracing adults, is worth starting in regions where the results are quickly dissipated in the bush. It would seem more realistic for the Administration to recognize that higher education should be provided as rapidly as possible for those ready to benefit by it: government cannot circumvent those accidents of location or history which result in some peoples being ready earlier than others.

The Minister's other defence of his policy was that the prerequisite for producing a university matriculant is twelve years of primary and secondary schooling even in Australia; this could hardly be reduced in New Guinea where students are learning in a foreign language about an alien culture. Hence, given the beginning of Administration primary schooling in the late 1940s, and of secondary schooling at the appropriate time about 1954-5, it would be difficult to expect the production of any matriculants earlier than about the present time, merely by devoting more resources to post-primary education. This was the Minister's more practical argument, though it seems to contradict his first argument to the extent that it suggests no deliberate slowing of any part of the programme. There could be disputing about the 'more or less' and the might-have-beens of the facts and figures of the last dozen years. And it is arguable that planning for university education should have begun some years earlier than it did.

None of these arguments alters the fact, however, that the supply of professional, administrative, and political leaders with higher technical or university education in the next ten years will certainly be much below what we would conventionally expect in a country taking on political and economic independence in that time. The more radical critics of present policy believe that such conventional expectations are unrealistic; that to define preconditions for self-determination means only to postpone it indefinitely; and that policy, instead, should be geared to a specified 'target date for independence'. The adoption of targets (which need not be publicized) would indeed be a salutary spur to the setting and testing of planned priorities for development. The Foot Mission's view that an educated *élite* is 'vital to any territory preparing for self-government' underlines the urgency of crash programmes (to tight timetables) of higher education and training. In practice, political change is certain to outrun the spread of formal education.

Displaying examples of new institutions. Unfamiliar social institutions are subtle phenomena, not to be easily understood by physical observation of their outward and visible signs. Any new visitor to New Guinea is reminded of this truth. New Guinea natives, like other people, have a lively curiosity, and it is a common experience, particularly in the remoter districts, to see a group of twenty or thirty native people, mostly men, standing all day outside the office of the patrol station, doing nothing but gaze intently at the mysterious comings and goings, shufflings of paper, conferences, pounding of typewriters, and other magical activities of the little band of Europeans within. Similar groups can be seen congregated around airfields, schoolhouses, and anywhere that Europeans pursue their inscrutable concerns. The gap between this kind of 'observation' and real comprehension has sometimes been dramatized by the rise of forms of cargo cult, in which the people imitated the outward forms of European behaviour without appreciating their real significance. Examples are numerous: drilling with wooden 'rifles'; setting up imitation 'offices'; planting shade trees and waiting for cocoa to grow beneath them; clearing airstrips in hope of an accession of aeroplanes.

For this reason, it seems optimistic to expect much 'political education' to be imparted by such measures as taking leading indigenes on tours of inspection of Australian Parliaments and local authorities and departments. Even the running commentaries and discussions which accompany these visits are likely to be marginal to real understanding.

Another example of this 'exhibitionist' approach was the building throughout the Territory in recent years of elaborate and expensive courthouses, of outlandish design, in and through which to show off the majesty of British justice. This curious experiment gained nothing in popularity from the facts that each of the new courthouses cost as much as two or three homes, or as several schools, was used not more than two or three days in a year, and indeed was held too sacred and seen to be too inconvenient to be put to other uses between sittings of the court.

More important, the 'justice' dispensed in these and other European courts has been very rapidly approximated in form and spirit to the European model. For example, native people have been baffled to see accused persons, whom they 'knew' perfectly well to be guilty, in their terms, of an alleged crime, being acquitted on technicalities of evidence or law, as adduced in conventional pleading by European defending counsel.

'Demonstrating our institutions' in these fashions could well prove a double-edged tool of political education.

Native Local Government Councils. The form of political education on which Australian policy has laid most stress has been the creation of institutions in which the native people can practise direct participation in responsibility, and the most elaborate effort in this field was the development of Native Local Government Councils. As 'native village councils', these were foreshadowed in the Papua and New Guinea Act of 1949; from the establishment of the first council at Hanuabada in 1950 the system was expanded until in July 1964 there were ninety-two councils representing about 921,000 people. For practical reasons—mainly the provision of a sufficient annual budget to support worthwhile projects—these bodies were never established at the 'village' level. For example, in 1957 the five councils in the Gazelle Peninsula represented from eighteen to thirty-three villages each, and from about 3,500 to 7,500 people. The 1956 estimates for the five ranged from £8,456 to £16,676. These figures remain typical today. The revenue came from direct taxation of indigenous residents of the council area, from fees, and from charges for services. Council membership was confined to New Guinea natives; on average there were thirty-five to forty councillors, elected every two years by native residents of the area over the age of seventeen who were liable to council tax.[2]

In September 1956 the Minister for Territories clearly stated that the councils were intended as instruments of political education:

A principle to guide us in government might be described as the representative principle . . . that a people should be able to choose those who will serve them in government and that those who are chosen should be answerable for their actions to the people. The representative principle leads eventually to responsible government. . . Though we start with local government councils, in time there will be a transition to larger representative bodies, perhaps to federations of local government councils: or to regional councils and then to federations of regional councils (Hasluck 1956b:7, 8).

[2] The new Local Government Ordinance of 1963 came into force on 1 January 1965. Councils then ceased to be prefixed 'Native' and could cover all members of their community. Corporations could be taxed and could vote; the voting age was raised to eighteen, and the functions and central supervision of councils were importantly amended. The text is confined to actual experience up to 1965.

In evaluating this objective, the functions of councils must be considered. They are corporate bodies, and had power to make rules (subject to revocation by a District Officer) on a specified list of matters, including 'games or pastimes' in which New Guineans might be defrauded, control of weapons and of practices likely to cause breach of peace, water pollution, disposal of waste, vermin and pests, the regulation of destruction of flora generally and of noxious or diseased plants in particular, hygiene, registration of births and deaths, movement of livestock (owned by New Guinea natives only), use of fire, measures against famine, flood, and pestilence, control of the cultivation of foodstuffs, and enforcement of native custom. There was a general provision that each council had 'such powers and authority as are conferred on it by native custom' where the custom did not conflict with the law or the 'general principles of humanity'; there is evidence, however, of hasty drafting in this clause, and it is doubtful if it was seriously considered to be workable; it has now been replaced by a clause allowing councils to recommend to the Administrator 'the enforcement, variation or abolition of any native custom' existing in the council area. In addition, with the approval of the District Officer, a council could engage in business, build works of benefit to the community, and 'provide, or cooperate with any Department of the Administration . . . or other body in providing any public and social service'.[3]

Impressive though this list may be, in practice it has not enabled the councils to become legislative bodies entrusted with political decisions of any significance. As the early councils began to experiment with their rule-making powers, it soon became obvious that the Administration would allow them little scope for the application of local custom or for its modification by case-law. Owing to doubts and hesitations in Port Moresby about allowing divergent rules on the same subjects to develop in different areas, there was at first great delay in approving council rules; the doubts were resolved in favour of uniformity; councils and supervising officers were perplexed by the difficulty of getting their rules passed, and this restriction on their autonomy tended to lower their prestige in the eyes of the native people. It seemed to many that the things they could do on their own initiative were negligible compared with the duties imposed on councils by the central government, which conceived them as bodies whose main responsibilities were tied to local works and services. This interpretation was confirmed by a Native Local Government Memorandum issued by the Department of Territories as early as 1952, which was much more modest and practical than that of the Minister already quoted. It said councils were intended:

[3] In practice, economic activities by Local Government Councils have, as a matter of policy, been consistently discouraged in recent years.

> To teach responsibility, enlist support for raising native living standards, to prepare for fitting into the Territory's political system, to face the facts that progress is inseparable from good order and industrious habits, and that services must be paid for.

The time had come, it continued, both to decentralize administration and to provide opportunities for the more ambitious natives who were beginning to expect provision of services without any native effort.

In this sphere councils have certainly done active and useful work and gained the rudiments of administrative experience for their members. They own trucks, trailers, and tractors; they build roads and bridges and schools and medical aid posts; some of them conduct economic enterprises in plantations, processing, transport and marketing of primary products, and employ a wide range of native servants from drivers and carpenters to clerks and coffee inspectors. In addition they provide a channel of demands from the local people for the extension of education, works, agricultural, and public health services.

Basically, however, the system as it has developed reflects the Australian conception of local government as mainly an administrative instrument of central government, rather than as an arena for experiencing and resolving important clashes of community opinion, which is the essence of politics. Although there are considerable variations in council initiative and activity, depending largely on the advice given them by different supervising officers, it has been observed that even 'in a politically conscious group', typical agenda items of a council meeting were: training of the assistant clerk; additions and improvements to the council chambers (building of a Council House is compulsory—to provide an immediate task for the first councillors); registration of births, deaths and marriages; opening of the market; and news of the council boat. The writer attended a meeting at Rabaul of representatives of all the councils in the area, at which the issues raised were of the same order: transport of medical supplies to the aid posts in the area; whether missions, rather than the parents, should be required to provide the children's lunches at their schools; whether the councils could get a government grant or loan to run a public refreshment-room at Rabaul market; and so on. This is not a criticism of the councils themselves, but of their adequacy as instruments of *political* education.

Intermediate representative bodies. The next level of political participation has been developed in a comparatively perfunctory way. From 1957, after long hesitation, a minority of native members was nominated to District Advisory Councils, which are mainly bodies of officials and non-indigenous private citizens meeting from time to time to be consulted by District Commissioners on matters of local interest. The same practice has been followed with the Town Advisory Councils that play a similar role in the larger urban centres. The Administration made it clear that native participation was to be essentially as observers, and since the ratio of natives to other members was about one to five, European interests tended to dominate the agenda of these bodies. Indeed, the power-lessness of native representatives has sometimes discredited them with their own people. In recent years, however, the numbers and effectiveness of native members on these bodies have both been increased. Meanwhile, autonomous elective urban government re-mains long overdue in the bigger towns of the Territory.

The Papua and New Guinea Act foreshadowed that native local government councils were to form part of a more comprehensive framework of representative institutions, including Advisory Coun-cils for Native Matters containing 'at least a majority' of (nominated) New Guineans, chosen from those who had given 'meritorious service' in the local government councils. In 1960 the Minister, on advice, concluded that tiers of area and regional councils, and the amalgamation of existing councils into larger units, would be preferable to any merely advisory bodies; but the idea of inter-mediate representative bodies, with their own funds, was set aside, at least temporarily, in favour of the enlargement of native repre-sentation in the Legislative Council by indirect election based on the local councils. This system was allegedly 'designed to make use of the sense of responsibility and education in political procedures which local government is intended to inculcate'. It is true that the system of election worked smoothly enough, and many of the native Legislative Councillors were drawn from leading local government council members—one of the few available reservoirs, indeed, of experience in European institutions of any kind.[4] However, after three years, that system was replaced by direct election based on a common roll, and the change may well be a realistic one. The arena of Territory-wide politics is in many ways distinct in content and quality from that of native local 'government' as it developed in practice.

Representation at the centre. The first representative governing body in the Territory was the Legislative Council of 1951-60, which replaced the Australian Governor-General in Council as the legis-lative organ for the Territory, under the Parliament of the Common-wealth. There was no provision for elected indigenous members of this Council; three indigenes were nominated as non-official mem-bers (the minimum number prescribed) and a fourth was nominated as an official member in 1960, the last year of its life. The elective element in the Council consisted of three non-indigenous members,

[4] Of present members of the House of Assembly from areas having councils, 43 per cent were Council members at their election in 1964.

chosen by electorates restricted to non-indigenous voters. Six private citizens were appointed from the expatriate community as non-official representatives. The remainder of the Council was made up of the Administrator of the Territory and sixteen appointed senior officials, thus ensuring an automatic government majority in the total Council membership of twenty-nine (Hughes 1959:209-29).

In 1960 the Council was reconstituted, providing for a non-official majority. The Administrator was retained as presiding officer; the number of official members was reduced to fourteen; and the number of non-official appointed members was raised to ten, of whom at least five must be indigenes (in fact six were appointed). In addition, the non-indigenous community was represented by six elected members, and six new places were provided for indigenes elected by their own people. Upon a system of indirect election, each of these members was chosen by an 'electoral college' for his electoral district, the members of which had in turn been elected by members of Native Local Government Councils or of communal groups in areas without councils.

The table below summarizes the constitution of the two Legislative Councils, and compares it with that of the House of Assembly:

Members	*Legislative Council*		*House of Assembly*
	1951-60	1963	1964
Ex officio			
Administrator	1	1	
Appointed			
Official	16	14	10
Non-official—			
Non-indigene	6	4	
Indigene	3	6	
Elected			
Non-indigene			
Restricted electorates	3	6	
Special electorates			10
Indigene			
Restricted electorates		6	
Race unspecified			
Open electorates			44
	29	37	64

In 1963, following recommendations of a Select Committee of the Legislative Council (which diverged in some respects from those of the United Nations Mission of 1962), the Council was replaced by a House of Assembly with, for the first time, a majority of elected members. The Administrator was excluded from membership of the House, and the official membership was further reduced, to ten. The elective element was substantially changed. In the restricted electorates for the two Legislative Councils, only members of the relevant racial group could vote or be elected. In the House of Assembly all elected members are chosen directly, on the preferential system, by the same body of voters, as registered for each electorate on a common electoral roll. This contains virtually all adults, indigenous and others, throughout most of the Territory except the few areas not yet completely under the sway of Australian law and order. Registration is compulsory, but voting is not. Each voter may vote twice: once for candidates for one of the ten special electorates, who must be non-indigenes; once for candidates for one of the forty-four open electorates, who may be either indigenes or non-indigenes. It can be seen that while this system guarantees the election of at least ten non-indigenes, it does not guarantee the election of any indigenous representatives. The House is elected for a maximum term of four years, but a general election may be initiated by the Administrator at any time within this period. Elected members of the House receive a remuneration of £950 a year plus daily allowances to attend sittings, travel expenses for touring their electorates, and postage and telephone allowances. Official members receive an allowance of £150 a year plus travel expenses.

The first elections for the House of Assembly were held over a period of four and a half weeks, simultaneously in all electorates, during February and March 1964. The previous months had seen the most intensive patrolling in history of all parts of the Territory, first to compile the electoral rolls and then to tell the voters, so far as possible, something of the meaning of the elections and of the technicalities of voting. Voting was by the preferential system, but it was not necessary for a valid vote that preferences beyond the first must be indicated. The vast majority of the electors being illiterate, they were allowed to indicate a single preference by a 'mark' or to ask the officiating officer to complete the paper for them (the 'whispering ballot'). Only one seat was uncontested, the North Markham special electorate, the unopposed candidate being Mr H. L. R. Niall, District Commissioner of Morobe District, who was subsequently elected the first Speaker of the House of Assembly. Just under three hundred candidates contested the other fifty-three seats. Although the ten special electorates had been, according to the Minister, especially created at native request to ensure there would be some European elected representation in the House, there were non-indigenous candidates in about twenty of the open electorates as well. In the event, Australians were returned in six of these, making a total of twenty-six European (including the official members) and thirty-eight indigenous members in the first session of the House. (Bettison, *et al.* 1965:*passim.*)

The value of the central legislature as a vehicle for political advancement depends in part on its functions and powers, which in turn affect the degree of acceptance and interest it elicits from the

New Guinea people. Ultimate legislative power rests, of course, with the Commonwealth Parliament in Canberra, but in recent years it has confined itself to enacting major constitutional reforms, mostly by way of amendments to the Papua and New Guinea Act, 1949-1963. Under this Act, which serves as the 'constitution' of the Territory, Parliament has delegated to the Legislative Council, and in turn to the House of Assembly, plenary powers to 'make Ordinances for the peace, order and good government of the Territory'. Bills for Ordinances mostly originate in the Territory and are ultimately approved by the Department and Minister in Canberra; but their agent, the Territory Administration, cannot legally force proposed legislation on the New Guinea House of Assembly. On a number of occasions important Bills were rebuffed by the old Legislative Council, and had to be withdrawn for reconsideration and improvements in line with the wishes of the local members. It would not be impossible for an Appropriation Bill to be rejected, thus hamstringing the Administration's programme. As the foregoing table shows, to avoid defeat on a division in the last Legislative Council, the Administration needed at least four non-official votes besides all the official ones. In practice it never had any difficulty in mustering a majority, being only once defeated in a division, and then on a comparatively unimportant matter. When certain proposed measures were obviously unpopular, it preferred withdrawal or amendment to an open trial of strength.

On the other hand, the Australian government in its various guises has retained a negative power of veto over New Guinea legislation it considers reckless or incompetent. An ordinance requires assent by the Administrator or, in certain specified cases, by the Governor-General, before it has the force of law. And even when an ordinance has been assented to by the Administrator, it may still be disallowed by the Governor-General within a period of six months. Reasons for withholding assent or for disallowance must be laid before the Commonwealth Parliament. In all these cases the effective power of veto lies with the Minister for Territories, who instructs the Administrator and advises the Governor-General. In addition, the Australian government has at its disposal the powerful sanction of providing something like two-thirds of the public revenue of the Territory.

It must be obvious, however, that a free use of the formal sanctions would be impolitic, and, as already seen, under the old Legislative Council it hardly proved necessary. The Administrator's power to withhold assent was used only twice, in each case to ensure purely technical amendments. From 1951 to the middle of 1962 the Governor-General's similar power had been exercised eleven times in all, and his power of disallowance twelve times—in a period in which the Legislative Council passed a total of about 750 ordinances. In the absence of political parties, or any other means of

ensuring a stable government majority in the new House of
Assembly, the situation remains essentially one in which the
Australian government has committed itself to securing the agree-
ment of New Guinea representatives, who from 1964 on are likely
to be mainly elected native people, to its legislative policies for the
Territory.

At the same time, it is necessary to remember that legislation is
not government. Australia's policy in New Guinea is carried out
through the daily actions of the Administration, which is still
entirely expatriate in its upper ranks. The cumulative effects of
administrative action and of Administration leadership confer upon
it the whole initiative in policy, and therefore in introducing
legislation necessary to carry out policy; and the Administration is
irremovable by any formal act of the legislature. This is still a long
way from responsible government.

The germs of responsibility. The essence of responsible government in the British tradition is that the controlling heads of the
administrative departments should be elected members of the
legislature and should owe their positions as executive heads to
the support of a majority of the legislature. In former British
colonies the traditional manner of moving from representative
colonial government to responsible self-government has in essence
comprised two steps. First the leading administrative heads of
departments, who formed (perhaps with other leading citizens) an
Executive Council to advise the colonial Governor and give legal
approval to executive orders and regulations, were given seats in the
representative assembly as official nominees. Second, the holders of
these executive offices were made 'removable on political grounds';
in other words, the offices were no longer held by appointed public
servants, but by elected politicians. (See Lynch 1964.)

In New Guinea the advance towards responsible government in
this central, crucial sense has been much more tortuous. Until 1960
there was a nominated Executive Council on traditional lines. In
that year, along with the Legislative Council reforms, this was
abolished and replaced by an 'Administrator's Council', consisting
of the Administrator (who had not been a member of the Executive
Council), three other official members of the Legislative Council
(the two Assistant Administrators and the Director of Native
Affairs), and three non-official members of that body (of whom two
must be elected members). The functions of the Administrator's
Council were advisory and regulation-making—and in practice
almost purely formal. Occasionally the Administrator would explain
some current or pending measure, but debate was rare and decisions
were not taken.

In 1961, moreover, the Minister set up in the Territory a non-
statutory, administrative 'Central Policy and Planning Committee',
consisting of the Administrator, the two Assistant Administrators,

and the Treasurer of the Territory (the Director of Native Affairs being added in 1964). This body was supposed to co-ordinate policy and administration, but contained no popular representative element. In the absence, also, of direct representation of most departmental heads, it may be doubted whether its role is as comprehensive or as influential as its name implies. The official rationalization is that the Administrator and Assistant Administrators, under the reorganization of 1961, each 'supervises' and is 'generally responsible for' a group of administrative departments, and between them they cover the lot (see Chapter 10). More significant for our present concern is the duality of the top executive structure, the absence of non-official participation, native or otherwise, in anything like real executive responsibility, and the fact that the wholly official Policy and Planning Committee continues as, if anything, a somewhat more effective and influential executive body than the partly representative Administrator's Council.

Into this situation the changes accompanying the establishment of the House of Assembly introduced two new complications. In the first place, without altering the official membership of three plus the Administrator, the non-official membership of the Administrator's Council was raised from three to seven, all of whom must be elected members of the House of Assembly. 'This reform,' said the Minister in Parliament, 'is part of a deliberate purpose of preparing for a future Territorial executive'; however, no change has yet appeared in the operation, as distinct from the membership, of the Council. In the second place, following a recommendation of the Select Committee, a 1963 ordinance provided for the appointment by the Administrator of not more than fifteen 'Parliamentary Under-Secretaries' from among elected members of the House of Assembly.[5]

The former Minister, the Administrator, and the Assistant Administrator (Services) made a number of disconnected statements on different occasions about the intended role of these Under-Secretaries: they would represent a stage in the development of responsible executive government; they would be trainees, getting an understanding of parliamentary procedure, administrative methods, departmental organization, and the formulation of policy; they would be attached to each of the 'main' departments 'to understudy those official members who act in the legislature in a role resembling Ministers'; they would be associated with departments *not* represented in the House, to supplement the official representation reduced from sixteen to ten by the latest constitutional reform; they would be consulted in policy-making, conveying public opinion to the Administration and portraying Administration thinking to the electorates.

[5] The maximum number may be increased by resolution of the House (Parliamentary Under-Secretaries Ordinance, 1963, s. 5).

After the 1964 general election, ten Parliamentary Under-Secretaries were chosen, all being indigenous members for open electorates, literate or more or less fluent in spoken English, and spread fairly evenly over the main regions of the Territory. In June they took a special oath of office, undertaking not to divulge official information. In July the Assistant Administrator for Services announced that they would have full access to files and other information, and would work closely with directors of Administration departments, to learn departmental administration, how executive decisions were made, and how policy was formulated. When they had a full understanding of these things they 'would be separated from the executive, and given offices in the House of Assembly building'. Seven of them were, for these purposes, 'attached' to the departments not directly represented in the House of Assembly (including the Department of the Administrator), and the other three were assigned to the Treasurer and to the two Assistant Administrators, all of whom are members of the Assembly.

It appears that Under-Secretaries retain their right, as members, to ask Questions, criticize Administration policy and actions, and even vote against the Administration, which, however, has asked to be consulted beforehand by an Under-Secretary thinking of venting open opposition. These understandings have not been put into writing, and only time can tell what infringements would incur the only formal sanction—the Administrator's power of dismissal. The salary of £1,300 a year, substantially more than that of ordinary members, is a strong inducement to loyalty; on the other hand, there is electoral risk in becoming an Administration 'yes-man', and on losing his seat an Under-Secretary forfeits office as well.

Five of the Under-Secretaries were also appointed as members of the Administrator's Council (the other two places for elected members of the House being filled by Europeans). With the permission of the presiding officer, Under-Secretaries who are not members of the Council may attend and be heard at its meetings. However, unless the role of the Council is transformed, the value of this participation would seem to be limited, whatever its future constitutional significance (though this also remains obscure). No Under-Secretary has been appointed to the Central Policy and Planning Committee, but some of them have been allowed to attend informal policy discussions, for example of the current works programme, considered as a salutary object-lesson in the allocation of finite resources between competing projects and regions.

Formal instruction. A Department of Territories propaganda pamphlet, compiled rather hastily in 1963, gives the following information:

> Special measures have been put into operation to overcome the lack of political experience among the native people. At each sitting of the Legislative Council fifteen leading Papuans and

New Guineans are brought as observers to Port Moresby for
political education. At the same time they receive special courses
of instruction in political theory and procedure. In 1962 a party
of twelve native leaders was brought to Australia to observe and
be instructed in the working of government there, at both the
parliamentary and local government levels. This was again done
with a larger group of native leaders in March-April, 1963 and
the procedure will continue. Special courses of instruction in
political procedures are given in all districts and at Port Moresby
(Territories 1963c:5, 6).

The pre-election programme to familiarize voters with their obligations at the polls has been mentioned: it was an heroic operation,
yet could scarcely be expected to impart much beyond the mechanical requirements of voting. Before the House of Assembly first met,
a seminar was held at Sogeri, near Port Moresby, to initiate the
newly elected members into some of the mysteries of parliamentary
procedure (Bettison 1965). Opportunities of this kind will certainly
increase. A series of seminars on New Guinea's political and
economic future, with substantial representation of native leaders
among speakers and audience, has been sponsored by the Australian
Association for Cultural Freedom, and another, on the recent World
Bank Report, by the recently-formed Council on New Guinea
Affairs, also a private organization. Among official efforts, the
P.N.G. Administrative College, established in November 1963
primarily to train an indigenous public service, has undertaken to
organize seminars on politics and government from time to time for
members of the House of Assembly and other political leaders.
Clearly, formal political education still lies mostly in the future.

INDIGENOUS POLITICAL DEVELOPMENT

It would be strange if the deliberate Australian measures for
political development had not been accompanied by some spontaneous indigenous political activity, not necessarily consistent with
Australian conceptions and intentions. There have been such
manifestations, but so far they have been tentative, disjointed,
scattered, and often short lived. In general, it is Administration
policy to encourage indigenous organizations and activities not
directly opposed to Australian measures, but it has not always been
easy to recognize in time the true nature of local developments or
to handle them constructively. On a topic so fugitive, any generalizations should be treated with reserve.

Cargo cults. Since European occupation there has been a long
history of outbreaks of quasi-religious movements having in common, as Gavin Souter (1963) puts it, attempts to answer one very
puzzling question: 'Why have we so little while the white man has
so much, and how can we improve ourselves?' The answer is usually
supplied by a leader who claims to be in communication with the

spirit world, and to have been told that Europeans have somehow diverted the cargo (material possessions, prosperity, and knowledge) intended by supernatural powers for his people. This is a highly plausible explanation to a stone-age people unable to see for themselves the material basis, the techniques, and organization which make possible the lavish productions of industrial civilization.

In recent years some movements of this general kind have taken a more rational turn. The Kabu Movement, or 'New Men', in the Purari River delta of Western Papua, and the movement led by Paliau on Manus Island to the north of the New Guinea mainland became, after an initial quasi-religious impetus, essentially secular organizations for self-improvement, involving total rejection of the traditional way of life and the adoption of Utopian programmes of social and economic change along European lines. Occasionally these semi-secularized cults have even included ideas of rebellion and local 'independence'. All have been inhibited, however, by the persistent influence of some fanatical cultists, by lack of the material resources and organizational skills to make anything like a reality of their dreams, and by the hesitancy of the Administration to help remedy these deficiencies. Practical advice and positive guidance, together with long-term technological education and training, would both capitalize on these spontaneous impulses towards progressive change and erode the foundations of the cargo cults, which lie deep in the people's system of beliefs (see Burridge 1960; Lawrence 1964; Maher 1961).

Politically, the cargo cults, by spreading beyond their point of origin, have been a potential influence for wider regional unity. But they have failed to breed institutions capable of sustaining this against the disruptive effects of local rivalries, mutual recriminations about thefts of doctrine, and the exploitation of these rifts by sometimes unscrupulous leaders seeking notoriety or petty power. And even when it is used creatively, leadership in New Guinea is traditionally insecure.

The cults also play a part in inter-racial politics. Often beginning auspiciously, for example with acceptance of Christianity as a talisman for the attraction of 'cargo', inevitable disillusion may convert them into a specific medium for the expression of latent anti-European sentiment. However, it seems premature to see the cults, as some observers have done, as the forerunners of a future nationalism. Nationalism elsewhere has usually been stimulated by resentment at the ruling power's oppressive policies or unwelcome presence. The paradox of New Guinea, as Mr Tom Mboya of the Kenya government observed to his own expressed amazement, is that in general the Australian Administration and its policies are welcomed as benevolent, at least in intention, and this seems to inhibit the very desire for independence which is a condition of the self-government those policies are intended to promote.

Mr Hasluck once sought to resolve this paradox by suggesting that his policies would promote a more healthy and permanent focus of unity than would traditional nationalism. It is impossible yet to forecast what form this might take.

Political reactions through Local Government Councils. An indirect effect of the native local government policy has not infrequently been to stimulate or bring to light spontaneous expressions of political aspiration or conflict. Some groups have shown jealousy at the establishment of councils in other areas before their own. Some groups have resisted the establishment of councils in their own areas from an objection to the special taxation which this formerly implied. The operation of councils has sometimes brought out latent antagonisms between local native groups, or between them and non-indigenous groups such as Chinese traders or the missions. The latter themselves in some cases have resented the rise of a rival power in their previous area of influence, for example when councils sought to introduce secular schools.

Another indirect effect of local government councils has been to provide a forum for the raising and discussion of political issues. These have extended to questions of land tenure and alienation, demands for native courts, educational policy, and other matters, not necessarily in conformity with the policy of the Administration, and not within the limited administrative competence of councils themselves.

This forum was extended when the Department of Native Affairs initiated a conference of representatives of councils in the New Guinea Trust Territory in June 1959. Discussions at the conference, said Administration officers who attended it, were marked by 'political maturity', and no fewer than thirty-three 'moderate and coherent' resolutions were passed for submission to the government. These did not elicit official replies till twelve months later, when about nine of the resolutions were acted upon by the Administration. But at the request of council members the Administration has sponsored three repetitions of this conference in different centres on a Territory-wide basis, and managed by delegates themselves. A notable feature of the most recent one, at Wewak in 1964, was the inclusion in a number of resolutions of calls upon members of the House of Assembly to help to further their purposes.

There have been critics who feared that the introduction of Western-style institutions at the grass-roots level of rural villages might raise particularly difficult problems of adaptation, and might even involve, at the pace now contemplated and adopted, 'a degree of coercion' to get people to merge individual village destinies into the larger whole of the council area. They point out, among other things, that where councils are established it is the practice to withdraw authority from the *luluais* or *tultuls* (native headmen or constables) who were previously government representatives in

the individual villages. Not every village can expect to be represented by a separate member in the new Council; in addition the
elections for these bodies tend to draw out younger men rather than
the traditional leaders. The latter thus have a motive for resisting
the introduction of councils, and critics add that when introduced
they eliminate one of the traditional contacts between government
and local village opinion. However, there is evidence that in some
areas a good deal of traditional influence persists behind the scenes,
restricting the autonomy of councils and putting a brake on rapid
change.

Other critics have been impatient with the practice of European
officers assessing the 'capacity' of a group to manage a council
before introducing it, arguing that 'until the people have the
institutions they will never know how to run them'.

Yet experience in many areas has belied these fears. One of the
critics, Dr David Bettison, himself wrote (1962) that the local
government councils 'are becoming the focus of interest of people
who hitherto have had suspicious attitudes, who spoke different
languages and who often engaged in warfare'. He also quotes the
development at Milne Bay (and could now quote the even more
dramatic case of the Gazelle Peninsula) where the people of several
adjacent council areas, formerly at enmity with one another, asked
for amalgamation into a larger council so as to co-ordinate activities
affecting the region as a whole. This kind of consolidation has been
repeated elsewhere, though in at least one instance, that of the
Orokolo and Vailala Councils in 1964, it subsequently broke down.

Whether all of the above tendencies were anticipated by Administration policy or should be classed as unforeseen native initiative is
immaterial. In either case they represent important political gains,
if it is true, as both the former Minister and some of his critics have
said, that 'the crux of the problem of political development is simply
. . . to create a sense of nationhood, of common loyalty and common
institutions in the place of a fragmented society of local loyalties'.

Welfare and industrial organizations. Within the past decade
certain unofficial organizations have provided imported opportunities for the development of native leadership, and one possible
base for indigenous political development.

Problems of housing and employment for immigrant workers in
Port Moresby led Mr Maori Kiki and his wife, with 300 members
of their tribal group, to found in November 1958 the Kerema Welfare Society, whose interest soon extended to wages and working
conditions. In one student's view this signified 'the beginning of
the transition to the political phase' (Healey 1962a). Spreading its
organization rapidly to the Gulf and Western Districts of Papua,
in 1961 the society was renamed the Western Welfare Association.
There is now also an Eastern Welfare Association.

Meanwhile, encouraged by the Minister for Territories to present a case to the Native Employment Board which was then investigating wage scales for native workers, the Keremas, Motu, and other groups in Port Moresby formed in 1960 a Papua and New Guinea Workers' Association, under the leadership of Dr Reuben Taureka. The Administrator asked Mr W. A. Lalor, the Public Solicitor and President of the Public Service Association, to help the Association and the Welfare Society to present their case. It resulted in agreement with the employers on an urban cash wage of £3 a week for unskilled workers employed other than in domestic duties, stevedoring, and shipping, in Port Moresby, Lae, and Rabaul.

Soon afterwards there appeared a Madang Workers' Association, which achieved a membership of 1,125 by the beginning of 1964. Workers' Associations were subsequently formed in Rabaul and Lae, then in Kavieng, Wewak, Goroka, and Wau-Bulolo. In face of these regional developments, the Papua and New Guinea Workers' Association was re-named the Port Moresby Workers' Association. Under the presidency of Mr Oala Oala-Rarua it conducted a recruiting drive in the middle of 1964 which raised its membership from under 500 to over 1,000, including general labourers, transport workers, carpenters, plumbers, and employees in retail stores, hotels, and clubs. Membership is open to workers in all industries in the Port Moresby Sub-District.

In 1961 a cash wage agreement was reached for the majority of unskilled workers in Madang, and separate wage agreements were made for stevedoring workers in Madang and Port Moresby. In 1963 the Madang Workers' Association succeeded in bringing their cash wage to the Port Moresby, Lae, and Rabaul level of £3 a week. Accompanying these developments, and scarcely keeping pace with them, has been the strengthening of the Territory Department of Labour, with the appointment of an Industrial Organizations Officer in June 1961 to help growing organizations, and the operation from March 1963 of ordinances to regulate industrial organizations and industrial relations.

There is a subtle combination of paternalism and control in the industrial legislation. The former is seen in the legal immunities granted to unions in respect of industrial action, including the right to strike, and in the provisions governing voting, the use of funds, and assistance to unions by Administration officers. The latter is represented by the provisions for compulsory registration of organizations, restriction of their objects to 'industrial matters', and denial of the right to affiliate with unregistered associations within the Territory. There is nothing to prevent registered associations from using voluntary donations for political activities, or from affiliating with each other or with trade union movements in Australia or abroad. Yet one senses a certain anxiety lest trade union organizations may be exploited for 'other than industrial purposes', and a desire to maintain close Administration scrutiny and control of their activities.

It would be natural to expect these organizations, which so far are wholly urban, to provide a focus and a forum for political discussion and preparation. The absence of representative municipal government leaves a political vacuum in the towns, which at the same time contain the more literate, articulate, and detribalized native populations and the seeds of social, economic, and racial discontent. The leaders of the Workers' Associations were well represented among the 1964 candidates for the House of Assembly, both successful and unsuccessful, and they are well aware of the relation between Australian trade unionism and political party organization. Industrial organization in each region of the Territory has begun with that hitherto unattainable ideal of Australian labour radicalism, the 'one big union', and so offers one of the most effective available means of fostering a sense of common interest among urbanized native people and of spreading political ideas. It is true that the Workers' Associations are beginning to organize 'industry branches', but this does not contemplate fission. The first Territory-wide conference of Workers' Associations was held at Madang in October 1964, resulting in the announcement early in 1965 of a New Guinea Federation of Workers' Associations.

These are at present only tendencies and possibilities. The welfare and industrial organizations have not yet engaged in overt political activity; at present they are more easily seen as a nursery than as a medium for such activity.

Political behaviour in the legislature. As national legislators, elected members of the new House of Assembly start with very little political or administrative experience indeed, and that entirely within New Guinea. Only seven of the fifty-four had served in any of the previous Legislative Councils. Four of the ten special electorate representatives and three of the six Europeans from open electorates had been Native Affairs Department field officers, most of them having subsequently become planters or businessmen, as were all the other European elected members but one, a clergyman. Of the thirty-eight indigenous members, thirteen are former presidents or vice-presidents of native local government councils, and one was a council clerk; twelve saw service with Europeans in the war, in the police, or in the Pacific Islands Regiment; five have had experience as schoolteachers. By occupation, six of the Highlands indigenous members were government interpreters; there are one or two planters and traders; the rest are mostly subsistence farmers.

As to formal education: no elected member has completed a full secondary schooling, but as experience elsewhere shows, this does not necessarily inhibit the political effectiveness of those brought up and literate in the culture to which the political institutions belong. It is the fact that parliaments belong to an alien culture and that the formal documentation of the House of Assembly is mostly in an alien tongue that makes lack of education a significant handicap for the indigenous representative. Some twenty of the thirty-eight indigenous members have received no formal education at all; four more have at most three years; so that nearly two-thirds of them are either illiterate or semi-literate, and very few would have even hearsay notions of the working of a modern legislature. With remarkable lack of imagination, the mechanics of the House, like those of the Legislative Councils before it, were, as a matter of Ministerial policy, so shaped as to perpetuate the complex and often anachronistic forms and procedures of traditional British parliaments. This hardly eases the task of New Guinea legislators of either race.

The language situation in the House is paradoxical. English, Police Motu, and Melanesian Pidgin are the official languages, and there is a simultaneous translation service. Full versions of Bills, orders of the day, reports, and other documents are supplied only in English, with condensed summaries in the other languages. Hansard, printed only in English, includes the stenographic record of the simultaneous translators' version of speeches in other languages—a cogent but far from verbatim account. On the other hand, while only one of the official members is really fluent in Pidgin, this is the only lingua franca available to half the members from the New Guinea islands, most of those from the New Guinea coast, and all but two from the Highlands (one of whom knows English as well, while the other speaks only 'place-talk'—local dialects). Nearly all the members from coastal Papua have both Motu and English, but as most of them and all the European elected members also have some knowledge of Pidgin, this has quickly become the medium for many speeches by members of all races—except the officials. The growing and durable importance of Pidgin, incidentally, is thus underlined by the practice of the central legislature.

It is not surprising that in the first two meetings of the House of Assembly, as previously in the Legislative Council, the indigenous members have played a much more modest part than their European colleagues, speaking more rarely in the discussion of Bills before the House, and then more briefly and with little subtlety on technical points. One or two, who happen to be outstanding in their acquirement of European manners, habits, and speech, seem able to grasp the essential principles of legislation closely affecting their people, and can debate cogently in English. At the same time, most of them are persons of some weight and consideration in their own districts, and are neither shy nor awkward on the occasions when they feel called upon to rise to their feet. In the House's second meeting the writer witnessed most of the elected members in turn delivering with poise and force (and in one or two cases with amusing irony) a brief speech in support of the remarkable resolution that:

> We, the elected representatives of the people of Papua and New Guinea, desire to convey to the Parliament of the Commonwealth of Australia, the Trusteeship Council and the General Assembly of the United Nations Organisation, the expressed wish of the people that they, the people, and they alone, be allowed to decide when the time is ripe for self-government in Papua and New Guinea, and the form that such government will take, and the people's further firm conviction that the road to self-government can best be travelled with one guide—and that guide the administering authority. . . .

It is in debates on the Address in Reply or on the Adjournment of the House that indigenous members usually speak, either on very general matters like this resolution, on severer enforcement of the criminal law, the drift to the towns, and the need for unity and education among their people, or, at the other extreme, on the parochial needs of their own electorates for government development of industries, roads, and markets.

Among indigenous members of the last Legislative Council, six of whom were nominated by the Administration, there was a somewhat higher average of experience and literacy. An analysis of the divisions in the Council between April 1961 and the end of 1962 showed that five of the six appointed indigenous members almost invariably supported the government; the sixth, and four of the elected indigenes, sometimes supported and sometimes opposed the government; while two of the elected indigenes voted against the government in all divisions, thus ranking themselves, in attitude though not in any organized way, with the six elected expatriate members who did likewise (and thus looked something like an Opposition). These facts, together with a close study of the debates and of the issues at stake in the divisions, led the observer to conclude that:

> The indigenes, particularly the elected indigenes, are sorting things out for themselves. . . To date they have been moderate, cautious and not very talkative, but nevertheless some elected indigenes have clearly differentiated between matters which seem to further their short term interests and matters which seem not to do so. . . They are neither tools of the Government or the Opposition, but are developing independent and politically sound views of their own (Sloan 1962:20-1; see also Lynch 1962).

Such a verdict seems somewhat premature, especially with the hindsight that only two of the members concerned have passed into the new House of Assembly. Yet this House has already witnessed manful gropings toward the rudiments of political organization. Elected members seemed determined not to jeopardize the prospect of national unity by overt groupings on regional lines (which some people had predicted), and there was no other discernible basis for 'political parties' at this stage. The Administration made no attempt to create a pledged government majority, and this may, consciously or otherwise, have been decisive in eliminating any thought of a united Opposition. Instead, at the second meeting of the House in September 1964, a private gathering of indigenous members chose a Leader and Deputy Leader of the Elected Members. (They were Mr John Guise, a Papuan, and Matthias To Liman, a New Guinean, respectively; Mr Guise forthwith resigned his post as an Under-Secretary, but asked to remain a member of the Administrator's Council.) These decisions were encouraged and accepted by the European elected members, who took part in later meetings of the group which chose two Whips and discussed parliamentary tactics for the floor of the House. The Administration at first responded by appointing two official members as Whips of its own, and to some extent the business of the House has begun to be arranged 'behind the Speaker's Chair'. However, these rudimentary measures have since been allowed to lapse, at least on the Administration side.

Formation of the Elected Members' Group offers the possibility of concerted action in the House by the substantial non-official majority, and could thus be a formidable restraint on Administration policy. But several incidents in its first week distinguished it from a regular Opposition party. It seized the idea of making—as a single gesture, not a continuous resistance—a show of its collective strength by amending or delaying an Administration measure; but it conveyed these intentions to the Administration Whips and also agreed to admit an Administration spokesman to its meeting to discuss the 'wisdom' of its particular choice of issues—hardly the behaviour of an exclusive party caucus. That its own members did not consider it a 'party' was shown by at least one attempt by a European member to form a 'definite political party'; the meeting he called was poorly attended and quickly disintegrated as soon as his object became clear. When an elected member introduced an amendment to a Bill without consulting the group as a whole, elected members decided to vote individually in the resulting division. The House in Committee divided equally and the amendment was lost on the casting vote of the chairman;[6] the mover was criticized in a subsequent meeting of the Elected Members' Group but his freedom of action was accepted—in short, there is no hint of a pledge.

Of course, what happens in the legislature is not the only

[6] The amendment occasioning this first Division in the new House would have added chewing-gum to betel nut as a substance not to be consumed in hotel and restaurant kitchens!

important index of political activity or sophistication. After all, the Legislative Council usually sat for only a few weeks in each year, and House sessions will not be much different at first. Between sessions, members will need to study the background of legislation and their constituents' opinions about Administration policy and actions, and to broaden their acquaintance with people, the country, and their problems. Indigenous members are undoubtedly active in these ways. And it seems likely that the mere fact of their membership of the central legislature is a greater stimulus to such activity than they would receive in any other way. By the same token, it may well be from the central legislature outward and downward, rather than from the local communities upward, that organized political groupings will be developed. The decisions made there will be important; it will be equally obvious that those decisions can be consistently influenced only by concerted action in the House. Common interests and conflicts of interest will become clearer there; and indigenous members will learn, as they could not at home, the meaning of representative national politics. They will also become conscious of the sweets of office, and realize that organization is a pre-condition of re-election. In all of these directions there are already some signs that the New Guinea politician is quick to read the lessons of experience.

CONCLUSION

Rather than to intone cut-and-dried formulae for the future, it seems better to conclude by re-emphasizing the dilemmas and uncertainties that face Australia in its policy of helping New Guinea to advance to responsible self-government.

A pervading dilemma lies between the impatience of the outside world to see this nearly last of colonial territories 'freed' from alien yoke and the patience demanded by the realities of the internal situation. These are realities of economic, social, and political underdevelopment that are due to Australia's neglect in the past, but that cannot be exorcized by resolutions in international bodies or the wringing of academic hands. Australia's creation of political institutions is at present certainly outrunning its economic and social measures and also its formal preparation of the New Guinea people for political responsibility. If those people 'catch up' and formulate their own political demands at even half the rate envisaged by the outside critics, so much the better.

A second dilemma is between the natural wish Australians may have to free themselves of the moral, financial, and defence burden which New Guinea in fact will increasingly impose, and the equally natural wish to ensure that New Guinea, even when self-governing, 'retains a close and friendly association with Australia'. It seems that our obligations are inescapable, whenever and in whatever form self-determination is claimed.

A third dilemma is exemplified by a statement of the former Minister for Territories, in which he said in one breath that an Australian aim is 'to retain what is best in native life and to blend it with the influences of Western Civilisation', and in the next that another aim is 'to replace paganism by the acceptance of the Christian faith, and the ritual of primitive life by the practice of religion' (Hasluck 1956a:11). He was much more realistic on a later occasion in saying that he did not expect the New Guinea people would accept Australian institutions and values ready made (Hasluck 1964:5).

A fourth dilemma lies between the policy of 'uniform development' and the tendencies and pressures towards early emergence, if not deliberate fostering, of a political *élite*. If 'uniform development' means withholding educational opportunities and accelerated political and administrative training from those who are now most ready for them, it would mean shirking immediate responsibilities but could not prevent the rise of an *élite* 'qualified' for leadership in other—perhaps less palatable—ways.

Finally, there remain the open questions about Australia's ultimate policy on responsible government. When is it to be? What form is it to take? Does it mean statehood within the Commonwealth of Australia, 'self-government' within some looser form of association with Australia, membership in a 'Melanesian Federation', 'independence' subject to Australian economic aid and defence undertakings, or union with West Irian under Indonesia? It has been Australian policy that the New Guinea people will decide all these questions 'for themselves in their own good time'. Can Australia afford to leave all these questions to the New Guineans, and is there time to leave it all to them? On the other hand, can Australia afford to ignore the fashionable world doctrine of 'self-determination'? We must seek clearer ideas in this misty, vital, dangerous area.

REFERENCES

A.B.C.
1963   Broadcast by the Rt Hon. Sir Robert Menzies at Port Moresby, 6 September.
1964   News Bulletin, Papua-New Guinea Service, 15 June.

A.C.C.   [Australian Council of Churches, Division of Mission].

1965   *Responsibility in New Guinea: Report of an Australian Ecumenical Visit.*

ANGAU
1942-6   *Report of Activities.*

ALLAN, C. H.
1951   'Marching Rule: a nativistic cult of the British Solomon Islands.' *Corona*, III, 93-100.

ANDERSON, J. L.
1963   'The Development of a Cattle Industry in the Territory of Papua and New Guinea.' *Australian Territories*, III, i, 15-28.

ANON.
1951   'Community Development through Rural Progress Societies.' *South Pacific*, V, 123-6.

ASHBY, E., and HARBISON, F.
1960   *Investment in Education.* The Report of the Commission on Post-School Certificate and Higher Education in Nigeria. Lagos.

AUSTRALIA, *see also* B.A.E., Labour and National Service, Territories.
1901   *Commonwealth Parliamentary Debates (C.P.D.).*
1907   'Report of the Royal Commission of Enquiry into the Territory of Papua.' *Parliamentary Papers*, Senate vol. I, 137-463. (Report appeared separately in 1906, pp. cxxx + 197.)
1921-40   *Report to the League of Nations [to the Council of the League of Nations] on the Administration of the Territory of New Guinea (N.G.A.R.).* Melbourne and Canberra.
1946-   *Report to the General Assembly of the United Nations on the Administration of the Territory of New Guinea (N.G.A.R.).* Canberra and Sydney.
1947-   *Annual Report to Parliament on the Territory of Papua* (by Minister for Territories).
1957   *Tariff Board Report on Rubber* (August 1955). Canberra.
1962   *Census Bulletin*, No. 16. Bureau of Census and Statistics. Canberra.
1963a   *Tariff Board Report on peanuts, peanut oil, and other edible vegetable oils* (December 1962). Canberra.

References   271

1963b   *Tariff Board Report on synthetic rubber* (December
                         1962). Canberra.
1964   *Tariff Board Report on passionfruit juice and
                         passionfruit pulp*. Canberra.

B.A.E.
1951   *An Economic and Cost Survey of the Copra In-
                         dustry in the Territory of Papua and New Guinea.*
                         Canberra.

BAKER, Tanya, and
  BIRD, Mary
1959   'Urbanization and the Position of Women.' *Socio-
                         logical Review*, VII, 99-122.

BARNES, J. A.
1959-60   'Indigenous Politics and Colonial Administration
                         with special reference to Australia.' *Comparative
                         Studies in Society and History*, II, 133-49.

BELSHAW, C. S.
1955   *In Search of Wealth*. American Anthropological
                         Association Memoir No. 80.

BERNDT, Ronald M.
1952-3   'A Cargo Movement in the Eastern Central High-
                         lands of New Guinea.' *Oceania*, XXIII, 40-65, 137-
                         58, 202-34.
1954   'Reaction to Contact in the Eastern Highlands of
                         New Guinea.' *Oceania*, XXIV, 190-228, 255-74.
1957   'The Changing World in New Guinea.' *Australian
                         Quarterly*, XXIX, 39-55.

BETTISON, D. G., *et al.*
1962   *The Independence of Papua-New Guinea*. Sydney.
1965   *The Papua-New Guinea Elections 1964*. Canberra.

BETTISON, D. G.
1965   'The Sogeri Seminar', in Bettison *et al.* (ed.), *The
                         Papua-New Guinea Elections 1964*. Canberra.

BLOOD, N. B.
1946   Extract of Report of Patrol by Captain N. B.
                         Blood, A.D.O., from Hagen to Ifitamin. Appendix
                         A. ANGAU, *Final Report of Activities.*

BROOKFIELD, H. C.
1958   'The Land', in J. Wilkes (ed.), *New Guinea and
                         Australia*. Sydney.
1960   'Population Distribution and Labour Migration in
                         New Guinea.' *Australian Geographer*, VII, 233-42.

BROOKFIELD, H. C.,
  and BROWN, Paula
1963   *Struggle for Land*. Melbourne.

BROWN, Paula
1963   'From Anarchy to Satrapy.' *American Anthropolo-
                         gist*, LXV, 1-15.

BURRIDGE, K. O. L.
1960   *Mambu*. London.

BRUYN, J. V. de
1951   'The Mansren Cult of Biak.' *South Pacific*, V, 1-11.

CHALMERS, Rev. James
1887   'New Guinea, Past, Present and Future.' *Proceedings of the Royal Colonial Institute*, vol. XVIII.
1895   Discussion on William MacGregor, 'British New Guinea', in *Proceedings of the Royal Colonial Institute*, vol. XXVI.

CHRISTIAN, C. S.
1958   'The Concept of Land Units and Land Systems.' *Proc. 9th Pac. Sci. Cong.*, XX, 74-81. Bangkok.
1964   'The Use and Abuse of Land and Water', in S. Mudd (ed.), *The Population Crisis and the Use of World Resources*. The Hague.

CHRISTIAN, C. S., and
STEWART, G. A.
1953   *General Report on Survey of Katherine-Darwin Region, 1946*. C.S.I.R.O. Aust. Land Res. Ser. 1.
1964   Methodology of integrated surveys. UNESCO Conference on principles and methods of integrating aerial survey studies of natural resources for potential development.

CLINE, M. G., *et al.*
1955   'Soil Survey: Territory of Hawaii.' U.S. Soil Survey (Ser. 1939), No. 25.

CORDEN, W. M.
1963   'Prospects for Malayan Exports', in T. H. Silcock and E. K. Fisk (eds.), *The Political Economy of Independent Malaya*. Canberra.

CROCOMBE, R. G., and
HOGBIN, G. R.
1963   *The Erap Mechanical Farming Project*. New Guinea Research Unit Bulletin, No. 1. Canberra and Port Moresby.

C.A.B.
1963   'New Guinea's Political Future', XXXII, 49-64, 8 July.
1964   'New Guinea Assembly', XXXIV, 97-112, 17 August.

DAVIDSON, J. W.
1951   'The Study of History and Government', in R. Firth *et al.*, *Notes on New Guinea*.

EPSTEIN, A. L.
1961   'Pacific Commentary: The Tolai of the Gazelle Peninsula.' *Journal of the Polynesian Society*, LXX, 492-6.

EPSTEIN, A. L., and
T. S.
1962   'A note on population in two Tolai settlements.' *Journal of the Polynesian Society*, LXXI, 70-82.

References   273

EPSTEIN, Scarlett
    1964   'Personal Capital Formation Among the Tolai of New Britain.' Ch. 3 in Raymond Firth and B. S. Yamey (eds.), *Capital, Saving and Credit in Peasant Societies*. London.

ESSAI, Brian
    1961   *Papua and New Guinea*. Melbourne.

F.A.O.
    1952-   *Monthly Bulletin of Agricultural Economics and Statistics*, vols. 1-13. Rome.

    1958-63   *Cocoa Statistics*, vols. 1-6. Rome.

    1959-63   *The Coconut Situation*. Commodity Reports Nos. 1-9. Rome.

    1960   *Tea—Trends and Prospects*. Commodity Bulletin Series No. 30. Rome.

    1961a   *Report of the Fourth Session of the F.A.O. Cocoa Study Group*. Rome.

    1961b   *The World Coffee Economy*. Commodity Bulletin Series No. 33. Rome.

    1962a   *Agricultural Commodities—Projections for 1970*. Commodity Review Special Supplement. Rome.

    1962b   *Review of the world cocoa economy and the work of the F.A.O. Cocoa Study Group*. Committee on Commodity Problems, Cocoa Study Group. Rome.

    1963a   *Commodity Review 1963*. Rome.
    1963b   *Fats and Oils Projections*. F.A.O. Group on Coconut and Coconut Products. Rome.

    1963c   *Fluctuations in world trade in coconut products*. F.A.O. Group on Coconut and Coconut Products, item V(b) for Fifth Session, F.A.O. Rome.

    1963d   *Report of the Sixth Session of the Cocoa Study Group to the Committee on Commodity Problems*. Rome.

F.A.O. and ECAFE
    1961   *Timber trends and prospects in the Asia-Pacific Region*. Geneva.

FIAWOOD, D. K.
    1959   'Urbanization and religion in Eastern Ghana.' *The Sociological Review*, VII, 83-97.

FIRTH, R.
    1955   'The Theory of "Cargo" Cults: a Note on Tikopia.' *Man*, LV, 130-2.

FIRTH, R., DAVIDSON,
  J. W., and SPATE,
  O. H. K.
    1951   *Notes on New Guinea*. Mimeographed. Canberra.

FISK, E. K.
    1962   'Planning in a Primitive Economy. Special Problems of Papua-New Guinea.' *Economic Record*, XXXVIII, 462-78.

    1964   'Planning in a Primitive Economy: From Pure Subsistence to the Production of a Market Surplus.' *Economic Record*, XL, 156-74.

GRAHAM, G. K.,
   CHARLES, A. W.,
   and SPINKS, G. R.
   1963   'Tea production in Papua and New Guinea.'
                                 Papua-New Guinea Agricultural Journal, XVI, Nos.
                                 2 and 3.

GRIFFIN, B. F.
   1964   'The Impact of Representative Government on the
                                 District Administrative System.' Paper delivered to
                                 the District Commissioners' Conference, Port
                                 Moresby, 9 September.

GROENEWEGEN, K.,
   and van de KAA, D. J.
   1962-4   *Some preliminary results of the Demographic Re-*
                                 search Project Western New Guinea (Irian Barat)
                                 E.E.C. Project 11.41.002. The Hague. 6 Parts.
                                 1962 Beneden-Waropen. (Pt I)
                                 1963a Nimboran. (Pt III)
                                 1963b Noemfoor. (Pt II)
                                 1963c Schouten Islands. (Pt IV)
                                 1964a Fak-fak. (Pt V)
                                 1964b Moejoe. (Pt VI)

GROVES, Murray
   1962   *New Guinea—Australia's Colonial Fantasy.* Chif-
                                 ley Memorial Lecture, Melbourne.
   1965   'The Machinery of the Government.' Third of six
                                 articles in the *Australian.* 8 January.

GUIART, J.
   1951   'Forerunners of Melanesian Nationalism.' *Oceania*,
                                 XXII, 81-90.
   1952a   'The Co-operative Called "The Malekula Native
                                 Company".' *South Pacific*, VI, 429-32.
   1952b   'The John Frum Movement in Tanna.' *Oceania*,
                                 XXII, 165-77.

HAANTJENS, H. A.
   1963   'Land capability classification in reconnaissance
                                 surveys in Papua and New Guinea.' *J. Aust. Inst.*
                                 agric. Sci., XXIX, 104-7.

H.A.D., *House of Assembly Debates*, see T.P.N.G. 1964c.
HASLUCK, Paul
   1952   'A Policy for New Guinea.' *South Pacific*, V, 11,
                                 224-8.
   1956a   *Australian Policy in Papua and New Guinea.*
                                 George Judah Cohen Memorial Lecture, University
                                 of Sydney.
   1956b   *Australia's Task in Papua and New Guinea.* Roy
                                 Milne Memorial Lecture. Perth.
   1962a   *Australian Policy in Papua and New Guinea.*
                                 Address by the Minister for Territories to Public
                                 Service Association of Papua and New Guinea at
                                 Port Moresby, 1 September.

References 275

1962b	'The Economic Development of Papua and New Guinea.' *Australian Outlook*, XVI, 5-25.
1964	*Present Policies and Objectives*. Address to the Summer School of the Victorian Council of Adult Education, Melbourne.

HEALY, A. M.
1961a	'Native Local Government in New Guinea.' *Journal of African Administration*, XIII, 165-74.
1961b	'Pacific Commentary: Some Peoples of Papua.' *Journal of Polynesian Society*, LXX, 485-91.
1962a	Native Administration and Local Government in Papua, 1880-1960. Ph.D. thesis (A.N.U. Library).
1962b	'The Foot Report and East New Guinea.' *Australian Quarterly*, XXXIV, 11-22.

HIDES, J.
1936	*Papuan Wonderland*. London.

HLA MYINT, U.
1962	'The Universities of Southeast Asia and Economic Development.' *Public Affairs*, XXXV, 116-27.

HOGBIN, H. I.
1951	*Transformation Scene*. London.
1958	*Social Change*. London.

HOUNAM, C.
1951	'Meteorological and climatic conditions over British New Guinea and adjacent islands', in *The Resources of the Territory of Papua and New Guinea*, vol. 1. (Department of National Development) Canberra.

HUGHES, C. A.
1959	'The Legislative Councils of Papua-New Guinea.' *Parliamentary Affairs*, XII, 209-29.

I.B.R.D.
1965	*The Economic Development of the Territory of Papua and New Guinea*. Baltimore, U.S.A.

INGLIS, J.
1957	'Cargo Cults: the Problem of Explanation.' *Oceania*, XXVII, 249-63.

INSTITUTE OF PUBLIC ADMINISTRATION
1954	'Some Notes on the Administration of New Guinea', compiled by the Queensland Regional Group with the aid of Col. J. K. Murray. *Public Administration* (Sydney), XIII, 38-43.

INTERNATIONAL RUBBER STUDY GROUP
1947-1962	*Rubber Statistical Bulletin*, vols. 1-18. *The Future of Natural and Synthetic Rubbers*. London.

JARVIE, I. C.
1964   *The Revolution in Anthropology*. London.

JENNINGS, Sir Ivor
1956   *The Approach to Self-Government*. Cambridge.

Journal of Public Service of the Territory of Papua and New Guinea.
JOYCE, R. B.
           The Administration of British New Guinea 1888-1902. Ph.D. thesis, Cambridge. (Typescript copy.)

KING, C. W.
1956   *Social Movements in the United States*. New York.

KLINGEBIEL, A. A.,
and MONTGOMERY,
P. H.
1961   Land capability and classification. Agric. Handbook 210. Soil Conservation Service, U.S. Dept. Agric.

KOUWENHOVEN,
W. J. H.
n.d.   *Mimboran*. The Hague.

LABOUR AND
NATIONAL
SERVICE,
DEPARTMENT OF
1964   *Labour Information Bulletin*, No. 1.

LAMBERT, C. R.
1957   'Local Government in Papua-New Guinea.' *South Pacific*, LX, 465-74.

LAWRENCE, P.
1955   'The Madang District Cargo Cult.' *South Pacific*, VIII, 6-13.
1961   'Some Problems of Administration and Development in Papua-New Guinea.' *Public Administration*, XX, 305-14.
1964   *Road Belong Cargo*. Aust. ed. Melbourne.

LEGGE, J. D.
1956   *Australian Colonial Policy*. Sydney.

LEWIS, W. A.
1962   'Education and Economic Development.' *International Social Science Journal*, XIV, 71-9.

LYNCH, C. J.
1961   'A New Constitution for Papua and New Guinea.' *Journal of Polynesian Society*, LXX, 243-9.
1962   'Appointed Members in the Legislative Council for Papua and New Guinea.' *A.P.S.A. News*, VII, iii, 1-5.
1964   *Towards a Parliamentary Ministerial System of Government for Papua and New Guinea*. An expanded version of a paper presented to the Papua and New Guinea Regional Group of the Royal Institute of Public Administration, at Port Moresby, on 3 December.

References

McARTHUR, Norma
1956   The Populations of the Pacific Islands. Part VII, 'Papua and New Guinea.' A.N.U. Canberra.
1964   'The Age Incidence of Kuru.' *Annals of Human Genetics*, XXVII, 341-52.

McAULEY, J. P.
1953   'Australia's Future in New Guinea.' *Pacific Affairs*, XXVI, 59-69.
1958   'Problems Affecting the Native Local Government Policy.' *South Pacific*, IX, 569-75.

MAHER, R.
1958   'Tommy Kabu Movement of the Purari Delta.' *Oceania*, XXIX, 75-90.
1961   *New Men of Papua*. Madison, Wisconsin.

MAIR, L. P.
1948   *Australia in New Guinea*. London.

MANNHEIM, Karl
1946   *Man and Society in an Age of Reconstruction*. London.

MEAD, Margaret
1956   *New Lives for Old*. New York.
1964   *Continuities in Cultural Evolution*. New Haven.

MILES, J. A.
1956   'Native Commercial Agriculture in Papua.' *South Pacific*, IX, 318-28.

MURRAY, Gilbert
n.d.   Gilbert Murray Papers. (National Library of Australia.)

MURRAY, J. H. P. (Sir Hubert)
1912   *Papua or British New Guinea*. London.
1920   *Review of the Australian Administration in Papua for 1907 to 1920*. Port Moresby.
1925   *Papua Today, or an Australian Colony in the Making*. London.

MURRAY, J. K.
1949   *The Provisional Administration of the Territory of Papua and New Guinea; its policy and its problems*. John Murtagh Macrossan Memorial Lecture, 1946, Brisbane.

N.G.A.R.
    Territory of New Guinea Annual Report, *see* Australia 1921-40, 1946-.

N.I.D.
1945   *Pacific Islands*. Geographical Handbook Series, IV, 97.

OALA-RARUA, OALA
1965   'The Development of the Public Service in Papua and New Guinea and the Role of the Public Servants.' Paper delivered to the Second Seminar on the Future of the Free Institutions in Papua and New Guinea. Australian Association for Cultural Freedom, 15 January.

P.A.R.

Territory of Papua Annual Reports, *see* Territories 1905-.

PUBLIC SERVICE
COMMISSIONER
(N.G.)
1958   *Public Service Handbook.* Port Moresby.

READ, K. E.
1958   'A "Cargo" Situation in the Markham Valley.'
                        Southwestern Journal of Anthropology, XIV, 273-94.

REAY, Marie
1959   *The Kuma.* Melbourne.

REED, S. W.
1943   *The Making of Modern New Guinea.* Philadelphia.

ROWLEY, C. D.
1957   'Local Government in New Guinea.' *South Pacific*,
                        IX, 437-46.
1958   *The Australians in German New Guinea 1914-1921.* Melbourne.

RYAN, d'A.
1961   Gift Exchange in the Mendi Valley. Ph.D. thesis,
                        University of Sydney.

SALISBURY, R. F.
1958   'An "Indigenous" New Guinea Cult.' *Kroeber
                        Anthropological Society Papers* No. 18, 67-78.
1962   *From Stone to Steel.* Melbourne.

SCHMIDT, F. H., and
FERGUSON, J. H. A.
1952   'Rainfall types based on wet and dry ratios for
                        Indonesia with Western New Guinea.' *Kemen-
                        terian Perhubungan Djawatan Meteorologi dan
                        Goefisik, Djakarta, Verhand. 42.*

SCHWARTZ, T.
1962   'The Paliau Movement in the Admiralty Islands,
                        1946-54.' *Am. Mus. Nat. Hist. Anthrop. Paper*,
                        XLIX, ii.

SINCLAIR, A.
1957   *Field and Clinical Survey Report of the Mental
                        Health of the Indigenes of the Territory of Papua
                        and New Guinea.*

SLOAN, B. P.
1962   'The Uncommitted Vote in the Legislative Council
                        for Papua and New Guinea.' *A.P.S.A. News*, VII,
                        ix, 20-1.

SOUTER, Gavin
1963   *New Guinea, the Last Unknown.* Sydney.

STANNER, W. E. H.
1953   *The South Seas in Transition.* Sydney.

References

TERRITORIES,
DEPARTMENT OF
1905-   'Territory of Papua, Annual Report' (*P.A.R.*) in
                       Commonwealth *Parliamentary Papers.*
1960-   *Australian Territories.*
1963a   *Abstract of Statistics: No. 3 Territory of Papua and
                       New Guinea Statistical Tabulations.* Canberra.
1963b   *Economic and Functional Classification of Public
                       Authorities Finances for Territory of Papua and
                       New Guinea 1958/59-1962/63.* Port Moresby.
1963c   *Progress of the Australian Territories, 1952-1962.*
                       Canberra.
1964a   *National Income Estimates for Papua and New
                       Guinea 1960/61-1962/63.* Canberra.
1964b   *Report of the Commission on Higher Education in
                       Papua and New Guinea* (Currie Report). Canberra.

T.P.N.G.
1950/1   Patrol Report No. 10, Kikori Sub-District, Gulf
                       District.
1951/2   Ibid. No. 8.
1956-63   *Overseas Trade.* Bureau of Statistics. Bulletins 1-8.
1959-63   *Rural Industries.* Production Bulletins Nos. 1-5.
1962   Legislative Council of Papua and New Guinea.
                       Select Committee on Political Development: *In-
                       terim Report.* Port Moresby.
1963a   *Annual Report of the Department of Agriculture,
                       Stock and Fisheries.* Port Moresby.
1963b   *Annual Report for the year ended 30th June, 1962,
                       to the Minister of State for Territories from the
                       Public Service Commissioner.* Port Moresby.
1963c   *Quarterly Bulletin of Oversea Trade Statistics.*
                       Twelve months ended June 1963.
1963d   *Report on the Operations of the Department of
                       Forests for the year ending 30th June 1963.* Port
                       Moresby.
1963e   *Survey of Indigenous Agriculture and Ancillary
                       Surveys 1961-62.* Papua.
1963f   *Legislative Council Debates,* VI, 10.
1964a   Administration Press statement No. 130: The New
                       Public Service Ordinance. Port Moresby.
1964b   *Annual Report for the year ended 30th June 1963,
                       to the Minister of State for Territories from the
                       Public Service Commissioner.* Port Moresby.
1964c-   *House of Assembly Debates,* vols. 1- . Port
                       Moresby.
1964d   'Income Taxation.' *Finance Bulletin* No. 3.
1964e   *Quarterly Bulletin of Oversea Trade Statistics.* Nine
                       months ended March 1964.
1964f   *Quarterly Summary of Statistics,* No. 20.

TRUPP, S. L. (ed.)
1962   *Millennial Dreams in Action: Essays in compara-
                       tive study.* Supplement II. The Hague.

UNITED AFRICA
COMPANY
1963   *Statistical and Economic Review.* April. London.

UNITED NATIONS
1963   *United Nations Coffee Conference, 1962: Summary of Proceedings.* E/CONF. 42/8. New York.

UNESCO
1953   'The Use of Vernacular Languages in Education.' *Monographs in Fundamental Education,* No. VIII. Paris.

U.N. TRUSTEESHIP COUNCIL
1962   *Report of the U.N. Visiting Mission to the Trust Territory of Nauru and New Guinea, 1962.* Document T/1597. New York.

van der MEULEN, J.
1962   *Fish Marketing in Papua and New Guinea.* Faculty of Agricultural Economics, The University of New England.

van WIJK, C. L.
1962-3   'The soils of Bougainville Island—their distribution and main characteristics in relation to agricultural development.' *Papua-New Guinea Agricultural Journal,* XV, 123-32.

VOGET, T. W.
1959   'Towards a Classification of Cult Movements: Some further contributions.' *Man,* LIX, 26-8.

WALLACE, A. F. C.
1956   'Revitalization Movements.' *American Anthropologist,* LVIII, 264-81.

WATSON, J. B.
1964   'Anthropology in the New Guinea Highlands.' *American Anthropologist,* LVI, ii, 1-18.

WEBER, Max
1947   *Theory of Social and Economic Organization* (translated T. Parsons). London.

WEST, F. J.
1956   'Colonial Development in Central New Guinea.' *Pacific Affairs,* XXIX, 161-73.
1958   'Indigenous Labour in Papua-New Guinea.' *International Labour Review,* LXXVII, 89-112.
1963   'Sir Hubert Murray: The Australian Pro-Consul.' *Journal of Commonwealth Political Studies,* I, 282-95.

WHITE, R. C.
1964   *Social Accounts of the Monetary Sector of the Territory of Papua and New Guinea, 1956/57 to 1960/61.* New Guinea Research Unit Bulletin No. 3. Canberra and Port Moresby.

WICKIZER, V. D.
1964   'International Collaboration in the World Coffee Market.' *Food Research Institute Studies,* IV, 273-304.

References

WILKES, John (ed.)
    1958   *New Guinea and Australia*. Sydney.

WILLIAMS, F. E.
    1930   *Orokaiva Magic*. London.
    1934   'The Vailala Madness in Retrospect', in E. E. Evans-Pritchard (ed.), *Essays Presented to C. G. Seligman*. London.

WORSLEY, P.
    1957   *The Trumpet Shall Sound*. London.

WURM, S. A.
    1960   'The Changing Linguistic Picture of New Guinea. *Oceania*, XXXI, 121-36.
    1964   'Recent Developments in Linguistic Studies on the Australian New Guinea Mainland.' *Papers in New Guinea Linguistics No. 2*, Linguistic Circle of Canberra Publications, Series A—Occasional Papers, No. 4, 1-17.

Index